1966

High Points
in the
History of Italian Literature

High Points
in the
History of Italian Literature

by
DOMENICO VITTORINI

DAVID McKAY COMPANY, INC.
New York

Library of Congress Catalog Card Number: 58-9803

Under the sponsorship of the Curtis Institute of Music

MANUFACTURED IN THE UNITED STATES OF AMERICA

VAN REES PRESS • NEW YORK

To Mary Curtis Zimbalist, whose interest in the arts and Italian literature in general, and in these essays in particular, has been of the greatest aid and encouragement in bringing them to publication.

Contents

Preface

THIS collection of essays touches, as the title indicates, upon the most outstanding points of Italian literature. Its component parts are chronologically arranged, and they span the whole development of the literature of Italy, from Dante to Benedetto Croce and Luigi Pirandello.

All of the essays have been previously published in periodicals primarily meant for scholars. We have translated those originally written in Italian and added to them those already written in English in the belief that the general public will find interest in them. We hope that, in the present upsurge of culture in the United States, this book will find its place on the desks of cultured persons.

We are very grateful to each of the following journals for allowing us to reprint these articles: *Italica,* the outstanding periodical in the Italian language, for "Dante's Contribution to Aesthetics," "Dante and Courtly Language," "The Court of Heaven," "Realistic Elements in Tasso's *Aminta,*" "The Realistic Approach in the Evaluation of Romanticism," "Realism During the Romantic Age," "Alessandro Manzoni and the Realistic Novel," "Italian *Verismo,*" "The *Novecento,*" "Grazia Deledda and Her Early Literary Contacts," "Benedetto Croce and Criticism"; *The Romanic Review* for "Francesca da Rimini" and "Giacomo Leopardi's *L'Infinito,*" published at a time when there was much controversy over the interpretation of both of these topics; *Publications of the Modern Language Association of America* for "Leonardo Bruni Aretino and Humanism"; *Symposium* for "Luigi Pirandello as I Saw Him" and "The Historical Reality of the *Dolce Stil Nuovo* [Sweet New Style]" as well as "Dante's Love Concept"; *Letterature Moderne* for "Lights and Shadows in the *Vita Nuova*" and "Benedetto Croce and Luigi Pirandello"; *Mod-*

ix

ern Language Quarterly for "Giambattista Vico and Reality," published at a time when Vico was still unknown in this country; *The Modern Language Journal* for "Salutati's Letters to the Archbishop of Canterbury"; *The Pennsylvania Literary Review* for "Pirandello and the Concept of Reality"; and, lastly, Appleton-Century-Croft for allowing us to reprint our chapter on "Modern Italian Drama" included in their book *Modern Drama,* edited by Barrett Clark and George Friedly and published in 1947.

We wish to take this opportunity to express our appreciation to Ronald Lombardi and, in a particular way, to Robert Melzi for having made the first draft of the translation of "Lights and Shadows in the *Vita Nuova*" and "Giacomo Leopardi's *L'Infinito*." We have carefully edited and revised these translations to our full satisfaction.

High Points
in the
History of Italian Literature

Dante's Contribution to Aesthetics

D ANTE has been and is universally acclaimed a great poet.
His place in the field of aesthetics, however, is less known
and deserves further study.

Croce, in his *Estetica,* gives but scant attention to Dante and
believes the latter's contribution did not go beyond applying to
poetry in the vernacular [1] the four senses: literal, allegorical,
moral, and anagogical.

In sharp contrast to Croce's indifference toward Dante as an
art theorist stands the admiration that George Saintsbury bestows
on the poet. In his *History of Criticism* [2] referring to the *De
Vulgari Eloquentia,* he states: "For myself, I am prepared to
claim for it, not merely the position of the most important critical
document between Longinus and the seventeenth century at
least, but one of intrinsic importance on a line with that of the very
greatest critical documents of all history." [3] He even goes so far
as to claim the superiority of Dante's concept of poetry over that of
Wordsworth, as expressed in the preface to *Lyrical Ballads:*
"The contrast of the *De Vulgari Eloquio* and the Preface to the
Lyrical Ballads is so remarkable that it may be doubted whether
there is any more remarkable thing of the kind in literature." [4]
Stressing the importance of Dante's distinction between diction in
prose and poetic diction, the English critic characterizes Dante's
attitude thus: "The critic's attention is evidently from the first
fixed not exclusively, but, from the point of view of his business,
mainly, on questions of form, expression, result, rather than on
questions of matter, conception, plan." [5] Even more specifically
and clearly he explains Dante's efforts thus: "It is upon style and
diction that he bends his whole strength, and that he exhibits his
most novel, most important, most eternally valid criticism." [6]
Much as we admire Saintsbury's enthusiasm and sustained bril-

3

liancy, we feel that he has confused Dante with the rhetoricians of his time. Saintsbury himself states that Dante was led "to abandon the devices of the regular rhetoric and to construct, half-consciously, no doubt, a new and real Higher Rhetoric of the vulgar tongue itself." [7] Form was of paramount importance to the rhetoricians of Dante's time. It may even be stated that, having reduced poetry largely to form, they were interested in the latter even more than Dante,[8] but, unlike their great contemporary, they were insensitive to or indifferent toward content.

The weakness of Saintsbury's interpretation of Dante's critical views is revealed in his essay "Dante and the Grand Style," an address delivered before the members of the Dante Society on May 3, 1905.[9] In it, Saintsbury narrows down his analysis of the *Divine Comedy* to what he himself calls "minute illustrations" [10] of stylistic devices. He attempts to explain the beauty of many of Dante's famous lines through stress on vowel sounds rather than through the picture that they evoke, the feeling that they express, or the ideas that they convey. Though Saintsbury quotes Matthew Arnold's famous dictum "The grand style arises, when a noble nature, poetically gifted, treats with simplicity or severity a serious subject," [11] he fails in his critique of Dante to consider the essential element of the "serious subject."

If we turn to critics who have written at a time closer to our own, we find that the attitude toward Dante as an art theorist has not changed. E. G. Parodi, an illustrious Dante scholar, reduces Dante to a painstaking stylist on the assumption that for the great poet "la bella poesia consiste nella complessità e perfezione degli ornamenti retorici." [12] Allan Gilbert, in his *Literary Criticism: Plato to Dryden*, shares Croce's belief that Dante "tells us nothing especially significant" in criticism.[13]

The neglect of the speculative fruits of Dante's mind is all the more regrettable that he is wont to bring a fresh point of view and outlook even when he accepts, on the whole, traditional ideas. There is a well-known and oft-quoted passage in the *Convivio* which may be responsible for robbing Dante of a prominent place as a theorist of poetry, but which, if properly analyzed, shows how original Dante's mind was. In this passage the poet declares: "Le scritture si possono intendere e deonsi esponere massimamente per quattro sensi." [14] It is this passage that led Croce to deny Dante any prominence in his *Estetica*. In the first place, Dante was not referring here to the task of the poet but to that of the critic or commentator of poetry. He repeated here, in general terms, the theory that was universally accepted in his day by men of learning and by such official agencies of culture as the universities and the Church. [15] In a book such as the *Convivio*, motivated as it was by political considerations, Dante, then in exile, had to conform to conservative views if he wanted to succeed in his effort to appear a man of learning, unjustly banished from his beloved Florence. [16] Nevertheless, his originality appears in the remarks that he chances to make on the four senses. Very revealing is the stress that he gives to the literal sense: "Sempre lo letterale dee andare innanzi, si come quello ne la cui sentenza li altri sono inchiusi." [17] Dante uses in this passage the term "literal meaning" much as a modern critic would use the term "action" or "content" of literature. He declares that he is primarily interested in the literal and the allegorical senses and only incidentally in the moral and anagogical ones. [18] In the discussion of the allegorical sense, Dante establishes a significant distinction between allegory as understood by theologians and allegory as interpreted by poets. In the example of Orpheus, who with his lyre tamed wild beasts, he points out the ethical significance of the myth and not the religious one, as a theologian would have done. [19] The distinction is most important in that it shows how lay thinkers such as Dante, even though deeply religious, were asserting their independence from theologians at the time when lay culture was trying to emancipate itself from the theological civilization of the preceding age.

The thesis that we wish to propose is that Dante's significance rests on his consideration of content as the determining factor of artistic form in poetry. It is through this fact that Dante leaves the precincts of rhetoric and enters the field of aesthetics. Both the second book of the *De Vulgari Eloquentia* and several passages of the *Divine Comedy* allow us to reconstruct Dante's theory of art. In the first book of *De Vulgari Eloquentia* he sharply divides the illustrious vernacular from the coarse dialects of the various regions of Italy; in the second book he draws an equally sharp distinction between courtly poetry and popular poetry. The example of an ugly woman bedecked in silk and gold, whose ugliness is accentuated by precious metal and exquisite material, shows how sharply Dante divided noble content and language from their opposites. To tragic or noble style he attributed deep thoughts (*gravitas sententiae*), magnificent and winged metrical form (*superbia carminum*), stately disposition of parts (*constructionis elatio*), and well-chosen and noble words (*excellentia vocabulorum*); to comic style, he reserved the ordinary vocabulary (*quandoque mediocre, quandoque umile vulgare sumatur*).[20] Dante conducted his investigation by using the Aristotelian terminology of tragic and comic styles, but the basis of his distinction was strictly ethical. Noble poetry was to deal with a noble content, that is, with life envisaged as a universal entity, a pure concept free from the whims and imperfections of what is accidental. It is on this basis that he concluded that courtly poetry should deal only with the useful (Salus), the pleasurable (Venus), and the rational (Virtus), "dum nullo accidente vilescant."[21] Through the consideration of the close relation between content and form, Dante reached a theory of poetry that makes the *De Vulgari Eloquentia* a truly significant book and testifies to the speculative quality of its author. Dante's theory can be expressed thus: *Poetry is conditioned by the subject matter that it expresses. A noble content needs a noble language and a noble metric form; a mediocre and common subject needs a mediocre and common language, written in simple rhyme.* This belief is the core of the *De Vulgari Eloquentia*. The other sections which deal with division and choice of words, with the number of syllables and variety of meters, are a consequence of this central intuition based on the ethical or vulgar content of poetry.

Did Dante follow this theory in writing the *Divine Comedy?* We believe that the poet follows the critic as much as this is the case in every poet, ancient or modern. Unquestionably there are parts in the *Divine Comedy* that go beyond any critical theorizing on poetry. To attempt to explain the whole of the *Divine Comedy* only in terms of the theories of the *De Vulgari Eloquentia* or the *Convivio* is like attempting to explain the universe in terms of what Ptolemy wrote in his *Almagest.* Poetry and theory of poetry in Dante's day, as in our own time, are related only in part. A critic can and should refer to a theory only when the poet gives evidence of having, for artistic reasons, made use of it. In the *Divine Comedy* Dante gives ample evidence of his concern with this theory. The structure of the *Divine Comedy,* its ethical life sense correspond to Dante's ideas as expressed in his theoretical writings. The aesthetic values of the three canticles, for example, were established by him on the ethical and spiritual values of their content. The invocations herein testify, with their rising tone, to Dante's feeling that a more noble form was needed to express the nobler reality that confronted him. If, in the *Inferno,* he invokes the muses, in the *Purgatorio,* besides the muses he invokes Calliope, the muse of epic poetry, and, in the *Paradiso,* he addresses a very elaborate invocation to Apollo himself. In his success as a poet in properly expressing the subject of the last cantica he even dreams of being crowned poet laureate and of opening a new era of poetry. To him the poetry of *Purgatory* was higher than that of *Hell,* and that of *Paradise* higher than that of *Purgatory.*

In the light of his theory, qualifications that he gave to poetry are very meaningful. Thus, in calling the poetry of *Hell* "dead" (*morta*), he not only referred to the fact that it dealt with souls who were dead in that the vision of God was denied to them, but he also took into consideration the aesthetic quality of his poetry. The statement "Or qui la morta poesí risurga" [22] at the very

beginning of *Purgatorio* implies that the poetry of the first
canticle, in that it dealt with Hell, lay in the abysmal depths of
the infernal regions. If Dante called the poetry of *Hell* "dead,"
he called "sweet" (*dolce*) that of the school of which he considered Guinizelli the father and himself the highest representative.
Later in life, while writing the *Purgatorio,* he spoke in an unforgettable way of the *Dolce Stil Nuovo* in his imaginary meeting with
a poet of the old school, Bonagiunta Urbiciani.[23] To him the
poetry of the *Vita Nuova* was *dolce* because it possessed a sublime unity between the inner harmony of its content, his lofty
love for Beatrice, and the musicality and perfection of the form
that her inspiration gave to it. Dante sought that unity throughout his artistic career even in later years when youth was only a
memory. In fact, echoes of the *Dolce Stil Nuovo* are found in the
Divine Comedy, the book of his mature years, under the guise
of the courtly language that Dante uses whenever he meets
characters deserving admiration or love: Francesca, Pier della
Vigna, Brunetto. The description of the divine forest at the top
of the mountain of Purgatory bears the characteristics of the
poetry of nature of the *Vita Nuova*, just as many of the women
whom he met and described in his immortal journey reflect the
exquisite qualities that he lent to the ideal woman of his youth.
This is particularly true of Matelda, whom he meets in the forest
of Purgatory before Beatrice appears. She is so delicately sketched
that she seems to have struck the unerring fancy of Chaucer. In
the *Knight's Tale*, the scene of Emily in the garden when she
appeared before the dismayed eyes of Palamon is definitely
reminiscent of the picture of Matelda drawn as she gathered
flowers and sang in the divine forest.[24]

The presence of exquisite words in the *Vita Nuova* and in the
central parts of the *Purgatorio* and the *Paradiso* was as logical as
that of low words in the *Inferno*, but had Dante not established
in the *Vulgari Eloquentia* that "most excellent poets" should use
only the exquisite words of the illustrious vernacular? [25] Why,
then, the very low words that are found in the *Inferno?* The

theorist in Dante was compelled to trail behind his poetic genius, but there was always compromise and never complete capitulation. Canto XXX of the *Inferno* in which is depicted the brawl between Maestro Adamo and Sinone, a brawl that Dante enjoyed to the utmost and which he presented with crude faithfulness, is a perfect example of this compromise. Dante, the theorist, conscious of having departed from his noble style, makes Virgil voice disapproval as the latter scolds him bitterly; but Dante, the poetic genius, had, nevertheless, intuitively reached realism and had abandoned himself to it.

The clearest example of Dante's concern with his theory is found in Canto XXXII of the *Inferno*. When the poet enters the circle of the traitors, he tarries as if to gage whether his poetic gifts are equal to the stupendous task that he has assigned to himself: that of describing the awe-inspiring grandeur of Cocitus. His opening words lament the fact that he does not possess jarring and raucous rhymes as would be befitting the wicked hole toward which converge the rocky slopes of Hell.[26] It is evident that here Dante follows the tenet that a ghastly reality, to be fully represented, must be expressed through common and jarring words. He gives additional proof of his concern with this principle when he invokes the muses to grant him such power as to make his poetic diction equal to the reality which he wishes to depict.[27]

Very significant to this effect is also the tercet in the *Purgatorio:*

Lettor, tu vedi ben com'io innalzo
   La mia matera; e però con più arte
   Non ti maravigliar s'io la rincalzo.

My reader, you clearly see how I raise
   The subject of my song; therefore, do not marvel
   If I strengthen it with greater art.[28]

Dante was now at the door of *Purgatory* and the artist was conscious that as the *matera* rose higher, his art, too, should soar to keep pace with it.

The fact that Dante speculated about art should cause no

wonder. Many and often-quoted passages in the *Divine Comedy* testify to his artistic awareness. He confided to his reader (and this in the *Paradiso*) that often, in art, the finished product falls short of the intentions of the artist because the material under his hands is rebellious or insensitive to the intentions of the molder.[29] He also speaks of the *abito dell'arte*,[30] the skill and technique of the artist, and of the *fren dell'arte*,[31] a check imposed on him by art as to the proportions of his canticles.

The examples in the first ledge of *Purgatory* have always interested us as documents of the clear consciousness possessed by Dante that art is representation of reality. The excellence of the examples engraved in the glistening marble of the first ledge of *Purgatory* is predicated on the ground that they are so realistically executed as to lead one to the illusion of facing an actual reality. Of the angel of the Annunciation, Dante says that one would have sworn that it said "Ave." In the example of David, the poet is so overcome by the perfection of the engraved figure that his hearing and sight are in conflict as to whether David was actually singing or not, just as his sense of smell and that of sight were uncertain whether the incense in the scene was real or not.[32] These examples all point to an unconscious naturalism on the part of Dante, which carried him beyond the theoretical positions voiced in the *De Vulgari Eloquentia*. It is hard to find a clearer document of realistic art than the statement in *Purgatorio:*

> Morti li morti e i vivi parean vivi.
> Non vide me' di me chi vide il vero.

> The dead seemed dead and the living seemed alive.
> He who saw actual life did not see better than I.[33]

It may not be amiss to consider briefly the value that Dante gives the term *vero* (true). It is certain that he often uses it in the traditional sense, referring to spiritual truth hidden under the veil of poetry. In the *Convivio* [34] truth is identified with the allegorical sense. Reality is in the allegory and it is to be sought behind the events narrated, which makes of poetry a "beautiful lie." In the *Divine Comedy*, too, truth is treated in a few instances in the same fashion.[35] But it is equally certain that Dante uses *vero* in our own sense, identifying it with the tangible and controllable world. If allegorical truth interested the philosopher and the teacher in Dante, the literal truth attracted the attention of the artist. In the third ledge of *Purgatory*, where the envious are punished, Dante sees, in a sort of ecstasy, visions embodying examples of meekness. He describes his awakening from his ecstasy thus:

> Quando l'anima mia tornò di fuori
>   Alle cose che son fuori di lei *vere*,
>   I' riconobbi i miei non falsi errori.

> When my soul returned outside
>   To the *true* things that are outside of it,
>   I recognized my non-false errors.[36]

Here the term *vere* evidently refers to the external and natural reality. These contrasting uses of this term seem to be contradictory, but they can be explained if we consider that Dante accepted phenomena as true in the tangible world, and gave a transcendental, though none the less true, value to the spiritual aspects of life.

In closing, it is our hope that we have succeeded in showing that, in the thirteenth century, one witnesses, side by side with the study of rhetoric, the dawn of aesthetics. If so, a new chapter should be added to the history of aesthetics by considering the contribution made in the thirteenth century. Such a study would make more understandable the existence of great poetry in the age of Dante. It seems, in fact, unbelievable that such significant poets as Guinizelli, Cavalcanti, and Cino da Pistoia could have appeared without any attempt being made at a theoretical study of poetry.[37] The reconstruction of Dante's art theory also vindicates for him the distinction of having extricated poetry from the narrow boundaries of the Trivium that he and his generation accepted and revered. In the Trivium and Quadrivium there was no place for poetry as individual creation nor for the new activities, such as medicine and law, that had evolved in the new society of the eleventh, twelfth, and thirteenth centuries. Dante, although educated according to the traditional curriculum, placed himself, quite consciously, through his theory of art, outside the cramming boundaries of the Trivium, and paved the way for the new learning of the Renaissance. He felt clearly and keenly the distance that separated him from the official rhetoricians of his time to whom he denied the right of calling themselves "literati." [38]

The Historical Reality of the
Dolce Stil Nuovo (Sweet New Style)

THIS brief note on the *Dolce Stil Nuovo* is meant to seek the specific and exact interpretation that can be given to the well-known meeting of Dante in the *Purgatorio* with a rhymester of the previous generation, Bonagiunta Urbiciani.

During these last years there has prevailed the tendency of doubting the historical value of the term *Dolce Stil Nuovo* as used by Dante in Canto XXIV of the *Purgatorio*. The most illustrious critic of Italian letters in America, Ernest Hatch Wilkins, in his *History of Italian Literature*, published in 1954, and Francesco Flora, a very authoritative student of Italian literature, in his *Storia della letteratura italiana* (1940–42), have cast aside the use of this harmonious denomination in qualifying the poetry of young Dante and of the Florentine poets of the last decades of the thirteenth century. Our aim is to see what meaning can be given to the term *Dolce Stil Nuovo* in the above-mentioned encounter and what consequences can be derived from such an interpretation.

Dante contrasted very sharply and passionately the verse of the new poets with that of the Sicilian school, represented by Notaio Jacopo of Lentini, as well as the later verse of Guittone of Arezzo, Bonagiunta Urbiciani, and others whom he does not mention. Thus, three well-defined poetic modes are presented in the episode: that of the Sicilian poets in the court of Frederick II, that of the followers of Guittone, and that of the poet himself and his friends. In Dante's estimation, the content of the poetry that appeared before that of the Florentine group was identical with that of Guinizelli, Cavalcanti, Dante himself, and their young friends. The difference that created a sort of un-

13

fathomable abyss between the old and the new poetry was the absence of sentiment in the love verse of the older generations.

Old Bonagiunta, by implication qualified by the younger poet as a mediocre songster, was compelled to declare:

> O frate, issa vegg'io, diss'egli, il nodo
> Ch'l Notaio, e Guittone, e me ritenne
> Di qua dal dolce stil nuovo ch'io odo.

> Brother, now I see the difficulty
> That kept the Notary, Guittone, and myself
> From reaching the Sweet New Style that I now hear.

He was made to acknowledge with mortifying modesty that Jacopo of Lentini, Guittone, and he himself were very formalistic and conventional, while the new poets had harkened to the voices of their heart so that in their verse there glowed the flame of true love.

There is no doubt that Dante looked here at the past, recalling the days of his distant youth. Its remembrance was so vivid as to lead him to revoke the figure of Guido Guinizelli, his model in lyricism, and to add words that revealed a contemptuous attitude toward those who had preceded him in writing courtly verse. It is also evident that Dante had in mind the type of poetry exemplified by the *canzone*, which constitutes the keystone of the *Vita Nuova, Donne ch'avete intelletto d'Amore* (Ladies who possess understanding of Love), the most renowned *canzone* that he had written before 1292, the probable date of the composition of the *Vita Nuova*.

Without any trace of false modesty and with the frankness that is characteristic of him, Dante forced the old rhymester to call him

> Colui che fuore
> Trasse le nuove rime, cominciando:
> *Donne ch'avete intelletto d'Amore.*

> He who brought forth
> The new rhymes, beginning:
> *Ladies who possess understanding of Love.*

The new poetics that Dante revealed to Bonagiunta are well known:

> Io mi son un che, quanto
> Amore spira, noto, ed in quel modo
> Ch'ei detta dentro, vo' significando.

> I am one who, when
> Love passes like a wind, takes notices,
> And gives faithful expression to what Love dictates
> within my heart.

It is logical to ask whether this poetic theory had illumined the poetry of Dante's youth or whether Dante was lending to the rhymes of former years the theoretical approach that he had reached in the years of his thoughtful maturity, at the time when he was enclosing in the sublime forms of the *Commedia* his ill-repressed outbursts of disdain, wrath, and hatred, using "raucous and jarring rhymes."

This is the *nodo*, the pivot of the question, and we hasten to add that we are taking into consideration only the theoretical aspect of the question, and not the poetic quality of the poetry of Dante's youth. The value of the latter will shine forever in the annals of poetic art as the reflection of a time in the poet's life in which, in the midst of theoretical uncertainty and technical experimentation, the young Dante wrote the divine sonnets *Tanto gentile e tanto onesta pare* (So exquisite and so stately seems my Lady) and *Negli occhi porta la mia donna Amore* (Love abides in my Lady's eyes), sublimations of a poetic world where every mind open to the charm and musicality of beautiful poetry will always find a haven of peace and joy. Who will ever doubt the beauty of the sonnet *Guido, vorrei che tu e Lapo ed io* (Guido, I should wish that you, Lapo, and I), an idyllic creation, free of every preoccupation of scientific, doctrinal, or philosophical nature? Who will ever forget the charm of the poem, lost among the *Rime pietrose* (Stony Rhymes), where the poet sings:

Per una ghirlandetta ch'io vidi,
Mi farà sospirar ogni fiore.

For a tiny garland that I once saw,
Every flower will make me sigh.

From a cultural standpoint three well-defined zones appear in Dante's works: the one that guided the composition of the *Vita Nuova*, in which is reflected the admiration and predilection of Dante for both classical and Provençal poetry; the section represented by the theories presented in the *De Vulgari Eloquentia*, written during the first years of the poet's exile; and that to be found in the *Commedia*, in which the fullness of his thought and his poetic power are clearly visible.

In passing from the *Vita Nuova* to the *Commedia* weighty changes are observable. In the *Vita Nuova*, the work of Dante's youth, the love concept therein expressed was lent to him by Guido Guinizelli. One finds the documentation of this in the sonnet *Amore e cor gentil sono una cosa* (Love and a gentle heart are one and the same thing).[1] Here Guinizelli was given the title of *saggio* (the man who knows), a reflection of the doctrinal concept of poetry. Theoretically speaking, the same love concept abided in the *Commedia*, though totally new aspects of his mind and genius appeared in the immortal poem. Here, although he called Guinizelli "father," Dante was so conscious of the significance of his work as to declare that he had surpassed both Guinizelli and Cavalcanti.[2] The old Guinizelli was declared to be not as original as Cavalcanti, the younger poet, and Dante's most intimate friend. In the *Commedia* Virgil became the master and model of the poet, his only author, and the one on whom he had patterned the style that had given him honor.

Entering more directly the field of aesthetic ideas, one must conclude that in the *Commedia*, in its theoretical aspect, Dante has departed not only from the aesthetic ideas of the *Vita Nuova*, but also from those exposed in the *De Vulgari Eloquentia*. In the latter book, Dante had concluded that content determines poetic form,[3] a theory that he repeatedly applied in the verse of the *Commedia*, but in reality, the great poem, to whose creation both heaven and earth had contributed, cannot be reduced entirely to the theories of the *De Vulgari Eloquentia*. In the *Commedia* the poet used not only "melodious rhymes," but also those "jarring and raucous" so that his "poetic diction would not be different" from the reality of the Cocytus that he was about to depict.[4]

If Dante had already formulated the theory of the "melodious rhymes" (*rime dolci e gentili*) when he wrote the *Vita Nuova*, he would most probably have included it in Chapter XXV together with the historical data on poetry that he gathered there. Judging from the philosophical and doctrinal character of *Donne ch'avete intelletto d'Amore*, one must conclude that, at the time of the composition of the *Vita Nuova*, his concept of poetry was still doctrinal. His ideal pattern of lyric poetry at that time was Guinizelli's *canzone*, *Al cor gentil repara sempre Amore, Siccome face augello in la verdura* (In the gentle heart Love always seeks shelter, as a bird does in the green forest). It is not without reason that the poet, in the years subsequent to the writing of the *Vita Nuova*, wrote the philosophical *canzoni* now collected in his *Rime*. He held them in such great esteem that he wrote for three of them a commentary in his *Convivio*. These *canzoni* were deeply philosophical, and in them, side by side with charmingly melodious verse, one hears lines expressing rigorous and ironclad syllogisms, bristling with concepts. There is too much reasoning, excessive eloquence, often even rhetoric, for us to apply to them the denomination of *Dolce Stil Nuovo*.

What we claim is that in the last years of the Duecento there still prevailed the identification of poetry and doctrine. If we observe the annals of the poetry of those years, we shall find that each great poet of that time penned a *canzone* in which Love was discussed with dialectical rigor. We quote several of these *tours de force* of poetical composition on which rested the fame of the poets. Guinizelli wrote the one already mentioned above,

Al cor gentil repara sempre Amore.[5] Dante was the author of the canzone, *Donne ch'avete intelletto d'Amore.*[6] Cavalcanti wrote the famous but obscure *Donna mi prega perch'io voglio dire* (A Lady requests me and I wish to sing).[7] If this be true, the term *Dolce Stil Nuovo* was created by Dante when he, in his mature age, looked nostalgically at the years of his youth and the verse then composed. In the years around 1295, when Dante and his friends sought in poetry a refuge from the bitter and even bloody political struggles in which they engaged, that name did not echo in the poetic circles of Florence. It resounded for the first time on the sixth ledge of the *Purgatorio* during the poet's conversation with Bonagiunta.

Even if one gives to the term *Dolce Stil Nuovo* the philosophical content that Dante gave to Love in the *De Vulgari Eloquentia* and in the *Commedia* (Love as fruit of spiritual perfection), theoretically and strictly speaking there was no trace of the universality of this concept in the *Vita Nuova* and in his early writings. One must go to the later philosophical *canzoni* to find the identification of moral perfection with perfect love. The so-called *sonetti del gabbo* (mocking sonnets in the *Vita Nuova*, in which Beatrice is portrayed at very close range, making fun of her trembling suitor with her women friends) and the sonnets exchanged with Forese Donati are very far from any universality of inspiration. The poet was too close to his experience as a youth whose love was not requited by Beatrice that he might feel love in the light of spiritual perfection, a height that he reached only when he could look at his experience with detachment and serenity.

The great lyric poetry of the end of the Duecento flowered spontaneously, independently of the theories of the time. Only later, while Dante was penning the diary of his soul in the *Commedia,* did the poet reach, through a sublime intuition, the conclusion that poetry is sentiment, a conclusion that the romanticists of the nineteenth century accepted as the central canon of their art. In speaking to Bonagiunta, this conclusion made Dante conscious of the contempt that he had always entertained for the abstract verse of the Sicilian poets and for the heavy and unpolished verse of Guittone of Arezzo. Probably such an intuitive view of poetry came to him from his own experience as a poet, when he realized that the real verse that he had written after the *Vita Nuova* was melodious and spontaneous, very different from that which included abstract thoughts and cold syllogisms.

These remarks on the famous encounter of Dante and Bonagiunta aim at offering a more accurate and rigorously historical approach to the poetic flowering of the late thirteenth century. Our conclusions do not question the beauty of the poetry of the Florentine group, but it is dutiful to recognize that if the term *Dolce Stil Nuovo* was fashioned by Dante only when the literary experiences of his youth were but a sweet memory, around 1300, there existed no theory that accompanied the poetry of the late Duecento. This was beautiful, simply because the Florentine group was formed of true poets. It owed its significance to the poetic instinct of two great lyric poets: Guido Cavalcanti and his greater friend Dante Alighieri.

Dante and Courtly Language

DANTE'S *De Vulgari Eloquentia* has generally been looked upon as a work of pure linguistics. We are proposing the thesis that it is an important book on aesthetics. For us, Dante offers in it a theoretical treatment of the nature of poetry, such as he realized in writing the *Vita Nuova* and his philosophical *canzoni*, works that corresponded to his concept of courtly poetry. We restate this theory, for *repetita iuvant*.

Did Dante possess a clear, theoretical idea of poetry? Does he not deserve, not only the place that he assigned to himself in the Limbus among the greatest poets that the world had known up to that time, but also a place among the writers on aesthetics, that posterity has not yet given to him? If we follow the conclusions of the great critic and historian of aesthetics, Benedetto Croce,[1] Dante's contribution to aesthetics did not go beyond the application of the four senses to any work of poetry: literal, allegorical, moral, and anagogical. George Saintsbury,[2] in his admirable *History of Criticism*, reduces Dante to a rhetorician, new, magnificent, and original, but a rhetorician nevertheless. We believe that Dante, in speaking of the four senses, refers to the function of critics and not to the nature of poetry. He discusses poetry in other passages of his works, but Croce has not taken these into consideration in the history of aesthetic ideas. As to the connection between Dante and the rhetoricians of his time, the poet draws a sharp distinction between rhetorics that has practical aims and is also applicable to prose, and poetry which antecedes prose and is superior to it. The *prosaicantes* (prose writers), according to him, derive from the *inventores* (creative poets), and not vice versa. So proclaims the poet in the beginning of the second book of the *De Vulgari Eloquentia*, precisely when he is about to formulate the problem of true poetry by investigating its nature and prescribing its forms as to content, language, and metrics.

Dante did not greatly admire either the rhetoricians, who reduced poetry to a mere stylistic exercise, or the men of letters of his time, whose souls were not kindled by the flame that glowed in his own. To the latter are addressed the flaying words in the *Convivo:* "E a vituperio di loro dico che non si deono chiamare litterati, però che non acquistano la lettera per lo suo uso, ma in quanto per quella guadagnano denari o dignitate; sì come non si dee chiamare citarista chi tiene la cetera in casa per prestarla per prezzo, e non per usarla per suonare." (And to their shame I say that they should not call themselves men of letters for they do not acquire knowledge for its own sake but to gain money and honors through it; precisely as he, who has a harp in his house in order to rent it out, and not to use it himself, should not call himself a harpist.) [3] He vents his contempt against the same literati when, in his *Inferno,* he assigns them to the circle of the sodomites:

> Insomma sappi che tutti fur cherci
> e litterati grandi e di gran fama,
> d'un peccato medesmo al mondo lerci.

> In short, know that they were all clerks
> and great and very famous literati
> filthy in the world of the same sin.[4]

Among these sinners he places the grammarian Prisciano and the innovator of juridical studies, Francesco d'Accorso.

Dante lived a very lonely and disdainful existence. His bitter solitude was engendered, not only by the political struggles in which he engaged, but also by the religious and literary clashes in which he became involved. A child of democratic Florence, he saw himself forced to make a common cause with the aristocratic Whites, whose political faith was not superior to that of the Blacks, the original party of his family. Although a most religious man, he was compelled to fight the papacy. In the field of art he was contemptuously aware of the contrast between the type of poetry that pleased the common people and that which enjoyed the favor of cultured persons. He felt that there was not much to choose between those who *turpiter barbarizant* (write poetry in a revolting and barbaric manner) and the cold and abstract type of poetry that Guittone had offered to the generation that preceded his own.

It seems to us that the central problem of the *De Vulgari Eloquentia* is not only that of proclaiming the vernacular a lofty medium of expression, but also, and especially, that of presenting the pattern of a new poetry that would be equidistant from both the banality of popular verse and the abstract poems of the admirers and followers of Guittone of Arezzo. Dante announces to the cultured men of his generation the importance of poetry. He feels widely separated from them in that they accepted only the disciplines enclosed in the Trivium and Quadrivium, the school curriculum of his time, to which poetry had not yet been assigned a place. His book is the first document in which the new generations born into the Italian vernacular claim the rights of poetry through Dante in the *De Vulgari Eloquentia*.

Compelled to choose between Latin, a most illustrious but dead language, and the vernacular which was still in its infancy and was spoken in rough and jarring dialects, Dante chooses the language of cultured persons, the language whose usage places one higher than counts and lords. But in so doing Dante goes beyond the simple consideration of language. He focuses his attention on the content of poetry and designates for the new poetry three fundamental themes: Salus, the safety of one's country, assigned to epic; Venus, Love, and moral perfection; and Virtus, reserved for lyric poetry. He adds to his statement one of those subtle and significant distinctions that allow great minds to accept universal terms without falling into generical classifications: "purchè [queste tre realtà] non siano rese vili da ciò che è accidentale in esse" (provided these three realities are not offended by what is accidental in them).[5]

Dante is clearly conscious that it is necessary to reject both the unbridled naturalism of popular literature and the abstract quality of the courtly poetry of those who had preceded him. The statement referring to the necessity of keeping the themes treated by courtly poets on a high level, away from the relativity that absolute realities acquire when they are steeped in the actual experience of human life, is evidently directed more against naturalism than against the abstractions of courtly poets. Dante openly declares himself against the abstract quality of the poetry of the high style of his time when, a few years later, he had his imaginary conversation with Bonagiunta Urbiciani, a poet of the old school, on the sixth ledge of *Purgatorio*. In the *De Vulgari Eloquentia*, a book directed to the learned people of his time, and, therefore, written in Latin, he could not speak of the magic afflatus of poetry, nor of poetry as a free expression of personal sentiment. His readers would not have understood him and would have accused him of being ignorant. He wrote his essay as a man of learning addressing himself to learned men.

The thesis that Dante fashions for himself in writing the *De Vulgari Eloquentia*, and that slowly but clearly emerges from his ironclad and subtle use of syllogisms, starts from the consideration of the harmonious relationship that exists between ethical and aesthetic values: "ciò che è buono si confà agli uomini degni, ciò che è migliore si confà ai più degni e eiò che è ottimo ai degnissimi" (what is good is becoming worthy men, what is better is becoming worthier men, and what is best is becoming the most worthy).[6] Dante believed that man is not moved by natural instincts, but that he acts according to reason.[7] In this he followed the classical approach and conceptual manner of thinking. He was classical without ever forgetting actual experience. He felt close to daily needs and obligations, and wrote as one who tried to harmonize natural instincts and reason by lifting the natural toward the height of the ideal. He calls this to live *rationaliter* (according to reason). Since there is a close relation among all the attributes and actions of man, it follows that rationality governs the realm of poetry, too.

The intrinsic value of the *De Vulgari Eloquentia* does not

rest on the fact that Dante calls the endecasyllable the meter most suitable to Italian verse, although history has confirmed this belief of his, nor on his detailed study of the Italian vocabulary, and his painstaking and subtle division of the various words into distinct categories: childish, effeminate, virile, harmonious, and many others. No doubt these conclusions of his keen and observing mind are admirable, but they do not constitute the living and truly new part of the *De Vulgari Eloquentia*.

The significant and original part of the essay consists for us in the fact that Dante looks upon poetry as an indissoluble whole: content and form, vocabulary and metric. He reaches this unified and intimate relationship by the mental habit of thinking clearly and fearlessly, a habit which guided him throughout his life and determined also his aesthetic ideas. His division of poetry into courtly and popular, into tragic and comic style, rests on his belief that beauty is related to ethics and ugliness to immorality. He establishes the identity of ethics and beauty in clear terms, and returns repeatedly to stress this identity. This is more than a purely aesthetic conclusion for the poet. He had followed the habit of clearly dividing good and bad all his life. When a mere youth it had helped him to mark his own path, a narrow road on which he advanced almost alone, and, later, during the years of his exile, it consoled his loneliness with the proud conviction of having created his own party, free from any tie with the Whites and Blacks.

The very significant corollary that he derives from the identity of ethics and beauty is the conclusion that, in the art of poetry, content determines form. A true and lofty poet can sing only of a lofty love. The new poetry that he envisages in the *De Vulgari Eloquentia* should relinquish vulgar love affairs to the immature and rough songsters of popular verse. It should possess depth of thought (*gravitas sententiae*), a grand style (*superbia carminum*), a winged metrical form (*constructionis elatio*), and nobility of vocabulary (*eccelentia vocabulorum*).[8] This theory clearly explains why he referred, in the *Purgatorio*, to the poetry of his youth and that of his Florentine friends as

Dolce Stil Nuovo (Sweet New Life). Sweet does not refer only to the harmonious quality of their verse, but it includes its content as well. Their poetry sang of a perfect love, Love with a capital letter, in perfection of form, by cutting away the angular nature of passion and giving to love the vaporous quality of dream.

This style referred especially to the content and form of the *Vita Nuova* where, at the very beginning, Dante proclaimed that he consciously wished to keep away from the *parlare fabuloso* (the type of art typical of popular poetry). In penning the *Vita Nuova*, a book dedicated to the memory of Beatrice and his love for her, he felt in an exalted mood and wished to transcribe only "the words that are written in my memory under greater headings." [9]

The term "courtly language," when applied to Dante, must be interpreted in the light of the documents that the poet has left to us. It must be used in a precise and restricted sense. Courtly language is synonymous for Dante with perfect language and poetry. It is the language capable of expressing the love of "gentle hearts." It is the language of love lyrics. It is not only the language therein used, but also the lyric itself; and not all lyric poetry, but only that of the *Vita Nuova* and of the *Canzoni morali*, written in the poet's youth. In fact, in the famous meeting with Bonagiunta, the Sweet New Style is identified only with the central *canzone* of the *Vita Nuova: Donne ch'avete intelletto d'Amore* (Ladies who have an understanding of Love), whose composition preceded the writing of the *Commedia* by several years. The lyrics quoted in the *De Vulgari Eloquentia* are taken from those of the Provençal poets and Dante's friends.

It is natural to ask whether the courtly ideal disappeared when Dante set out to write his *Commedia*, a work that aimed at encompassing a vaster world, infinitely vaster than the one used in the verse of his youth. In the *Commedia*, the poet was face to face with a quite different artistic problem and task: the consideration of the awesome countenance of evil, that in the *Vita Nuova* had been consciously excluded from his art. In the

Commedia, Dante accepts, it is difficult to say whether consciously or unconsciously, the words that in the *De Vulgari Eloquentia* were specifically excluded: *femina, corpo, mamma, babbo,* and many others of a much lower nature.

This fact should not lead us to conclude that in the *Commedia* the theory of courtly language outlined in the *De Vulgari Eloquentia* is completely repudiated. That theory echoes in many parts of the poem and casts its diaphanous shadow over its verse.

The *Commedia* is the meeting place of numerous and most different currents and trends. The reader sees them in the poem in very clearly differentiated strata. The poet makes use of them as he feels the need of them in terms of the subject matter that he treats. One finds in the *Commedia* the traditional statement of the didactic aim of poetry, poetry as the veil of truth, poetry as a pleasing and tuneful lie. But there are also sudden and unexpected outbursts of poetical intuition such as that revealed to Bonagiunta concerning the value of spontaneity in poetry.[10] There are even more extraordinary aesthetic anticipations in the *Commedia.* Thus, in the Cocytus, Dante offers a definition of art that seems to be an echo of contemporary naturalism. It is amazing to read this line in *Inferno* XXXII:

Sì che dal fatto il dir non sia diverso.

So that my poetic diction may not be different from the actual reality.[11]

The term *vero* (true) is ever present in the poet's mind, and it echoes repeatedly in the *Purgatorio.* In describing the examples of punished pride engraved on the floor of the ledge where the sinners slowly walk under enormous weights he writes:

Non vide me' di me chi vide *il vero.*

He who saw the actual model did not see better than I.[12]

The poet is perfectly aware of the function of art in reproducing as closely as possible the details of actual reality. The reader, however, will find even in the *Commedia* remains of the theory presented in the *De Vulgari Eloquentia:* content determines the form of poetry. When Dante is about to enter Cocytus, he is so dominated by the horror of the place that he breaks forth into the unforgettable lines:

> S'io avessi le rime ed aspre e chiocce
>   come si converrebbe al tristo buco
>   sovra il quale pontan tutte l'altre rocce,
> I' premerei di mio concetto il suco
>   piu' pienamente: ma poichè non l'abbo
>   non senza tema a dicer mi conduco.

> If I had at my disposal jarring and raucous rhymes
>   as are befitting the awesome hole
>   where converge all other rocks,
> I should squeeze out the juice of my concept (express)
>   more fully: but since I don't have them,
>   not without fear I set out to write my verse.[13]

It is very evident here that Dante realizes and proclaims the close relation existing between the awesome grandeur of the *Inferno* and the poetic form that it is required of the poet who set out to express it. There the melodious words, the sweet rhymes used in expressing a lofty love yield their place to jarring and raucous rhymes, necessary to express the fearful atmosphere of the place. The content has become infinitely wider in the *Commedia,* but the theory of the *De Vulgari Eloquentia* has remained intact. The line quoted above, "so that my poetic diction may not be different from the actual reality," receives clarity from the theory of the close relation between content and form, even if one admits that Dante reached out toward us men of today, encompassing a wider sphere than that found in the *De Vulgari Eloquentia.*

The influence or residuum of the theory of the *De Vulgari Eloquentia* is also reflected in the value that the poet assigns to the three canticles that compose the *Commedia.* He calls *morta* (dead) the poetry of the *Inferno* when in *Purgatorio* he states: "ma qui la morta poesì risurga" (let now the dead poetry rise again).[14] To him the poetry of *Purgatorio* is higher than that of *Inferno* because its subject matter is loftier. It follows that, to the poet, the poetry of *Paradiso* touches the pinnacle of poetic significance, precisely because of the loftiness of content of the third canticle.

An evident proof of this evaluation can be found in the invocation of the three canticles, which acquire a higher and more winged tone and character as the poet passes through the three kingdoms. In the *Inferno*, Dante asks for the help of the Muses; in the *Purgatorio* he invokes that of Calliope, and in the *Paradiso* he proclaims that Apollo himself is his helmsman.

The poet is very conscious of the ascending character of his art, and this can be widely documented in the poem. In *Purgatorio* one reads:

> Lettor, tu vedi ben com'io innalzo
> La mia materia; e però con più arte
> Non ti meravigliar s'io la rincalzo.

> Reader, you clearly see how I raise
> My subject matter, and, therefore,
> Do not marvel if I strengthen it with greater art.[15]

Even the *Inferno* offers numerous examples of courtly language. The second canto is truly that of the court of heaven, where much of the action is pictured by the poet. Lucia, who addresses Beatrice, Beatrice who speaks to Virgil, and Virgil who feels the charm of Beatrice's eyes, especially when tears shine in them and increase their luminosity, are typical examples of courtly life expressed in courtly terms and situations. The presence of these elements creates an oasis of pure lyricism in the horror of the infernal landscape every time the poet encounters persons dear to him and, especially, in the case of Francesca and Pier della Vigna; the former an exquisite flower of femininity, the latter a courtly poet of renown. When Dante meets Brunetto, he expresses affection and veneration for him, but the meeting is not couched in the courtly mode.

On the other hand, Dante is constantly "courtly" when he addresses Virgil:

> O sol, che sani ogni vista turbata,
>   tu mi contenti si quando tu solvi,
>   che non men che saper, dubbiar mi aggrada.

> O sun, that heals every perturbed eyesight,
>   you make me so satisfied when you solve
>   my doubts that it is infinitely pleasing to me to
>   doubt not less than to know.[16]

These words remind the reader of those addressed by Virgil to Beatrice:

> Tanto m'aggrada il tuo commandamento
> che l'ubbidir, se già fosse, m'è tardi.

> Your command is so pleasing to me
> That to obey, had I already obeyed, seems late to me.[17]

Courtly poetry is naturally more visible in *Purgatorio*. One may even venture the hypothesis that the divine lines at the very beginning, expressing the beauty of the sky or the quivering of the sea, may have had their distant genesis in the poet's consciousness that the content of the second canticle was characterized by perfection. It was not without reason that the poet excluded from nature every change in his *Purgatorio*. He thought of it platonically as of a world that knew neither the *corruptio* nor the *mutatio* of earthly things.

The summit of *Purgatorio* is a magnificent fresco executed with delicate touches of courtly poetry: the divine forest, Lia, Matelda, the seven maidens who surround Beatrice, dressed in red as she was when Dante saw her in his childhood. All this is a delicate reflection of the world presented in the *Vita Nuova*. Dante weaves those memories on the warp and woof of the poem as he continues in it, modified and deepened, the story of his love for Beatrice. In the *Vita Nuova* Beatrice was presented as she mocked him with her women friends. In the *Commedia* she loves the poet. She openly admits to Virgil:

> Amor mi mosse che mi fa parlare.

> Love urged me who moves me to speak.[18]

Courtly poetry reaches its highest point in *Paradiso*, where Dante revises in a most original manner the love concept developed by the Provençal poets and followed by the courtly poets who preceded him.

In this sense, and in this sense only, the *Commedia* can and must be considered the continuation of the *Vita Nuova*. In fact, to poetry in the *Commedia* is assigned the original function, already exercised in the *Vita Nuova*, of exalting the beauty of Beatrice, the new beauty acquired in the mind and soul of Dante, after her death.

Beatrice, in the *Commedia*, does not lose her human attributes, although a higher spiritual function is assigned to her and to her love. Dante describes her *sorrise parolette brevi* (the short words said with a smile),[19] a laconic and original form, the beauty of which is very hard to render in translation. The smile of Beatrice keeps in *Paradiso* all the charm that the poet admired on earth. There are so many references to Beatrice's human attributes that it becomes useless to quote them. Suffice it to recall the invitation to the poet not to gaze too intently in her eyes, adding that

> non pur ne' miei occhi è Paradiso.

> Paradise is not in my eyes only.[20]

to see to what a large extent Beatrice has remained human in the last canticle.

The poet has kept the exalted beauty and charm of Beatrice through the function that he assigned in the *De Vulgari Eloquentia* to poetry of grand style, a synonym of courtly poetry for Dante.

The courtly derivation of the form assumed by Beatrice in the *Commedia* can be seen with evident clarity in the lines in which Beatrice is likened to the Guinevere of the Arthurian cycle:

> Beatrice, ch'era un poco scevra,
> Ridendo, parve quella che tossio
> Al primo fallo scritto di Ginevra

> Beatrice, who was standing at a certain distance,
> Laughed and resembled the one who coughed
> At the first capitulation of Guinevere that had been recorded in writing.[21]

Beatrice is definitely modeled on courtly womanhood. She is very lofty, yet human, too, and it is very difficult to understand how some critics, even in our day, can see in her the symbol of theology or, even worse, of Christ, Saviour of men, as Beatrice had been the savior of the poet.[22] Aside from the fact that Dante, at the top of the mountain of *Purgatorio*, definitely links Beatrice to the young woman whose love he celebrated in the *Vita Nuova*, he refers to her as the *Sponsa de Libano*, the bride from Heaven, a proof that Beatrice was still the woman who died in 1290, whose "ten-year-old thirst" the poet wanted to assuage by keeping his eyes riveted on her. Even more compelling are the lines in *Paradiso* that refer to Beatrice's love:

> S'io fiammeggio nel caldo d'amore
> Di là dal modo che in terra si vede,
> Sì che degl'occhi tuoi vinco il valore,
> non ti meravigliar.

> If I envelop you in the flame of my love
> To a greater degree than known on earth,
> So that I dazzle your eyes,
> Do not marvel.[23]

All these references and still many more take the reader back to the courtly world so dear to the poet since his early youth. Every objective student of Dante is compelled to notice that the courtly concept of love and poetry endured in the *Commedia*, although the poem assumed vaster and deeper forms than before. The courtly concept can be likened to a luminous vein of precious metal that was visible in the early verse of the poet and never disappeared from his more mature works.

Dante's "The Court of Heaven"

An Interpretation of the Second Canto of the *Inferno*

THE second canto of the *Inferno* opens with a most beautiful description of twilight. Light yields insensibly to the falling evening shadows; the brilliance of the setting sun gradually turns into darkness, and the calm and peace of the moment invite men and animals to rest.

In the first canto Virgil had prospected to his pupil the main phases of their journey into the Beyond, for if Dante wanted to reach the luminous peak of the mountain that arose before him he was to follow Virgil's dictates. Dante had indulged in the illusion that he could reach that summit alone, through his natural forces, unaware that these, identified with the basic instincts of human nature, could only lead him back to the confused maze of the forest. In a sudden outburst of enthusiasm Dante had accepted Virgil's invitation and had set out after him. But soon after, he had experienced awe before the difficult enterprise and, rather than openly confessing it, he boastfully, in the second canto, breaks into an outpouring of erudition, following the false dialectical process of one who feels the need of complicating the matter involved and raises his voice more and more as he tries to persuade others of a truth that he himself does not feel. Dante recalls to Virgil the journeys of Aeneas and St. Paul in the classical and Christian traditions, and uses philosophical terms (*il chi* and *il quale*) in referring to the personality and quality of the two great visitors to the Beyond. He declares his familiarity with the relationship between the Roman Empire and Christianity, concluding with false or ill-directed modesty that he does not see any reason why he, Dante, should undertake the long and arduous journey.

Virgil allows him to talk on for almost twenty lines (10 to 36), and then nails him with the cold and pitiless words:

> Se io ho ben la tua parola intesa,
> L'anima tua è da viltate offesa.

> If I have clearly understood your words,
> Your soul is tainted with cowardliness.

Commentators, all absorbed in their interest in explaining the historical references in the episode, have not seen, as far as we know, the ironical attitude that Dante takes toward himself, nor have they stressed the psychological value and the dramatic tone of this most human scene.

Virgil, after unmasking his pupil's fears, encourages him to continue his journey by offering him positive and personal reasons for doing so. He says that up in Heaven, in the "court of Heaven," three "ladies" have taken to heart Dante's safety: the Gentle Lady, Lucia, and Beatrice. The Gentle Lady, upon seeing that Dante was struggling in vain "on the flood where the sea itself cannot win" and that he was descending again most precipitously toward the dark forest, had called Lucia "an enemy of anyone who was cruel," and had recommended the poet to her. The latter had hastened to Beatrice who, in turn, had hastened to the Limbus to ask for Virgil's help.

Critics, old and new, have given an entirely religious meaning to this scene. The Gentle Lady is the Madonna; Lucia is identified with the Saint from Syracuse, the protector of eyesight, to strengthen which contention the fact is adduced that Dante suffered from trouble with his eyes; Beatrice is divine science, or theology. This interpretation is contrary to the text, and deprives it of the poetic quality that Dante gave to it.

If the theme had been developed by Dante according to the religious motif only, one would find it hard to understand why the poet has insisted so much on Beatrice's beauty,[1] and on her courtly manner of speaking.[2] Nor would it be understandable why

Beatrice appears circumfused by love, as bears witness the line:

Lucevan gli occhi suoi più che la stella

Her eyes shone more than the star

where *la stella*, by general agreement, refers to the star of Venus, and, hence, to love. Even without the specific reference to the "court of Heaven," it is evident that the whole episode is conceived and developed according to the ways of speaking and feeling of the *curialitas*, the courtly life that, according to Dante, embodied the ideal pattern of superior life in both the ethical and artistic fields.

This motivation is especially proven by the meeting of Virgil and Beatrice. The Roman poet, as soon as he sees the beautiful woman, is not only chivalrously moved to pray her to give him commands, but, having heard the reason of Beatrice's visit, hastens to say to her that but to hear her commands is to obey. Even if he had already obeyed her, he adds, it would have been too late.[3] It is difficult not to recognize courtly language in those words and in those with which Beatrice answers Virgil. She has hastened to Virgil, "relying on his courtly manner of speech," in which phrase *onesto* has the customary meaning of dignified and beautiful. After Beatrice has spoken, so says Virgil,

Gli occhi lucenti lagrimando volse,
Perchè mi fece del venir più presto:

She turned her eyes shining with tears,
Because of which she made me swifter in coming.

To the same aulic atmosphere refers the final argument with which Beatrice implores the help of Virgil:

Quando sarò dinanzi al Signor mio,
Di te mi loderò sovente a lui.

When I shall be in the presence of my Lord,
I shall often boast of knowing you.

Not different is the impression produced on the reader by Beatrice when she tells Virgil that she "was seated with the ancient Rachel." One seems to find oneself in those lofty atmospheres where "love and courtesy flourished," the memory of which was always dear to and present in the noble soul of Dante.

All of these moods that are woven into the episode are far from being religious and theological. Dante develops his subject matter here by giving to it the form of the *curialitas*, in the same way that in the fourth canto of the *Inferno* he gives poetic rendition of the Christian Limbus by placing it outside of Hell, in a lofty castle surrounded by seven orders of walls (the seven liberal arts), where dwell the great spirits of the ancients as well as that of the Arabic Averroës.

The artistic problem that confronted Dante at the beginning of his journey was to give poetic life to the concept of Paradise, that was abstract in the poetic field. He had not yet thought of the spheres where later he assigned the Blessed.[4] He did this in the third canticle just as he developed the grandiose plan of his *Inferno* as he wrote it. Here, in the second canto, he speaks in a generic manner of the "court of Heaven," and, in the light of courtly life, he develops a motif that had already appeared in the *Vita Nuova:* Beatrice surrounded by young women as beautiful and courtly as she.[5] This was a mellow reflection and a sweet memory of the poet's faraway youth, from which rise gentle figures of women dear to his heart and sacred to his memory.

It is worth mentioning that these women reappeared at the summit of the mountain of Purgatory, precisely as Dante was about to see Beatrice again. It is there that such figures as Lia, Matelda, and the ladies in waiting of Beatrice pass as light as a dream. There is no doubt that Dante wished to give a symbolic meaning to these ladies as he coldly theorized about poetry. But that he, as a poet, yielding to the impetus of his creation and describing so beautifully these young women, obeyed this rhetorical criterion is an opinion possible only in the brains of rhetoricians of yesterday and of today. For us, these young women are the evocation and reflection of the girls known at the time of his lonely yet happy youth. In evoking them, the poet continued a motif that appeared very frequently in the *Vita Nuova*. Had he not confided to *donne gentili* (courtly ladies) the greatness of his love? He tells us in the eighteenth chapter of the *Vita Nuova*, when one of them asks him: "To what end do you love this lady, since you cannot bear her presence?" that it is "the most novel aim of this love." Equally in the famous *canzone, Donne ch'avete intelletto d'amore* (Ladies who have an understanding of Love), Dante confides to them:

> I' vo' con vui de la mia donna dire,
> Non perch'io creda sua laude finire,
> Ma ragionar per isfogar la mente.

> I want with you to speak of my lady,
> Not because I believe that I may finish her praise,
> But only because I wish to give an outlet to my mind.

Even more explicitly, he addressed himself to the gentle ladies in the *canzone* composed on the occasion of Beatrice's death:

> E perchè me ricordo ch'io *parlai*
> De la mia donna, mentre che vivia,
> Donne gentili, *volentier con vui*,
> Non vo' parlare altrui,
> Se non a cor gentil che in donna sia.

> And because I remember that *I spoke*
> Of my Lady, while she was alive,
> O gentle ladies, *willingly with you*,
> I don't wish to speak with anyone else
> Except with a gentle heart that is within a lady.

In the *Vita Nuova*, as well as elsewhere, Dante set forth in a clear light the relationship of affectionate and sincere intimacy that bound him to his friends and to their ladies. In the sonnet *Guido, vorrei che tu e Lapo ed io* (Guido, I should wish that you and Lapo and I) the poet manifests the secret longing that Guido Cavalcanti, Lapo Gianni, and he be placed on a tiny vessel, together with their ladies, and that a gentle breeze move them on to the open sea where they will speak only of love.

These documents show us who were those who formed the group of poets of the *Dolce Stil Nuovo* (Sweet New Style) in the poetry at the end of the thirteenth and the beginning of the fourteenth centuries. These poets were persons of lofty sentiments who were urged by an affinity of feeling and thinking to isolate themselves from the many among whom they lived in order to realize a mode of existence that persons of the middle class could neither understand nor live. There returns to our minds the sonnet of Cavalcanti to Dante [6] and those of Dante to Cino da Pistoia,[7] in which the poets reproach their friends for the vulgarity to which they had abandoned themselves.

In the light of these facts, it is difficult to see in the *Donna Gentile* the Virgin Mary, as commentators want us to do. It seems to us that Dante attempted to reflect in the *donna gentile* the vague memory of one of those girls who must have seen with grief the manner in which young Dante was living. He was one of those men whose existence was a continuous attempt to fly skyward, only to fall earthward, like a bird with broken wings. This interpretation of the Gentle Lady is strengthened by the fact that the expression *donne gentili* constantly recurs in the *Vita Nuova*.

For the same reason, it does not seem to us that Lucia is the martyr from Syracuse, but rather the fluctuating remembrance of a girl known in the tormented youth of the poet. In the episode that we are discussing, Lucia is entrusted to care for Dante by the Gentle Lady who speaks to her thus:

> Ora ha bisogno il tuo fedele
> Di te, ed io a te lo raccomando.

> Now your faithful one needs you,
> And I recommend him to you.

If one accepts the curial interpretation of the episode, "faithful" must be related to the *fedeli d'amore* (faithful servants of Love) and not to the devotion that Dante may have felt for the Saint. Furthermore, if the *Donna Gentile* were the Madonna, it would seem very strange to find her placed in a secondary position to Lucia, not to mention the position she would have toward Beatrice.

The case of Lucia is made easier to interpret by the fact that she reappears in the *Purgatorio* (Canto IX) where she takes the sleeping Dante and carries him in her arms from the valley, where he spent the night, to the door of Purgatory. Virgil relates thus what has happened during his sleep:

> Dianzi nell'alba che precede al giorno,
> Quando l'anima tua dentro dormía,
> Sopra li fiori, onde laggiù è adorno,
> Venne una donna, e disse: I' son Lucia:
> Lasciatemi pigliar costui che dorme,
> Sì l'agevolerò per la sua via.
>
> . . . .
>
> Qui ti posò; e pria mi dimostraro
> *Gli occhi suoi belli* quell'entrata aperta;
> Poi ella e il sonno ad una se n'andaro.

> Before, in the dawn that precedes the day,
> When your soul was asleep within you,
> Over the flowers that adorn that place,
> Came a lady who said: I am Lucia,
> Let me take this man who is asleep,
> And thus I shall ease his ascending way.
>
> . . . .
>
> Here she placed you; and first was showed to me
> By her beautiful eyes that open entrance;
> Then she and your sleep vanished.

If we interpret Dante's sleep as his tarrying in his ascent toward purification because of the weakness of his flesh and Lucia as the one who makes his ascent easier, the function of Lucia in both episodes is very clear, without any need of invoking a religious interpretation.

What is true of the *Donna Gentile* and of Lucia is even truer of Beatrice whose poetic rendering must not be made heavier by identifying her with theology, just as the episode in the entire second canto of the *Inferno* must not be weakened in its poetic value by seeing in Lucia the illuminating grace of the Lord and in the *Donna Gentile* the Virgin Mary. Beatrice, here, as in all of the *Commedia*, is the poetic rendering of the Florentine girl whom Dante loved with an unrequited love. The only difference between the Beatrice of the *Vita Nuova* and the Beatrice of the *Commedia* lies in the fact that now Beatrice loves Dante while in the *Vita Nuova* she does not. Beatrice's attitude toward Dante before she admitted her love for him is clearly brought out in our episode by Lucia when she enjoins her to help him:

> Chè non soccorri quei t'amò tanto,
> Che uscìo per te della volgare schiera?

> Why don't you help him who loved you greatly,
> Who arose because of you above the common crowd?

These words seem to superinduce in us the memory of Dante's days when he was deprived of Beatrice's love and when his life was illumined by the sympathy of the gentle ladies.

This interpretation binds together in a closer unity the *Vita Nuova* and the *Commedia*. If we accept the hypothesis that the "court of Heaven" is the poetical transformation of the "court" that has known the dolorous love of Dante in his youth, the second canto develops and transforms the fundamental situation of the *Vita Nuova:* the unrequited love of Dante for Beatrice. Now Beatrice, blessed in Paradise, requites the love of the poet because she knows its beauty and greatness. In effect, she admitted to Virgil:

> Amor mi mosse che mi fa parlare.

> Love moved me that makes me speak.

This situation, too, is closely bound with Sonnet XLI of the *Vita Nuova*, where the thought of Dante, all aflame with griev-

ing love, rises toward Heaven and sees Beatrice in the glory of
Paradise.

In the *Commedia*, Dante's love is shared by the once-rebellious
Beatrice. Now the gentle ladies do not laugh any longer, nor
does Beatrice make fun of her lover, the timid and strange poet
who loved her so much and in vain. Now the *benedette anime*
(blessed souls) of the *Vita Nuova* have become the *donne
benedette del Paradiso* (blessed ladies of Paradise), and they help
him to render perfect the courtly love that in the youth of the
poet had been only pain, loneliness, and often a literary formula.
With the help of the three ladies Dante can now undertake the
journey of his spiritual ascent for which he had constantly
longed, an elevation that, in the fusion of both past and present,
became the fundamental motif of Dante's journey into the world
of the Beyond.

Lights and Shadows in
Dante's Vita Nuova

IT IS well known that the *Vita Nuova*, written after the death of Beatrice, is a book of memories in which Dante rethinks the events of his youth in the light of what that young girl meant to him or, at least, of what he believed she meant to him after the episode of the *Donna Gentile*.

The meeting with the latter took place immediately after the first anniversary of Beatrice's death. The struggle between the pale image of the dead girl and the young woman who attracted the poet and enveloped him in an ardent upsurge of love and passion lasted "several days," to quote Dante. If the final words of the *Vita Nuova*, referring to Beatrice, "I hope to utter praises of her such as were never uttered of any other woman," are understood to be not only a promise of writing the *Divine Comedy*, but also an indication of a complete and absolute return to the love of the early youth of the poet, one is led to believe that the work was written around 1292. At least the prose was written at that time, for the poet had been setting his feelings in verse since 1283, the date of the first sonnet *A ciascun alma presa e gentil core*.

Three planes of reality are projected in the *Vita Nuova*: that of "actual" life, that is, the relations that Dante actually had with Beatrice and other women; that of poetry, which reflects those experiences relatively closely to the time in which they occurred; and that of prose, which reflects them as Dante felt them after the death of Beatrice.

Critics, by using the terms *reality*, *realistic*, and *realism*, find considerable difficulty in differentiating between man's actual experience and its subsequent phase, when actual experience becomes art material. Paradoxically, actual life is not "real in art" until the poet relieves it in his stirred soul and causes it to blossom forth into sentiment, thought, and beauty by infusing into it a new life, a life that is real in the artistic plane. Art transforms the "actual" into the "real," to clarify the thought of De Sanctis and Croce, through the variations which life undergoes in being transposed from the level of experience to that of artistic expression. It seems, therefore, preferable to make use of the term "actual" to indicate the experience of the man in the poet, and the term "real" to refer to the changes that experience undergoes in the artistic works of the poet.

The plot of the *Vita Nuova* is very simple, and the action that develops in it emerges very clearly through the delicate shadings that the poet consciously gives to it. Dante fell in love with Beatrice at the age of nine; this love grew greatly when he was eighteen. Love filled the poet's life, but not to the extent of excluding from his heart interest in other young women, so much so that in the city he was criticized beyond the bounds of courtesy. Beatrice refused to greet him, but he continued to write poems about his great love for her. First, he sang of the effects that love had upon him; then, in search of "new material," he emerged from his egocentricity and exalted Beatrice's beauty and virtues. Beatrice died, and the poet's entire world sank into darkness. About a year after her death, Dante, sitting in his garden and thinking of the dead girl, beheld a young woman at a window gazing upon him with infinite tenderness and compassion. He fell in love with her and wrote poems for her which revealed to her his passionate sentiments. Dante was fully conscious that he was betraying Beatrice by yielding to that love, but that feeling came to him in all its naked truth only when he wrote the prose for the *Vita Nuova*. Beatrice's victory acquired the seal of reality through the words quoted above, which, even if repeated unendingly, will never lose the charm that glows in them.

Dante expressed his love in the forms that the Provençal tradition offered and prescribed at that time to poets of the grand style: the woman endowed with angelic perfection, the marvelous effects which she had on the one who loved her, absence or, at least, suppression of passion, perfect love born of admiration and worship of a woman's spiritual and physical qualities that were capable of raising the poet to God. These forms of courtly love in the *Vita Nuova* are accompanied by many conventional elements: Dante sees Beatrice for the first time when both are only nine years old; he sees her again after nine years, at the ninth hour of the day; he dreams of her rejecting his love "at the first hour of the last nine hours of the night." It should be observed that all these farfetched devices are found in the prose which, in terms of actual experience, is infinitely more conventional than the poetry. In the prose, Dante tells us that on the ninth day of his illness, he had in a dream a foreboding of Beatrice's death. Beatrice died on the ninth day of June, the ninth month of the year 1290, a date that the poet fabricated by invoking the help of foreign calendars. Beatrice appeared to him in the dream "almost in the ninth hour." In the nineteenth chapter the poet even explains to the reader why the number nine returns so persistently in the life of his lady: "to make it known that she was a nine, that is, a miracle whose root is found only in the wondrous Trinity."

This is the unimportant part of the *Vita Nuova* which, in varying degree, is found in all courtly poets of the time. It constitutes what poets of the grand style absorbed from the culture of their epoch. The living part is found where convention is broken down by a sincere and piercing cry in which the poet's torment has been so powerful as to break through the fetters of the traditional forms and to emerge from them in all its human truth. It is thus that were written the unforgettable pages of the little book in which the poet goes beyond the culture and doctrine of Dante, man of the thirteenth century.

It is natural to wonder to what point the "actual," that is, the historical and literal truth of Dante's love affairs has penetrated the convention of courtly love that envelops the *Vita Nuova* and makes of it one of the most perfect texts of ideal love. Only an attentive and objective reading of this work will enable us to answer such a question. Since the prose was written later and in a different mood from that which inspired the poetry, it is legitimate, in fact, dutiful, to read the poems independently of the prose. Only thus will we be able to see how the true experience of Dante as a man was reflected in vivid contrast on the two different planes of poetry and of prose in the book of Dante's youth. This way of reading will allow us to see how the poetry has preserved many fragments of true life which the prose attempted to exclude or eclipse when the poet looked in retrospect at the love affairs of his youth and saw them as a heap of extinguished ashes, without body or reality, in sharp contrast with the vivid light that enveloped the memory of his love of Beatrice. In showing these contrasts, our desire is not to be disrespectful of the poet, but only to know Dante better as a young man and to bring into relief the artistic process that guided him when he penned the *Vita Nuova*.

Nothing leads to a better understanding of authors than to know their aesthetic ideas; not those prevalent during their lifetime, which they may or may not have followed, but their specific tenets, and especially those that one can reconstruct in the work that one wishes to study. In the beginning of the *Vita Nuova*, precisely in the second chapter, the poet wrote: "Since to dwell on passions and deeds of such an extreme youthfulness seems to be a type of literature worthy of the people, I shall leave them; and, omitting many things which could be taken from the pattern whence these derive, I shall come to those words which are indelibly written in my memory under more important headings." This is the artistic creed of the poet at the time he composed his *Vita Nuova*. He believed that the contemplation and depicting of passions were not worthy of his art, for they represented the relativity of man and not the ideal and rational part of him. This latter part was found in the depths of his being and constituted the "more important headings" of the poet's life. What he omitted in the book of his youth was the element of passion, the memory of other loves, whatever they may have been, that accompanied his love of Beatrice. He left the elements of passion to the *fabula*, to popular art that was interested in sensuality, unbridled laughter, and loose metrical forms.

This was the plan which he had proposed for himself, but it is quite true that it was never possible for him to carry it out in full. Had he succeeded, the *Vita Nuova* would not be the first psychological novel in Italian literature. Traces of the human love are numerous, and they are still visible in the *Vita Nuova*. By way of example, the poem *Con l'altre donne mia vista gabbate* (XIV) shows us that Beatrice laughed at the poor poet who could not control his trembling with emotion as she approached him. The prose attributes the mockery to the other women, who were with Beatrice, and not to her, lessening in this way the impact of the situation and presenting it in the prose on a more ideal plane than the one projected in the poem.

The divine sonnet *I' mi sentii svegliar dentro lo core* (XXIV) loses much of its charm in the prose by a play on words of the name of Giovanna, Cavalcanti's lady, and the name Primavera, given to her by her friends because of the freshness of her beauty. In the sonnet the poet had written that he felt an unusual joy awakening in his heart in the guise of water gushing from a spring. His heart had unconsciously had the presentiment of the approaching of Beatrice and Giovanna. But in the prose Dante begins to rave about the fact that Giovanna bore that name because she walked ahead of Beatrice, not differently from St. John, who was the forerunner of Christ. And it was precisely for this reason that the girl had received the name of Primavera. She will come first (*prima verrà*), preceding Beatrice. Here the courtly system seriously damaged the poem or at least detracted from the poetic resonance that remains with the reader after having perused it.

The episode of the *Donna Gentile* is also presented on two different planes. Although both poetry and prose unite in revealing to us the struggle in the poet's heart between the image of Beatrice and the fascination of the *Donna Gentile* who showed compassion and love to the grieving poet, the prose removes every vestige of humanity from the poet's feelings. In the poem, in a very human way, the heart of Dante as a man is shown as it slowly surrendered to the young girl's love. The poet confesses its capitulation, "and then he sighs." The struggle between heart and soul, instinct and reason, is beautifully developed in the sonnet *Gentil pensero che parla di vui* (XXXVIII). But in the prose the need of conforming to the schema of courtly love causes reason to triumph, surpressing the heart's longings, and the poet calls the *Donna Gentile's* thoughts "most vile." Actually, the sonnet addressed to the young girl is replete with love for her, and Dante reveals in it all his sentiments with the melody and grace that are typically his when he listens to the voice of his heart. The above-mentioned examples should convince us of the effective and real existence of the two planes of reality reflected in the poetry and the prose.

These contrasts can be seen and documented even more readily in the sonnets dedicated to women who were called "women of the foil." Following the custom of Provençal poets who, in order to conceal the identity of the lady who was the object of their love, pretended to dedicate themselves to serve another lady of the court, Dante tells us that he concealed his love for Beatrice through three women to whom he gave homage and for whom he wrote sonnets on various occasions. It should be observed that the convention of the "woman of the foil" does not suit Dante very well. Such a woman was the victim of the understanding of two lovers who wanted to keep their relationship a secret, and who would agree as to which woman the lover would court in order to throw off all the suspicions of the people of their courtly group. It is natural for the lady not to be troubled by the feigned courtship which the man bestows on another woman. If this be so, it is not understandable why Beatrice, instead, was angered to the point of refusing her greeting to Dante when the poet dedicated his attentions to the three "women of the foil." Moreover, such understanding presupposed a true love or passion between two lovers, while in Dante's case only one was in love, the poet himself. The real truth of the matter is quite different. Dante met the three young ladies, fell in love with them, and wrote poems about them which, later, while composing the prose of the *Vita Nuova*, he was determined to reduce to the schema of courtly love by forcing them to express his homage to Beatrice. In the prose, through devious ways, he succeeds, at least in part, in his very difficult task. But it was not possible to destroy or remove the initial and substantial contradiction between his feelings for the three young girls and his love for Beatrice. The attentive reader will discover such a contradiction with lucid clarity, and he can conclude only that when Dante assembled the poems which constitute the central part of the *Vita Nuova*, those loves, of whatever nature they might have been, had become meaningless to him. At that time the only and true reality was his love for the dead Beatrice. Even the *sirventese* that Dante, in the sixth chapter, tells us that he wrote in honor of the sixty most beautiful women of Florence, does not place Beatrice at the top of his thoughts, for she occupied only the ninth place, which most certainly must not have flattered her vanity as a woman.

The prose in the fifth chapter refers to the woman in whom Dante concealed his love for several years. Their relationship was born out of mere chance, when, one day in church, Dante's eyes, which were turned in Beatrice's direction, met with those of this woman. Dante relates that "immediately I thought of making this woman a foil for the truth; and I showed so much attention to her that those who discussed me believed her to be my secret love. With this woman I succeeded in hiding myself for several years and months." There is no doubt whatsoever that, according to the prose, this woman served only as a mask for his love for Beatrice. In the seventh chapter we are informed that, since this woman had to leave Florence, Dante felt obliged to write a sonnet in which he proposed to "make a complaint about it." If he had not shown grief, the poet tells us, "people would have immediately noticed my concealment." But the poem contains this verse:

Sì che, volendo far come coloro
Che per vergogna celan lor mancanza,
Di fuor mostro allegranza
E dentro de lo core struggo e ploro.

Thus, wanting to be like those
Who for shame hide their loneliness,
Outwardly, I display happiness
While within I cry, consumed by longing.

These words tell the very opposite of what the occasion of the woman's departure called for. The poet should have displayed sorrow instead of "happiness." The prose tells us that the sonnet was included in the *Vita Nuova* "because my lady [Beatrice] was the immediate cause of certain words which are found in the sonnet." In reality, what the poet writes in the prose shows him struggling desperately to attain unity of love in his *Vita Nuova*, but the attempted union between the actual and the artistic reality shows lacerations and breaks. One can only repeat that Dante's love for the "woman of the foil" was no longer alive when he wrote the prose of the *Vita Nuova*, though it had been a real love.

Even the sonnets in the eighth chapter fit very imperfectly into the schema of courtly love. The two sonnets, which are very beautiful, are none other than the expression of the poet's grief over the death of a young girl whose beauty and gentleness Dante admired. Love itself, personified, cries over her death, and the poet sees Love standing, his head bowed, over the beautiful image of the dead girl. She possessed a gay nature, and possessed that which, with the exception of honor, merits the highest exaltation in a woman—beauty. The poet sings that Death

di pietà nemica,
Di dolor madre antica,
Giudizio incontestabile, gravoso,

hai partita cortesia
E ciò chè in donna da pregiar, vertute;
In gaia gioventute
Distrutta hai l'amorosa leggiadria.

> enemy of pity,
> Ancient mother of grief,
> Heavy and unquestionable judgment,
>
> you have destroyed courtesy
> And what is praiseworthy in a woman, virtue:
> In her gay youth
> You have destroyed the lovable charm.

In the prose the poet informs us that the two sonnets are included in the *Vita Nuova* because he remembered that "he had once seen her," the young deceased person, in the company of his gentle lady, Beatrice. In the prose, the poet's feelings are denied to the young woman and are directed toward Beatrice. Even if the poet cried, he states, he did so only because he once saw her in Beatrice's company, and if he proposed to "say several words regarding her death," he did so in compensation for having seen her in his lady's company. Yet, the memory of the young girl and her death are very much alive in the poems. In the prose they are obscured by the literary preoccupation to which the poet has subjected himself.

Chapter nine leads one to similar conclusions. Here, too, it is impossible to harmonize the poetry and the prose. The poetry, studied, as we have suggested, independently of the prose, shows us the end of a love affair, while a new interest appears in Dante. Basically, it shows the poet's passing from an old to a new love. According to the poetry, Dante tells us that he left the city against his will. Naturally enough it was Florence, but the poet does not mention it by name, preferring the romantic haze of the unknown. He was on horseback, he informs us, and he encountered Love dressed in a pilgrim's clothing like the poet. Love, too, was dispirited and unhappy with the sadness that accompanies the end of every human experience. Love reflected the poet's mood; it was the poet himself—his heart aglow with love. Love informed him that he was taking his heart "to serve a new pleasure." The poet transfused himself to such an extent in the thought of the new love that he felt completely identified with it. In spite of all the efforts displayed in the prose, the sonnet has nothing to do with Beatrice. Perhaps it would be more accurate to say that Beatrice has nothing to do with the sonnet. If Dante's love for Beatrice had been more alive in his heart at the writing of the sonnet, one cannot understand why Love was so sad, spiritless, and so full of sighs. Dante's feelings for Beatrice were not really in danger. The love which becomes obscured in the sonnet is that which he felt for another woman when a new interest was aroused in the poet's heart, and he freely sang of its joy:

> Allora presi di lui sì grande parte
> Ch'elli disparve, e non m'accorsi come.

> Then I took from it such a great part
> That it disappeared, without my awareness.

The prose tried in vain to change the sonnet's meaning. Referring it to the occasion when Dante left Florence, possibly for a military expedition, the prose attributes the poet's sadness to the fact that he will no longer be able to see Beatrice, but this element is completely foreign to the sonnet's theme. This poem remains strictly love poetry, strangely and violently inserted in the magic circle occupied only by his love for Beatrice. It is because of such contrast that the idealistic pattern of the *Vita Nuova* is cut across by elements that show us the love theme plunged in the immediacy of life, without transportations of any kind. This part forms a beautiful underground spring that flows silently but powerfully under the conventional framework of the *Vita Nuova*.

Who can ever forget the words with which Dante described the curiosity of friends and gossipers who wanted to know who the woman was that had destroyed him so, and he "smilingly looked at them and said nothing"? Of course, the most perfect sonnets in the *Vita Nuova*, *Tanto gentile e tanto onesta pare* and *Ne gli occhi porta la mia donna amore*, are rooted in the idea of perfection which was so dear to the Provençal and courtly poets.

However, that idea became luminous and beautiful only because it was enriched by the human tenderness that it acquired in passing through Dante's soul. It is due to this fact if the blinding light of the absolute, diffused throughout the work, is often made varied, arising from the remembrance of actual life, life as actually lived. Who will complain and accuse the poet for not having adhered literally to the cultural precepts of his time? The soul of true poets is too great to remain constrained and oppressed by the narrow circle prescribed by the culture of their times.

Dante's Concept of Love

THE aim of this essay is to study Dante's love concept as revealed in the *Vita Nuova* (New Life), the *Convivio* (The Banquet), and the *Divina Commedia* (Divine Comedy).

We shall be guided by what Dante tells us in each of his three works, and we shall not allow ourselves to be influenced by any preconceived conclusions concerning his love concept. It is a simple matter to reduce a man to a formula, but, actually, it is inhuman, abstract, and often useless to do so. It is preferable to see the poet's ideas as an integral part of his life, a solution, or an attempt at a solution, of particular moments of his existence. Nor do we wish to reduce Dante's love concept to that of the courtly tradition of his time. This can only be, as it was, a starting point, from which he moved on as does every great poet in the moment of his artistic creation. Therefore, we do not desire either to force Dante within a preconceived system of love or to steep him in the courtly tradition.

We are guided in our discussion by the difference that exists between culture and art. Culture is looked upon here as something a poet receives from the atmosphere in which he is born and lives; and art, which is original creation, as an activity that needs new attitudes and directions. Those who follow this distinction seek more diversity than uniformity in the works of a poet that reflect various moments of his existence.

The historical school, which deserves so much praise for a serious and documented study of Dante's works, often offers the drawback of wishing to reduce Dante the poet to the culture of his time by presupposing that the culture of an age constitutes a determined and homogeneous block rather than a whole of different tendencies. A critic, applying this absolute and unitarian concept of the culture of a given time, quotes from various authors in order to document what he wishes to see in a determined work of the poet, a dangerous procedure, unless it is accompanied by the certitude on the part of the critic that Dante actually knew a definite book.

The three pivotal points of these considerations will be, as we have stated, a careful study of the three major works of the great Italian poet: the *Vita Nuova*, the *Convivio*, and the *Commedia*. In a special way we shall dwell on the thirtieth and thirty-first cantos of the *Purgatorio* and the poetic figuration of Beatrice in the *Paradiso*.

Dante lived a "courtly" life previous to his exile in 1302, and he sought refuge in it after Florence drove him away from his Baptistery, his "bel San Giovanni." There is no doubt that he generally followed the Provençal concept of love, in spite of the harsh words with which he refers to the widow of Nino Visconti and the sonnets exchanged with Forese. This concept was a part of the poetic culture of his day, followed by the poets of the *Dolce Stil Nuovo* who were all members of the White Party. Either one wrote according to the popular manner whose realism, lack of form, and barbaric rhymes displeased Dante, or one belonged to the group of chosen minds for whom Love was a spiritual reaction expressed in "sweet rhymes." Content and form were intimately united in Dante's poetics.

Michele Barbi, in his introduction to the *Convivio*,[1] attempts to remove every contradiction between the *Vita Nuova*, the *Convivio*, and the *Commedia*, reducing to an oversimplified form the genesis of the three works. Barbi does not take into consideration that logic can also be *a posteriori*, and then, in its absolutism, offends life that does not flow placidly and peacefully among meadows flowering with asphodels. Aristide Marigo, too, in his learned article *Amore intellettivo nell'evoluzione filosofica di Dante* (Intellective Love in the philosophical evolution of Dante), following Giulio Salvadori,[2] concludes that in the *Vita Nuova* "the description of the reactions of the soul, traditional subject matter of erotic lyricism, is closely connected with the solution of the problem of knowledge."[3] For Marigo, the *Dolce Stil*

Nuovo began "at Bologna where studies of philosophy are fervidly pursued, and where ancient wisdom is less subjected to theological interpretations," [4] thus giving a value of absolute certainty to a very contingent fact, and creating a critical determinism without any philosophical basis.

For us, the *Dolce Stil Nuovo* represents the development, original and personal in the various poets, of the theory of courtly love with close connections with the Provençal tradition. To bring into play the averroistic current in order to explain the poetry of Cavalcanti and the mystic currents to explain that of Dante is to look at the problem from an external vantage, leaving a great amount of liberty to the will of each critic.

There is perfect agreement among critics as to the brief plot of the *Vita Nuova:* the meeting with Beatrice at the age of nine and at eighteen years of age, her salutation to the poet, her ceasing to speak to him, the presentiment of the death of the young woman, her death, the brief obscuring of Dante's love for her because of the passion that suddenly flared within the heart of the poet for the *Donna Gentile.* These events are translated in the *Vita Nuova* through the Pythagorical numbers of three and nine, and through other ideas generally accepted by the poets of high style, such as the angelic woman, the unity of love, the justification of love as a force that leads man to God. On the whole, the short plot of Dante's book is woven with courtly love and a great deal of convention, but also with sudden outcries of true feeling that reveal the most personal aspects of the poet's character.

In his love concept, as presented in the *Vita Nuova,* Dante keeps himself closely tied to courtly tradition and presents to us a love circumscribed by virtue. Out of respect for this tradition, he writes concerning sensuality: "And since to dwell on passions and deeds of such an extreme youthfulness seems to be a type of literature worthy of the *fabula,* I shall leave them aside." [5] He very urgently informs us that passion was totally absent from his love for Beatrice. He says so in the prose of the *Vita Nuova,* but the reader, in perusing his first sonnet written, if we believe the poet, when he was eighteen years of age in 1283, cannot help asking himself whether the poet does not insist so vigorously on the absolute spirituality of his love precisely because he wished to exclude from it his inevitably sensuous reaction to the beauty of Beatrice. And why, if it were not so, would he have imagined that Love appeared to him and

> ne le braccia avea
> Madonna involta in un drappo dormendo?

> in his arms he had
> Madonna enveloped in a cloth and asleep? [6]

Even the prose, written in 1292, in which the sonnet is set, has kept the reflection of this sensuality: "Ne le sue braccia mi parea vedere una persona dormire nuda, salvo che involta mi parea in un drappo sanguigno leggeramente" [7] (In his arms seemed to me to see asleep a naked person, except that she was lightly enveloped in a crimson cloth). The poet constantly makes Herculean efforts to force his love within the formula of courtliness, thus doing violence to the literal truth of the situation. We have already seen how Dante sacrifices to this ideal the women of the foil.

From courtly tradition Dante borrows his custom of rendering actual reality through a vague halo, reached by not mentioning by name the places or persons to which he refers. A clear example of this is in Chapter XXIII when he refers to his half-sister by the terms "donna pietosa e di novella etate" (compassionate Lady, very young in years). Likewise, in the last sonnet dedicated to the women of the foil, he refers to Florence by the term "sopradetta cittade" (above-mentioned city). [8] Only here and there the character of conventionality is broken by a sincere and lacerating cry in which the reader realizes that the poetic expression has become fused with the torment of the heart of the poet. At other times Dante's genius draws away subconsciously from tradition, and then his art levels down toward a realism that surprises the reader, as when Beatrice is described to us when she laughs with her friends at the poet. [9] However, it is useless to deny that the basic tone of the *Vita Nuova* is conventional, but it is equally true that the poetry that will live forever is that born by breaking the conventions that tradition offered the poet.

In his above-mentioned introduction, Michele Barbi presents the *Convivio* as a work of pure doctrine corresponding to the mature age of the poet. Barbi represents more fully than any other critic a reaction to Witte [10] and to Vossler [11] who wished to see in the *Convivio* an intellectual and even a religious crisis in Dante. We deny the existence in Dante of the rationalism of the type of the nineteenth century, but we believe and declare that the doctrine of love contained in the *Convivio* is of a different nature from that in the *Commedia*, and especially that in the *Paradiso*,[12] where it is characterized by a contemplative element and by Platonism.

Although the existence of doctrine in the *Convivio* cannot be denied, nevertheless it is useless to try to remove the dissonances and downright clashes that exist between it and the *Vita Nuova* and between it and the *Commedia*. It is impossible to see on the same human and poetic plane the love for the Gentle Lady in the *Vita Nuova* that makes of it the first psychological novel in Italian literature, and its negation in the *Convivio*, where Dante tells us that it was not love for a woman, but love for philosophy. Dante is so definite in his likes and dislikes as to make it difficult for us to cavillate when we discuss his attitudes. He is a poor witness for the defense lawyers. If we follow Barbi when he enjoins us to explain Dante with Dante, we find that the poet has not made the differentiation, inferred by Barbi,[13] between the woman of the *Vita Nuova* and that of the *Convivio*. Dante explicitly declares that almost three years after Beatrice's death "quella gentile donna, cui feci manzione ne la fine de la *Vita Nuova*, parve primamente, accompagnata d'Amore, a li occhi miei e prese luogo alcuno ne la mia mente" (that Gentle Lady, whom I mentioned at the end of the *Vita Nuova*, accompanied by Love, appeared to my eyes at first and took some place in my mind),[14] and later relates again his falling in love, adroitly and slowly changing the human and beautifully youthful countenance of the Gentle Lady into the dignified and august one of philosophy. He tells us the reason with blinding clarity: "Dico che pensai da molti, diretro da me, forse sarei stato ripreso di levezza d'animo, udendo me essere dal primo amore mutato; perchè a torre via questa riprensione, nullo migliore argomento era che dire quale era quella donna che m'avea mutato"[15] (I say that I thought that by many, behind my back, I should be perhaps accused of levity of mind upon hearing that I had changed from my first love; whereupon, to remove this accusation, there was no better argument than to say who was the woman who had changed me).

The *Convivio* most clearly shows this most human preoccupation, if one agrees with us, that Dante was struggling against his political detractors who were "cruel and pitiless" in a quite different manner from the ladies whom they courted in society. Here it was a question of defending one's reputation that, as Dante informs us, had fallen very low. There is no doubt for us that in the *Vita Nuova* Dante was referring to a woman with whom he was temporarily in love when he wrote about forgetting Beatrice for the time being. In fact, in commenting upon the sonnet *Gentil pensiero che parla di voi* (A gentle thought that speaks of you), Dante wrote: "E dissi questo sonetto, lo quale comincia: 'Gentil pensiero,' e dico 'gentile' in quanto ragionava di gentile donna, chè per altro era vilissimo"[16] (and I said this sonnet, which begins "Gentle Thought," and I say "gentle" in that it spoke of a gentle lady, for, as to the rest, it was most vile). So that sad episode appeared to him later when the fire of passion was extinguished and he had returned to the love of Beatrice. The nature of this "most vile" love was forgotten when he wrote the *Convivio*.

On the *Convivio* is projected the shadow of his exile, and this is the truly living part in it, the part that urges Dante to write unforgettable pages in which he narrates his peregrinations and confesses to us his loneliness, and then breaks forth into the lament: "Veramente io sono legno sanza vela e sanza governo, portato a diversi porti e foci e liti dal vento secco che vapora la dolorosa povertade" [17] (Truly have I been a ship without sails and without rudder, carried to diverse ports, mouths of rivers, and shores by the dry wind that dolorous poverty blows). His greatest enemy is the "infamy" that persecuted him so unjustly with the danger of robbing him of his livelihood. With a smile that curves his lips toward spurning this world, he lingers to describe with bitterness the nobility of fame that grows so easily with our friends and infamy that assumes monstrous proportions with our enemies.[18]

I repeat that there is no doubt that the *Convivio* is a book of doctrine, but the primary reason why Dante wrote it was to put an end, as he himself says, "to the great infamy and danger" that pursued him in his exile. He was like Boethius who wrote his *De Consolatione Philosophiae* in order to excuse "sotto pretesto di consolazione la perpetuale infamia del suo essilio" [19] (under the pretext of consolation the perpetual infamy of his exile). Even more clearly, Dante stated: "Movemi timore d'infamia.... Temo la infamia di tanta passione avere seguita, quanta concepe chi legge le sopra nominate canzoni in me avere signoreggiata" [20] (I am moved by fear of infamy.... I fear to have followed the infamy of such a great passion as he who reads the above-mentioned *canzoni* believes to have mastered me). He struggles valiantly to remove this infamy, showing that "non passione ma virtù sia stata la movente cagione" (not passion but virtue was the moving cause).

In the *Vita Nuova* Dante rejected sensuality because of the noble aspirations of his soul and an aesthetic principle. Here, under the cold maxims, there is a struggle for life: "ischiudere ogni falsa opinione da me, per la quale fosse sospicato lo mio amore essere per sensibile dilettazione" [21] (to cut off every false opinion of me, through which it could have been suspected that my love was for a sensuous delectation). It was but natural that Dante's love concept in such a situation remained *disumanato* (deprived of its human quality), and in a very different sense in which it was in the *Commedia*. The verse: "Questi mi face una

donna guardare" (This makes me look at a woman) is commented upon thus by the poet: "ove si vuole sapere che questa
donna è la Filosofia; la quale veramente è donna piena di dolcezza,
ornata d'onestade, mirabile di sapere, gloriosa di libertade, sì
come nel terzo tratto, dove la sua nobiltade si tratterà, fia
manifesto. E là dove dice: 'Chi veder vuol la salute, faccia che li
occhi d'esta donna miri; li occhi di questa donna sono le sue
dimostrazioni, le quali, dritte ne li occhi de lo 'ntelletto, in-
namorano l'anima, liberata da le contradizioni" [22] (where one must
understand that this woman is Philosophy, who truly is a woman
full of sweetness, ornamented by stateliness, admirable for knowledge, glorious for freedom, as will be manifest in the third
treatise where her nobility will be discussed. And there where it
says: *He who wishes to see his own salvation must look into the
eyes of this woman*, the eyes of this woman are her demonstra-
tions, which, straight into the eyes of the intellect, make the soul,
freed of all contradictions, fall in love). He even reaches the
point of placing the love of Philosophy before the love of Beatrice.
And he does so in no uncertain terms, going so far as to state
that he felt that the love of Philosophy occupied a larger place
in his heart than did that of Beatrice.[23]

No matter how hard one tries, one will never be able to take
away from the *Convivio* many of the abstractions from the love
concept of the poet. We do not blame him, of course. But we do
blame his enemies who forced him to give a political answer to a
political accusation that aimed at damaging the reputation of the
great and impecunious man.

The "true" revelation of what actually happened in his life is
found in the *Commedia*, the book of intimacy and the autobiography of his soul; the true answer, if one admits the principle
that a later document wipes out and nullifies the previous utterances of what concerns the "objective" truth of the events. The
most limpid mirror is found in Dante's confession at the summit
of Purgatory and precisely in the Earthly Paradise where he,
purified of the weight of the flesh through the vision of evil in

both the Inferno and Purgatory, reacquires the original perfection of man and becomes worthy of gazing into the eyes of Beatrice.

The narrative of what actually happened after Beatrice's death is violently contrary to what Dante had written in the *Convivio*. Here we read that he used to go "dov'ella [la Filosofia] si dimostrava veracemente, cioè ne le scuole de li religiosi e a le disputazioni de li filosofanti. Sì che in picciol tempo, forse di trenta mesi, cominciai tanto a sentire de la sua dolcezza, che lo suo amore cacciava e distruggeva ogni altro pensiero" [24] (where it [philosophy] showed itself most truly, that is to say in the schools of religious people and in the discussions of philosophers. So that in a very short time, perhaps in thirty months, I began to feel so much of its sweetness that its love drove out and destroyed every other thought). But Beatrice knows that the truth is quite different. And she "regal in her rebellious act" accuses Dante of having been unfaithful to her. It is of no use to quibble; the time to which the poet refers in the two works is the same, that after Beatrice's death:

Sì tosto come in su la soglia fui
    Di mia seconda etade e mutai vita,
    Questi si tolse a me, a diessi altrui.
Quando di carne a spirto era salita,
    E bellezza e virtù cresciuta m'era,
    Fu'io a lui men cara e men gradita;
E volse i passi suoi per via non vera,
    Imagini di ben seguendo false,
    Che nulla promission rendono intera.

As soon as I was on the threshold
    Of my second age, and I changed my life,
    This man relinquished me, and gave himself to others.
When from my flesh I had become pure spirit,
    And my beauty and virtue had increased,
    I became to him less dear and less acceptable;
And he turned his steps on the wrong path,
    Following false images of good,
    Which render no promise in its entirety.[25]

What the nature of this betrayal was is said later on when Beatrice, woman even to the point of being moved by jealousy, shouts to Dante:

> E quali agevolezze o quali avanzi
>   Nella fronte degli altri si mostraro,
>   Perchè dovessi lor passeggiare anzi?

> And what greater promises and qualities
>   Showed themselves on the forehead of others,
>   That you should pay courtship to them? [26]

We are far from singling out this contradiction in order to indict the poet. Indeed, we see in his confession not only that of the lover, which is addressed to Beatrice, but that of the poet and man, which is addressed to all of us. He wished to confess that when he was young he was too earthy and carnal to be able to love according to the norms of courtly love. And now, only when the passing of years has deepened in him the meaning of the values of life, has he become capable of perfect love.

Dante resumed in the *Commedia* the theme of love, clinging to the facts, as related in the *Vita Nuova*. These were for him a living reality under the poetic veil that enveloped them without minimizing or destroying them. In fact, in the *Commedia* he refers to Beatrice as being the same girl whom he saw, loved, and sang to in the *Vita Nuova*. She was the same girl whose love "m'avea gia trafitto, Prima ch'io fuor di puerizia fosse" [27] (had transfixed me, Before I were out of my childhood). Beatrice is attired as she was in the *Vita Nuova* and produces on him the same effects that she exercised on him as she was wont to do in his youth: "sicchè d'amor sentii la gran potenza" (so that I felt the great power of love).

To identify so clearly the Beatrice whom the poet meets on the summit of Purgatory with the girl of whom he sang in the *Vita Nuova* is another proof of the absurdity of Barbi's thesis, which states categorically that Dante "annetteva all'esser filosofo il dovere di comportarsi ad ogni età seconda che la ragione richiede; e come le rime d'amore, e le passioni che le ispirano, sono convenienti o giustificate nell'adolescenza, così ad età matura conviene 'pur virilmente' poetare" [28] (attached to being a philosopher the duty of behaving at every age according to the requirements of reason; and as love rhymes, and the passions that inspire them, are becoming to and justifiable in adolescence, so it is required to write poetry "more virile" at a later age). If this were true, one would find it difficult to explain why Dante returned to the love of a woman, be it spiritualized like that of Beatrice, in the last years of his life, and dedicated to it the last thoughts of his mind and the last throbbing of his heart. The progression established by Barbi does not exist in Dante. The *Convivio* was written with a polemic spirit. The *Commedia* remains a book of intimacy. Dante is still a "servant of Love" in the *Commedia*, but he undertook a journey that superficial poets of the courts had never been able to undertake. Beatrice is still his "Lady," but she is the Lady who loves him. There is in the *Commedia* the remembrance of the physical charm of Beatrice together with that of her friends whom Dante had invoked to do honor to her, and whose fresh beauty now adorns the slope of Purgatory and the Earthly Paradise.

The women of the foil have reacquired their physiognomy and they perform a function close to that which the poet gave them: to serve as intermediaries between himself and Beatrice. Had these maidens not appeared near Beatrice in the *Vita Nuova?* Had they not tried to console the grieving poet? Had he not confided to them his unrequited love? And here is Lucia, Lia, and Matelda, who reappear in the *Commedia* without any fear of offending the purest love of Dante for Beatrice. Her friends on earth have now become her maidens in the world of perfections, where love can be revealed without danger of being spotted by earthly considerations.

The *Commedia* represents another phase of the poet's life, a life more thoughtful and pensive than the one projected in the *Vita Nuova*. The *Commedia* is illumined by two lights, Virgil and Beatrice: Virgil, the symbol of the elevating power of poetry; Beatrice, the symbol of intellectual love. The *Commedia* was the book over which Beatrice presided, just as Aristotle, "the master of those who know," presided over the *Convivio*.

In the *Commedia* Dante develops and deepens the love concept of the poetry of his youth by giving to it a philosophical character. In the *Purgatorio* Love appears to him as an innate force that bends man toward the object by which he feels attracted. From it depends "ogni buono operare e il contrario" (every good deed and its contrary), and it is

> sementa in voi d'ogni virtute
> E d'ogni operazion che merta pene.

> a seed in you of every virtue
> And of every deed that deserves punishment.[29]

In the second canticle Love assumes always new forms as the mind of the poet returns to meditate on this great force. Yet, he never dissociates his thinking from his human experience. Even before meeting Beatrice, as he climbs the slopes of Purgatory, Dante has a dream in which the impure thought of the *femmina balba* (the stammering old female), "who turned Ulysses away from his delectable path," disturbed his mind. The victory of the lady, "holy and swift," shows the victory of the poet's idealism over the seduction of the flesh that rises from the forbidding darkness of the night.

The search as to what Love really was, was so insistent that, after having discussed its nature in the seventeenth and eighteenth cantos of the *Purgatorio*, he returned to it in the twenty-fifth, exposing in it the generation of man in terms extremely scientific and realistic. Thus the *Purgatorio* reflects Dante's thoughts on Love considered as a cosmic force and as an individual experience. Without this assiduous and passionate work of Dante's thought on Love it is difficult to understand his confession to Beatrice, in the thirty-first canto, of the wanderings of the poet after her death.

He unveils there his whole soul, proclaiming his love, perfect and pure, for the woman whom he knew in his youth. Only after his long journey through the horrors of the *Inferno* and the sufferings of the *Purgatorio* does Dante realize, in his thoughtful maturity, that Love, according to the ideal of the poets of Provence, has become a deep and living reality. It is there, at the summit of the mountain of Purgatory, that he offers to Beatrice the love that he has not been able to offer her on this earth.

The *Commedia* is radiant with love. It is, indeed, essentially a love poem in which Dante kept the promise made to Beatrice at the very end of the *Vita Nuova*, that he would say of her what had never been said of any other woman.

It must not be believed that Beatrice in the *Commedia* assumes the abstract form of a symbol, even if critics have seen in her theology or revelation. Her profile in the *Commedia* is much stronger and more concrete than in the *Vita Nuova* where the pearl-like color of her forehead passes lightly in the guise of the souls that the poet believed reflected in the transparency of the Heaven of the Moon. Beatrice is thoroughly humanized in the *Paradiso*. Her smile has virtually tried the ingenuity of the poet in his attempt to render it in numberless ways. It is a great blunder to imagine that Beatrice's body has left no trace in Dante's memory, nor, consequently, in his book.

Nor is it to be believed that the love concept, resumed in the *Commedia*, became a diaphanous or an anemic mysticism. It was the mysticism of a man who was very severely tried by experience and who matured in a life of grief that would have broken any other man.

The basic ideas of the *Vita Nuova* reappear in it, but transformed. Thus the Provençal principle, that Love leads man to God, reappears here, too, but lives again in the light of all that Beatrice, so frail a remembrance in terms of the human, had been in reality for him during the years of his exile. Beatrice becomes in the *Commedia* a synonym of truth or, at least, the one who leads Dante toward absolute truth, that is God:

Quel sol, che pria d'amor mi scaldò il petto,
   Di bella verità m'avea scoverto,
   Provando e riprovando, il dolce aspetto.

That sun, which first warmed my breast with love,
   Of beautiful truth had discovered to me,
   By proving over and over again, the sweet countenance.[30]

Love in the *Commedia* has gone beyond the human; it has become a flight above the earthly conditions of man, a conquest of the immutable values of truth, whose degrees of continuous ascent are symbolized by Dante and Beatrice rising through the sphere of Paradise. It may not be amiss to note that in the *Convivio* the seven spheres had been the symbol of the seven liberal arts, of the trivium and the quadrivium. The highest point of the ascent through Paradise is reached in the last canto when the love of Beatrice, through the mystic St. Bernard, allows Dante to see the innermost nature of the universe:

Nel suo profondo vidi che s'interna,
   Legato con amore in un volume,
   Ciò che per l'universo si squaderna:
Sustanza ed accidente, e lor costume,
   Quasi conflati insieme per tal modo,
   Che ciò ch'io dico è un semplice lume.

I saw that in its depths penetrate,
   Bound with love in one volume,
   What through the universe is unfolded
   In multiplicity of forms:
Substances and accidents and their ways,
   Almost perfectly blended together, in such a manner
   That what I write gives but a feeble glimmer of its
      actual reality.[31]

The *Paradiso* is the kingdom of absolute faith reached through the love of Beatrice. It is Beatrice who keeps alive in him the faith that to live is to pass through "the large sea of being," and that the shadow of God is projected over the universe. In the

Vita Nuova Dante had identified Love with Beatrice. In the *Paradiso* the theme of Love is resumed but in proportions that make it embrace cosmic Love. The last line of the *Commedia* reveals the unity between God and Love, between Love and universal life, and it gives us one of the first revelations of the hidden God of whom Pascal spoke.

Francesca da Rimini and the
Dolce Stil Nuovo

THE episode of Francesca da Rimini (*Inferno V*) is beset by a deep contradiction. Francesca, as a sinner, is in the second circle of Hell, where those who have yielded to lust are tossed about by a raging storm, but in the episode she stands as a glorification of Love. Does Dante glorify the sinner in her? If so, why should he have placed Francesca in Hell? If not, why should he have presented her in the light of sympathy which is diffused around her? Here lies the contradiction which we wish to solve.

The apparent inconsistency has been felt by several critics who have dealt with it according to their interpretation of the episode and of Dante's entire poem. Dall'Ongaro evades the issue by saying that it is a "sublime contradiction." [1] Foscolo believes that Dante's attitude toward Francesca was actuated by his gratitude to her family, as he had been a guest of her father, Guido da Polenta, and of her nephew, Guido Novello. Ginguené goes further and states that Paolo and Francesca are not really damned. [2] Francesco de Sanctis faces the issue but solves it in a way that needs a brief discussion. "Those two go together," states the great critic in rejecting Ginguené's theory, "and they love each other even through eternity, not because they are not damned, but, indeed, because they are damned." [3] He explains his attitude by pointing out that in Hell all earthly conditions are made eternal and remain unchanged, as in the case of Filippo Argenti and Capaneo. True, but sin in the case of the latter two is their penalty. Filippo Argenti had yielded to wrath and through wrath he is punished. Capaneo had defied God and his own curses are his punishment. Virgil rebukes him thus:

> O Capaneo, in ciò che non s'ammorza
> La tua surperbia, se' tu più punito;
> Nullo martirio, fuor che la tua rabbia,
> Sarebbe al tuo furor dolor compito.

> O Capaneus, in that your pride is not softened
> You are greatly punished;
> No punishment, except your rage,
> Would be a befitting pain to your furor.[4]

"There is not the slightest detail on which the word 'sin' is not written," [5] concludes De Sanctis, using the presence of sin to fashion a Francesca not different from a woman of contemporary fiction and seeing in Dante a forerunner of the realistic writers. Living in the age of naturalism and reacting against the emptiness of the decadent romanticism, De Sanctis tinged his criticism of Dante with his realistic aesthetic belief to the point that, to him, Francesca is the first real woman who has appeared in Italian literature, one who has eclipsed Beatrice and Laura, who are, to him, mere concepts of a feminine ideal. Benedetto Croce follows entirely De Sanctis's point of view, emphasizing even more the presence of passion in the episode. "Their love was a true love, complete and real, soulful, sensuous, with gentle and delicate aspirations, the ecstasy of beatitude; languor, abandon, perdition." [6]

To us, however, Francesca is Beatrice's sister and, if this can be proven, we propose to draw conclusions about Dante and his art which are very different from those of the above-mentioned critics. Francesco De Sanctis tried to remove the contradiction in the episode by glorifying Francesca's sin; we, on the other hand, shall try to show how Dante glorified Francesca in the name of Love as the *Dolce Stil Nuovo* conceived it.

When we find Dante in the circle of the lustful ones, he sternly and objectively points out the sinners who are punished in it:

Intesi ch'a così fatto tormento
Enno dannati i peccator carnali,
Che la ragion sommettono al talento.

I understood that to such a torment
Are damned the carnal sinners,
Who submit reason to instinct.

A storm rages in an atmosphere "mute of every light," and it
tosses the spirits in the midst of shrieking cries, moans, and
laments. Dante wants to know the names of the sinners and
Virgil mentions Semiramis, Dido, Cleopatra, Helen of Troy,
Achilles, Paris, and Tristan. There is a vast difference between
the way in which Dante refers to the sinners as an abstract
moralist and his attitude toward the great lovers of antiquity and
history. He is, to be sure, severe with Semiramis:

Che libito fe'licito in sua legge,

Who made libitum licit in her laws,

but when Virgil mentions Dido:

che s'ancise amorosa

who killed herself for love

and Helen and Achilles, Cleopatra, Paris, and Tristan, Dante's
heart fills with pity and he is almost overcome:

Pietà mi vinse e fui quasi smarrito.

Compassion overcame me, and I almost fell in a swoon.

It seems that the key to the whole episode lies in this changed
state of mind that gradually lets the episode drift away from the
main narrative and gives to it a unity of its own. We, too, as we
read, forget the sinners and the entire circle where lust is punished.

As Dante listens to Virgil mentioning the great lovers of antiquity, he is no longer looking at their sin; he feels himself lost in the dream and beauty which are diffused around them. This attitude is quite natural in one who evokes memories of the great lovers of the past and looks at them through time which shrouds in solemn silence the deeds of man. Sin sinks into oblivion and only the noble transport of the human heart remains. The language itself in referring to the celebrated lovers has changed, and the strength of the first lines of the canto is followed by a musical sequel of *terzine*, light and luminous. Of Dido he says that *s'ancise amorosa* and of all the other shadows that

> Amor di questa vita dipartille.
>
> Love departed them from this life.

These *terzine* serve not only as a background to the episode, but they also show the change which has taken place in Dante's mind. In the presence of the great lovers of history, that which appeared lust to Dante, the moralist, has become love to Dante, the dreamer. A dreamer is not necessarily the man, and even less, the poet, who is ignorant of the negative and relative sides of human nature. He is the man, and especially the poet, who ignores the negative and relative in the name of what is positive and absolute in the deeds of man, rising to love's loftier levels and forgetting the weakness of the flesh.

In the *Vita Nuova* Dante's life exists, so to say, on two planes, on one side his stormy and passionate youth, on the other the sublime love for Beatrice. Beatrice represented for him an ideal embodiment of love which was marred and offended by the presence of other women in his life. To us the women of the foil are not a mere imitation of a literary device used by the Troubadours, but real women for whom Dante did not feel the same platonic love that Beatrice awakened in his heart. Were it not so, Beatrice would not have denied him her greeting, as Dante tells us:

And for this reason, that is to say, for this widespread rumor that seemed to cast on me the infamy of vice, that most gentle lady ... denied me her greeting which was all my beatitude.[7]

When Dante meets Forese in Purgatory, we learn from the poet's own lips how turbulent his youth had been, and we still possess an insulting sonnet written by the lofty poet of mysticism about Forese's wife. A fundamentally different Dante from the lover in the *Vita Nuova* appears in the *Rime Pietrose* in which he sings of his violent passion for a woman to whom he refers as Pietra. Guido Cavalcanti, in one of his sonnets, with tenderness and concern, grieves over the manner in which his dear friend, Dante, wastes his youth. In the *Vita Nuova* there is but a faint echo, and well disguised, of this turbulence, while Dante's youth appears suffused with the light that Beatrice casts on it. The *Vita Nuova* represents a frantic projection in the world of the absolute, a flight to a lofty plane in order to forget the tormenting struggle of a sensuous youth. Dante is plainly conscious of this projection into the realm of the absolute as we can see from a passage in the very beginning of the book:

and since to dwell on passions and deeds of such extreme youthfulness seems a sort of language worthy of fable, I shall leave this aside and ... shall come to those words that are written in my memory under more important headings.[8]

In his quest for a higher plane and a nobler style, shunning the lowness of the *fabula*, Dante chooses to relate the more important events of his life that refer to his love for Beatrice. In this fashion he leaves out the struggle that he underwent to curb his violent and passionate nature. Had he not done so, he would have realized an aesthetic canon that became the accepted basis of art only in the nineteenth century. Love, with its relative characteristics, Love in its becoming, does not appear in the *Vita Nuova*. Still less does it appear in the *Commedia* where Beatrice, radiant with the beauty of immortality, leads him to the very pinnacle of human perfection, which is the contemplation of

Truth and of God. Dante saw in Beatrice Love, pure Love, because he had in his soul the power to forget her body and to replace it by a spiritualized being. To imagine him ignorant of the human side is to follow in the footsteps of Biscioni, Rossetti, or of Perez, who saw in her only an allegory and not a real person. Dante presents his love for Beatrice after he has purified it of all elements of passion. His story begins on the luminous threshold of the Ideal, leaving out what appeared negative to him and what might disturb his dream. If we do not keep this in mind the *Dolce Stil Nuovo* and almost the entire *Commedia* lose their meaning and value for us.

Dante's century was an age of sublime synthesis, in which all aspects of life were harmonized. In the early centuries of the Christian Age asceticism had despised the human body. In the thirteenth century, on the contrary, mysticism accepted all the earthly realities and lent them a spiritual significance. Dante, in the *Vita Nuova*, gave us the luminous tangibility of Beatrice's beauty, and his theory was that we are attracted by the tangible and bodily charms, but that we must rise through them to the contemplation of the absolute and eternal beauty. His love for Beatrice was interwoven with the moral problem of his youth, and Beatrice stood before him as the giver of a moral rhythm to his life. Love was to him spiritual affinity between gentle persons and, as such, it was sung by all the songsters of the *Dolce Stil Nuovo*. It is the same with Francesca da Rimini as with Beatrice. Dante saw in her the lover, he gave her his own feelings, and only a luminous, gentle lady stood before him. This shows that in the *Commedia* there remained the same attitude toward love as had been expressed in the *Vita Nuova*, the marvelous book which grew under the influence of the ideals of the *Dolce Stil Nuovo*.

It has been the custom to point out that a gap exists between the *Vita Nuova*, expression of Dante's idealism, and the *Commedia*, embodiment of Dante's realism. This leads to the question: was Dante a realist and in what sense was he a realist? Dante's reality was in the conscience of man and not in the world of senses. He was a Neo-Platonist. The great value of the *Commedia* lies in the fact that it portrays Dante's victorious journey to a moment of supreme inner quietude sought in vain through an active and stormy life, through war, politics, through the study of philosophy and science, and only found in the secret chamber of his heart where his dreams abode under the gentle light of Beatrice's love. This transcendental attitude permeates the whole of the *Commedia*. In it life is looked at from a distance. It is a meditation on life which results in a tragic indictment of Evil, in the ghastly punishments of Hell, and in a glorification of Good, in the bliss of Paradise. The *Commedia* was written during Dante's exile, and it bears the scars that experience had left in his heart. Dante was a disillusioned and grieving man. Offended by actual life, he sought refuge in an ideal world. Hence his constant projection toward the past, when beauty and chivalry reigned, his indictment of the present sordid misery, and his losing himself in the light and harmonies of Paradise.

Love does not fundamentally change in the *Commedia*. It becomes more human in a Dantesque and universal sense as it is laden with all the weight of the sorrows of the poet's life. Love is more human, not because it acquires any element of passion, but because it is the only solace of the sorrows of a great soul. In many passages Dante discusses love. In the *Purgatorio* he gives a definition of it which can be summarized thus: love is our bending toward an object of loveliness. Love is followed step by step from its incipient stage to its highest development. His analysis takes into account, with the accuracy of a modern psychologist, all the elements, bodily as well as spiritual, which create this mysterious power. Love is awakened in us through our senses, but it develops into a spiritual phenomenon, because our desire is a spiritual movement.[9] Dante's intellectual and universal reaction is never dissociated from the actual experience of life, so that his idealism stands on a concrete basis. We find in this theory the same conception as expressed in the *Vita Nuova*, the love that Dante felt in the pure countenance of Beatrice, in the light of

her eyes, in the radiance of her smile. When Dante meets
Beatrice on the top of Purgatory, she reproaches him for having
yielded to passion after her death. Her words rehearse Dante's
theory that we have just illustrated.

> Mai non t'appresentò natura od arte
> Piacer, quanto le belle membra in ch'io
> Rinchiusa fui, e sono in terra sparte; [10]

> Never nature nor art offered to you
> A pleasure as great as the beautiful limbs
> In which I was enclosed, which now are scattered over
>   the earth.

Body and soul are here presented in a sublime unity, and pleasure
is again spiritualized through the pure beauty that shone in
Beatrice. The treatment of the concepts of "pleasure" and
"beauty" interests us all the more that they appear in the episode
of Francesca. It was the *bella persona* of Francesca that revealed
love to Paolo's heart, just as Dante came to know love through
the *bella membra* of Beatrice. Francesca, in requiting Paolo's
love, shared the same *piacere* which gave Dante the joy that
consoled and uplifted his heart in the days of his youth as well as
during the stormy adventures of his manhood. The parallelism
found in the two episodes shows beyond any doubt that Dante
attributed to Paolo and Francesca the same kind of love that
existed between him and Beatrice.

Francesca is not the only idealized woman in the *Commedia*.
Indeed, Dante's poem is a marvelous garden where these flowers
of feminine loveliness bloom. Pia, Piccarda, Lia, Matelda, Cos-
tanza, Cunizza express the embodiment of the feminine ideal
such as Dante patterned after Beatrice or after his own dream.

Many reasons must have contributed toward Dante's idealization of Francesca. He must have seen and known Paolo during
the time that the latter was *capitano del popolo* at Florence in
1282. Paolo is described by all commentators as handsome and

given to the gentle cult of art. What more natural than to idealize his love for Francesca of whom Dante describes *la bella persona?* Love, according to the code of the *Dolce Stil Nuovo*, had nothing to do with the marriage ties of the lady or man. It was a humble worship that realized its goal in a poetical vent of lofty feelings. How gentle and delicate are the words and thoughts that Dante lends to Francesca! Peace and love hover over the whole episode and they spread a gentle light, a hush of mystic silence over the mysterious search for love that torments man. In that silence every toil, every contradiction disappears, and Dante's mind feels again that peace which Francesca wishes him and which he had experienced in Beatrice's presence; Beatrice, who made everyone chaste and cast a veil of longing melancholy on the soul of man.

At the time that Dante wrote the *Commedia* the sad happening of the death of Francesca and Paolo belonged already to the past, and the lovers had taken their place for the love poets near Tristan and Iseult. They, too, had made the supreme sacrifice of their lives for love.

Dante's stern moral sense, however, condemned Francesca to Hell because she, being married to Gianciotto, had felt love for Paolo, his brother. No admiration, no affection, no sympathy ever stood in the way of Dante's moral sense. Ulysses, Brunetto Latini, Farinata, Ugolino are all persons whom Dante admired greatly but whom he placed, nevertheless, in Hell. He glorified them not for the sin for which they are punished, but for other attributes that he admired in them. As to Francesca, Dante vindicates the nobility of her love for Paolo when she relates to him the story of that love.

Paolo and Francesca are pictured in the episode against a background of courtly life which Gabriele D'Annunzio has reconstructed in his play so magnificently and so perfectly. They are reading a book of courtly love, the romance of Lancelot. Unknowingly they feel lost in an atmosphere of love. The simile of doves comes to Dante's mind. As doves glide toward their nest carried by their longing, so Paolo and Francesca answer the call

of the poet, who begs them to come to him in the name of the love
that gently carries them:

> O anime affannate,
> Venite a noi parlar, s'altri nol niega.

> O souls who know the pangs of love,
> Come to speak to us, if you are not impeded.

Dante forgets altogether the circle, the sinners, and the punishments. He addresses them as *anime affannate*, referring to *affanni
d'amore*, and thus using the terminology of love poetry. It is the
love of the *Dolce Stil Nuovo* as we can see from the mention
of *cor gentile* and *dolci sospiri*, *dolci pensieri*, and from the personification of Love; a personification and a terminology which
lead us back to the doctrine of love of that school. "It is as
natural for a gentle heart to love as for a bird to hasten to the
verger," had said Guinizelli, and Dante had clarified that thought
in his sonnet:

> Amore e cor gentil sono una cosa.

> Love and the gentle heart are the same thing.

Benedetto Croce notices the presence of these concepts, but
thinks that they are placed there to induce Paolo and Francesca
to their sin.[11] On the contrary, their presence in the episode
shows that, for Dante, Francesca's love for Paolo was a natural
movement, natural in a superior order of concepts. Love, which
to the songsters of the *Dolce Stil Nuovo* was the supreme power
in the universe, echoes in the episode:

> Amor che a cor gentil ratto s'apprende.
> Amor che a nullo amato amar perdona.

> Love that to the gentle heart quickly clings.
> Love who to no one, who is loved, forgives not to
>   love back.

If we forget that this conception of love is diffused around Paolo and Francesca, we are easily led astray. G. G. Parodi, another modern critic, sees in Francesca "a woman who loves that way, with all herself and forever," and "what does Francesca know of duty and of wrong? What do excuses matter to her?" [12] He bases his conception of Francesca on Dante's line, "Amor ch'a nullo amato amar perdona." Parodi's conception of womanhood does not exist in Dante. What meaning have the words "it is a necessity to requite with love him who loves" severed from the philosophical background that Dante gave to them? To understand the episode, we must imagine it in close and immediate relation with the *Dolce Stil Nuovo*. Dante is simply above the excuses and wrongs in the question. He thinks only of love, and in that name he bids Francesca to tarry and speak to him. Again, how could Dante have spoken to Francesca of a love that reminded her of a sinful relation? While Dante, in the midst of the infernal storm, ponders over their tragedy, he feels in it only a pure and mysterious affinity between two noble and gentle souls. Francesca had discovered love in her heart in response to Paolo's delectation in her. Their love was made of *dolci sospiri*, and it prompted them to read together the courtly romance of Lancelot. Dante delicately portrays their love as existing unknown to them. "Soli eravamo e senza alcun sospetto," Francesca tells him, and it is this feeling that makes the poet declare the two lovers innocent and wronged, in no uncertain terms. Dante calls them *anime offense* and bows his head in pity and sympathy, meditating on the beauty of their love. His chief anxiety is to know from Francesca how love was revealed to them:

> Ma dimmi: al tempo de' dolci sospiri,
> A che e come concedette Amore
> Che conosceste i dubbiosi desiri?

> But tell me: at the time of sweet sighs,
> To what purpose and how did Love grant you
> That you came to know the unrevealed longings?

One day they were reading together how Lancelot, the gentle and timid lover, was kissed by Guinevere, and Paolo's lips sought hers. This moment of supreme ecstasy was shattered by their death. In the episode three stages of their love are considered: the *dubbiosi desiri*, when love was diffused in their lives without their being conscious of it; the revelation of it through their reading Lancelot's romance; and their tragedy, *il doloroso passo*. Love was about to become passion and Dante called on Death to keep that love on the heights that Beatrice had assigned to it. The atmosphere of *fabula* was about to envelop the two lovers in its prose and he jealously snatched them from it to raise them again to the regions of his lofty poetry where they abide in the luminous beauty of the episode.

Dante's sympathy was so stirred by Francesca's story that he arbitrarily created for the two lovers a vague state that differentiates them from the other sinners. Paolo and Francesca are not violently tossed by the storm like other sinners, but they are gently wafted by their love.

> que' due che insieme vanno
> E paion sì al vento esser leggieri!

> those two who go together
> And seem so light in the wind!

Their love endures even through eternity, and Paolo will never be divided from Francesca. Even the laws of Hell are broken as the storm, that Dante has just said never ceases, subsides around Francesca.

> Mentre che il vento, come fa, ci tace.

> While the wind, as it does, is silent here.

In the light of this interpretation, Francesca, while condemned by Dante, the moralist, for having loved Paolo, is redeemed by Dante, the poet, for the nobility of her love. It is her innocence that gives a meaning to her resenting the way in which her life

was taken. Likewise, it is her innocence that makes her voice echo
in the silence and lull of the infernal storm when she cries,

> Caina attende chi vita ci spense.

> Caina is waiting for him who took our lives.

What meaning would these words have on the lips of an adulterous Francesca?

By following this interpretation we can also remove a vulgar
meaning from the passage:

> Quel giorno più non vi leggemmo avante,

> That day we read no further,

which is construed by critics to convey a veiled allusion to a
tryst between her and Paolo. Could the Francesca we have known
in the episode speak in such a manner? Could such a remark from
Francesca be followed by the closing lines of the episode?

> Mentre che l'uno spirto questo disse,
> L'altro piangeva sì che di pietade
> Io venni men così com'io morisse;
> E caddi come corpo morto cade.

> While one spirit said this,
> The other wept so that with compassion
> I fell in a swoon, as if I were dying;
> And I fell as a dead body falls.

We interpret those words as a clarification of the *doloroso passo*,
their death: "We read no further because death claimed us in
that very moment."

Furthermore, by considering the episode somewhat isolated
from the main narrative, we can account for the fact that the two
lovers do not share altogether the lot of the other sinners and for
the subsiding of the storm. We can also understand why Caina,

the circle of traitors, is waiting for Gianciotto, and, above all, we can see why Dante is so passionately sympathetic with Francesca.

The remembrance of the love that Dante felt for Beatrice had never abandoned him. It shone like a beacon above all his sorrows and disappointments, even to the last years of his life during the bitter days of his exile, when Francesca's countenance smiled on him. The conception of love which he lent to Francesca forms a link between Beatrice and her, between the *Vita Nuova* and the *Divina Commedia*, the first and last chapter of Dante's life.

Salutati's Letters to the
Archbishop of Canterbury

A Note on Humanism in the Fourteenth Century

THE study of the three letters that the Italian humanist and statesman, Coluccio Salutati, addressed to Thomas Arundel, Archbishop of Canterbury, constitutes a modest contribution to a better knowledge of the contacts between Italy and England at the end of the fourteenth century and at the very beginning of the fifteenth. They prove that the Church, trade, and culture continued to be very active factors in the relations between the two countries as they had been in previous centuries. The three letters cover a period of time of four years, from 1399 to 1403, and they give us a glimpse of the conditions of England and Italy in those years, while casting a revealing light on Coluccio's temperament and on the nature and forms of his Humanism.

Thomas Arundel, Archbishop of Canterbury, was caught in one of the many violent political storms that lashed England during the reign of Richard II and in which the Archbishop was a very active participant. Richard II was attempting to increase his royal authority by the process of centralization that independent lords naturally resisted. Three families were especially active: Gloucester, Warwick, and Arundel. In 1397 Richard II, with the help of the French, struck at his enemies. Thomas's brother ended his life on the gallows and the Archbishop by an act of Parliament was deprived of the archbishopric of Canterbury. Thomas Arundel, after a sojourn in France, sought refuge in Italy and went to Rome to ask Pope Boniface IX not to recognize the edict that deprived him of his seat. The Pope, to avoid a break with either side, compromised by giving Thomas Arundel the archbishopric of St. Andrews in Scotland. Before returning to England, the Archbishop visited Florence and met the Chancellor of the Republic, Coluccio Salutati.

Coluccio was already advanced in years when he met the Archbishop in Florence, around the year 1398. The first letter that the Chancellor addressed to Thomas Arundel bears the date of August 30, 1399.[1] It was carried to England by a member of the Archbishop's household who had been an eyewitness of the event that Coluccio described. The letter deals with the religious revival of the Bianchi or Whites that took place during the months of August and September in 1399. The detailed account of what happened on that occasion bears witness to the deeply religious fervor of Coluccio Salutati. Florentine citizens, described as "prone to violence and vengeance," [2] are said in the letter to have turned to God and to religion: "All have donned the sackcloth, sing hymns, and visit the holy shrines. Having been marvelously converted, all have turned to penitence. They fast, abstain from meat, and, even if they are persons of high lineage and rank, they go barefoot through the city, visit the religious places, and weep over their sins with humility and devotion." [3]

The religion of Salutati assumes a most orthodox form in this letter. Not only does he speak about miraculous happenings in generic terms borrowed from St. Matthew's gospel,[4] but he also refers to the sweat of blood that had covered four images of Christ within the territory of the Republic. Coluccio even sent to the Archbishop a copy of the letter pertaining to this supernatural event, that had been received by the Council of the Florentine Republic.

This revival must have struck Salutati most deeply because he refers to it also in a letter to a friend and contemporary of his, Pietro Turchi.[5] His attitude toward that religious event, as expressed in this letter, is the same as the one revealed in the letter to the Archbishop of Canterbury: extreme piety and complete orthodoxy.

In the face of the repeated expressions in Salutati of a religious faith that to many might even seem extreme, it is surprising to

notice the insistence with which Francesco Novati tried to mini-
mize the religious enthusiasm of Coluccio.[6] The great historian
and critic, to whom we owe the matchless edition of Salutati's
letters, goes to great pains in quoting laws and ordinances enacted
on that occasion by the city council which point to an objective
attitude toward religious revival on the part of some of Coluccio's
contemporaries and superiors. Ordinances, however, being acts of
government, can concern themselves only with the order and
safety of the city and not with the religious meaning of the event
in question. They possess a questionable value in documenting
the personal feelings of those who witnessed the revival.

Novati's attitude has been that of many critics who have studied
the Humanism of the fourteenth century and have colored it
with their personal leanings to the point of transforming the
Humanists into a sort of late nineteenth-century positivistic
thinkers. If we judge by the testimony of Salutati's contemporaries, nothing is further removed from the truth. The traits of
the cultural life of the fourteenth century documented by Salutati's letters are borne out especially by the often-quoted passages
from Petrarch's work as well as by Boccaccio's statement about
his age in the fourteenth and fifteenth books of his *Genealogies of
the Gentile Gods*.[7] For us these three poets and scholars represented the new spirit that was the Renaissance, but transcendentalism and ascetism were still integral parts of the new pattern that
civilization assumed in their age. Religion was an essential part
of the cultural world and classicism and Christianity coexisted
very harmoniously in the minds of the men of that time.[8] It
is true that secular civilization was gradually assuming clearer
forms, but the Church was still a very strong factor in the
civilization of the fourteenth century, and individual religious
faith was not affected by the new belief that the Church should
not interfere with the internal affairs of the state. Marsilio of
Padua's *Defensor Pacis* (1324) was a significant document of
the consciousness of the role and nature of the secular state
then dawning, but it was the exception and not the rule in its
unorthodox attitudes in matters pertaining to dogma. Dante's

De Monarchia gives clear evidence of the sharp distinction that most intellectual men drew between the Church as a political entity and the Church as a religious institution. Viewed from the perspective of the fourteenth century, Marsilio stands out definitely as a rebel, and his extreme positions in matters of dogma become greatly toned down, if one remembers that he was writing from the standpoint of Ludwig of Bavaria against Pope John XXII, and defending state rights against the encroachment of the Curia. Thus the transcendentalism expressed in Salutati's letters was in accord with the predominant spirit of the age. The solemn and gloomy aspects of Italian cities of those days, with their narrow, winding, and ill-lighted streets, were the result not only of economic and military necessity but also of a vague detachment from the joys of life in keeping with the religious teaching of spurning the gifts of the earth. These conditions form a suitable background to the disdain for the material side of life constantly expressed by Salutati in his letters.[9] The study of the classics, in whose writings, he, like Petrarch and Boccaccio, sought a moral lesson, was a large part of the secluded and austere existence that he lived. It never occurred to this generation of Humanists to identify classicism with a pleasure-seeking or even pragmatic mode of life. The materialists and libertines of their time were their enemies, as they were of asceticism and Humanism.

The second letter that the Chancellor of the Florentine Republic addressed to the Archbishop of Canterbury bears the date of April 4, 1401.[10] In it Salutati entrusted to the care of the English prelate, a friend and neighbor who had left Florence and had gone to England for reasons of trade, a common practice for enterprising Italians especially at a time when the advancing tide of Islam was closing the East to their activity.[11] Salutati's friend was Antonio Mannini, and Coluccio referred to him in very endearing terms, calling him *vicinum et fratrem meum*, (neighbor and bosom friend). Mannini, as Novati has established, was an ambitious merchant who was in England in the days of political turmoil under Richard II, and again returned there in 1441.[12]

Salutati had set for himself a very difficult task in writing a letter to the Archbishop of Canterbury in behalf of his friend. Mannini, in his adventurous and perhaps meddlesome life, had taken sides against the Archbishop of Canterbury during the rebellion under Richard II. He had even gone to Rome to serve the cause of the new incumbent in the see of Canterbury. Coluccio was supposed to plead for his friend and see to it that he would be forgiven by the Archbishop and restored to the favor of the latter. The skillful diplomat of the Florentine Republic did this most adroitly. His letter is a document of his political tact. In it he begins by rejoicing at the safe return to England of his friend, the Archbishop of Canterbury. He hopes that he did not incur any hardships during the stormy days of the revolution. Indeed, he hopes that out of the evil and horrible experience he will reap benefits for himself since "bonis omnia cooperantur in bonum" (everything turns out well for worthy people). He cannot refrain, however, from adding that it is a mark of nobility to be forgiving, and that it is better to receive offense and injuries than to inflict them on others. Having thus prepared the ground, Coluccio recommends his friend, adding that if Mannini found himself on the opposite side during the revolution, he was ordered to do so by the King, and compelled by the pressure of the Archbishop's enemies.

After having discussed this somewhat official business, Coluccio, as he was wont, passed to personal and cultural matters that show us what intellectual ties linked the two men. Coluccio begs his friend to see to it that he, Coluccio, receives St. Augustine's treatise, De Musica. Since Salutati refers to this work in a very laconic manner, it can be deduced that the two men must have spoken about it when the Archbishop was in Florence. This supposition is confirmed by the third letter that we shall analyze presently. The conversation of the two friends, undoubtedly carried on in Latin during the Archbishop's visit to Florence, throws light on the intellectual side of their friendship, which, if we believe what Salutati writes in this letter, must have been very intimate and deep. To convey to the Archbishop the depth and warmth of his feeling toward him, Coluccio quotes from Terence: "Dies noctesque me ames; me desideres" (Love and long for me day and night).[13]

Coluccio also asks his friend whether he would be interested in reading his own treaty on the nobility of law and medicine, a book that, as Salutati informs us, grew out of a dispute with a physician. If he is interested, Coluccio will have a copy made for him. We know of Petrarch's attack against the physicians of his time, and this letter documents the irreconcilable antagonism that existed between the Humanists and the scientists of this time.

By studying Salutati's literary form we can detect in his writings one of the main traits of Humanism, that of embellishing literary diction with classical imagery and parallels. In the days of Petrarch and Coluccio Salutati, Humanism aimed at this goal, while scientists clung to cold facts and unimaginative diction. The discrepancies between the pattern of thinking of the Humanists and the scientists were more formal than substantial, though the more objective attitude of the latter toward reality was to lead, in the following century and especially in the Cinquecento, to the establishment of the method of scientific investigation on which rests the science of our age.

From Coluccio's third letter,[14] written on January 29, 1403, we learn that the Archbishop had not taken the trouble to send an answer to Coluccio about St. Augustine's book during the two years that had elapsed from the date of the letter that we have just examined. However, in 1403 the Archbishop had sent to Florence a member of his household, whose name is latinized by Coluccio into Nicolaus Lucefrus, with the task of copying Salutati's book, *De nobilitate legum et medicinae*. Coluccio wants to make a gift of his work to the Archbishop and, therefore, promises to have a copy made and sent to him. At the same time he asks again for a copy of St. Augustine's six books, *De Musica*.

We are informed that when the Archbishop was in Florence, Coluccio had asked him whether he owned that work and, upon receiving an affirmative answer from the prelate, Salutati had expressed his ardent desire to have a copy made for him. The open and naïve expression of Salutati's longing for St. Augustine's book is an additional proof that for him there was no chasm between classical and medieval books, between the civilization of classical Rome and that of Christian Rome. He was ardently interested in both. The perusal of Salutati's letters shows that only in the following century, in such men as Leonardo Bruni, Niccolò Niccoli, and Lorenzo Valla, there began a clear-cut separation between classical and medieval culture. Such a departure can be amply documented,[15] but it refers more to individual attitudes, even poses at times, than to a split in the whole cultural field of the fifteenth century. It is even more uncritical to suppose such a split in the age of Salutati, as critics are wont to do.

The main purpose of the present letter to the Archbishop of Canterbury was a practical one: to help financially the monks of the convent of Santa Maria degli Angeli that the prelate had visited during his stay in Florence, and whose exemplary life he must have admired on that occasion. These brothers, according to Salutati, were in great financial straits for having bought a property close to the convent, a purchase that was made necessary by the fact that an adjoining residence was a source of danger and scandal to the monks. Will he not help, then, in a measure whose necessity and nobility must be evident to his humanity and prudence? Coluccio's diplomatic skill stood him in good stead. In the stately form of his Latin diction he circumvents every objection that might arise in the Archbishop's mind. Let not the Italian brethren be deprived of assistance by the fact that in England there are monks who, too, are needy and undoubtedly will ask help from the noble prelate. The English monks have the generosity of the Archbishop at their disposal all the time. Coluccio, like the good Humanist that he was, strengthened his eloquent plea with historical parallels. He reminded the Archbishop how

Ptolemy of Egypt and the King of Tyrus helped Solomon to build his temple. Besides, are they not all brothers in Christ?

The reference to the Archbishop's visit to the convent, a visit that perhaps implied hospitality for the foreign prelate, gives us an inkling on Thomas Arundel's sojourn in Florence, his interests and contacts. If we add to the religious interest the intellectual aspects of the relationship that united the two distinguished friends, we shall have a fairly accurate picture of the fourteenth-century Humanism, as exemplified in England by a powerful Churchman and in Italy by an outstanding statesman and man of letters.

Leonardo Bruni Aretino
and Humanism

THE work of Leonardo Bruni Aretino that bears the title of *Dialogi ad Petrum Histrum* [1] lends itself admirably to illustrate the change that intervened around 1400 in the attitude toward Humanism of such outstanding men of the previous century as Dante, Boccaccio, Petrarch, and Salutati, and that of the younger generation represented by Niccolò Niccoli, Roberto de' Rossi, and the author of the *Dialogi*, Bruni Aretino.

This important booklet appeared at a historical moment when Italian life, especially epitomized in the Florentine republic, was undergoing very radical changes, slowly relinquishing the democratic Commune and drifting more and more toward the despotism of the Signoria. Two generations are placed face to face in Bruni's work, that of the Moral Humanism of the fourteenth century and that of the Aesthetic Humanism of the following century. The book clearly reflects the much faster tempo that history and life were assuming in comparison with that known to men of the older generation, represented in the *Dialogi* by Coluccio Salutati.

The term Humanism is here referred to the classical section of the cultural background of Western civilization from the early centuries of the Christian era to the eighteenth century—the dawn of the Romantic age. The new civilization that sprang like a young and not too strong shoot at the foot of the gigantic plant of Roman civilization, culturally speaking, kept many traits that classicism bequeathed to it. Such men as Cassiodorus and Boethius, two outstanding authors of the Christian age, were nurtured in classicism. In fact, classicism was the only culture known to them and to men of their age, until, in the eleventh and later centuries, a new civilization dawned, characterized by a new language, a new theory of state and society, a new attitude toward religion, in short, a new life.

Western civilization has enjoyed periodic returns to classical sources. The first, and it can hardly be called a return, was the contact that the Fathers of the Church had with classical authors. The works of the classics, notably Plato and Aristotle, were read by those who molded Christianity in its beginning, by absorbing into its very fabric the ideas of the classical thinkers which were consonant with it. Boethius translated Aristotle in the sixth century. Plato and Aristotle constituted the pillars of twelfth-century culture at Toledo, Spain, Chartres, France, and Palermo, Italy. The *De Civitate Dei* by St. Augustine, in the fifth century, and the *Summa* by Thomas Aquinas, in the thirteenth century, could not be conceived without the close connections that their authors enjoyed with the works of the above-mentioned classical thinkers. We believe that the Humanism of the early centuries of the Christian era should be denominated as *Religious Humanism*. It flourished at a time when the Christian Church was the central factor in the history of civilization.

As civilization developed and life assumed a more definite lay character, the books of the classics were reread with aims other than religious. Thus Dante, Petrarch, Boccaccio, and Salutati sought in these books a moral lesson, looking in them for guidance and light in ennobling morally the conduct of the lay individuals of their time. This phase of Italian thought was accompanied by the gradual downfall of the Communes, a process lamented by such noble-hearted citizens of Florence and the Italian republics as Dante, Franco Sacchetti, and Salutati.

With Leonardo Bruni Aretino, Humanism assumed an aesthetic character in that in him, and in many other men of letters of the fifteenth century, every concern yielded to that of form and beauty. This is amply and clearly documented by the *Dialogi*. We propose to use this book in order to conclude that the Humanism of the fifteenth century, as represented by Poggio Bracciolini, Lorenzo Valla, Marsilio Ficino, Pico della Mirandola, Jacopo Sannazzaro, and others was *aesthetic*. This new type of Humanism was especially promoted by the Signorie of the various Italian cities, and it contributed to a new literature and a different civilization.

Leonardo Bruni Aretino (1370–1444) was among the first to look upon classicism as an integrating factor in molding the new Italian civilization that he dreamed would replace that of the fourteenth century. In this sense his importance in the history of Italian culture is very great, and the historians of Italian literature have constantly focused their attention on him.[2]

A careful examination of his *Dialogi ad Petrum Histrum* will reveal to us the deep gap that separated Leonardo Bruni from the Humanists of the previous century. The deciding factor in this split was the different traits that Bruni saw in the culture of Coluccio Salutati and those that he sought and desired in the men of culture of his own generation.

The *Dialogi* appeared in 1406[3] and they refer to a discussion on the relative merits of the civilization of the fourteenth century and those of the new one that was dawning in Florence at the very beginning of the Quattrocento. It is a sort of *Querelle des Anciens et des Modernes* in reverse, for here we find the exalted praise of the greatness of the past and the complaint over the want of significance in the present Florentine life.

The discussion is supposed to have taken place during the Easter week of the year 1401[4] in the home of the learned and universally beloved Coluccio Salutati, chancellor of the Florentine republic, and a great admirer of classicism. Other interlocutors were Niccolò Niccoli, Roberto de' Rossi, Pietro Sermini, and Leonardo Bruni himself, all four representing the younger generation.

Bruni wrote these dialogues in order to inform a very dear friend of his, Pietro Vergerio of Capodistria, then absent from Florence, of the interesting and rather heated discussion that took place between Coluccio Salutati and Niccolò Niccoli. Salutati had attacked the lack of eloquence in the younger set of his time, and Niccoli had sprung to its defense, censoring the uncouthness and mediocrity of the modern age in comparison with the greatness and splendor of the classical period. Coluccio had patiently listened to Niccoli, and then he had called to the attention of the young orator the fact that one could not very well accuse of mediocrity an age that had produced three arresting figures such as Dante, Petrarch, and Boccaccio. Niccoli, like the ardent paladine of classicism that he was, had returned to the attack by expressing a deep contempt for the mediocrity of the three poets mentioned by Coluccio, stating that, in terms of culture, they were truly wanting.

Coluccio had listened to the fiery statements of young Niccoli with a smile of almost commiseration, and the discussion, so typically Italian, had come to an end for that day. The four young interlocutors took leave of Coluccio while the glory of the setting sun enveloped in its golden light the city of Florence, beautiful in the magnificence of its marble palaces.

On the following day, so Bruni tells us in the second dialogue, Salutati, Niccoli, and the author meet in the splendid gardens of Roberto de' Rossi. Among them was also another interlocutor, Pietro di Ser Mino, better known under the name of Sermini, a youth very devoted to classical studies who later took Salutati's place as chancellor of the Florentine republic. Before them spread the city of Florence in all its splendor, astir with activity and intense life.

In the memory of all echoed the injurious words that Niccoli had addressed to the majestic figures of the three Florentine poets. It was but natural for their conversation to drift toward the continuation of the discussion of the previous day. Half jokingly and half in earnest, Salutati entrusted Niccolò Niccoli with the task of defending Dante, Petrarch, and Boccaccio. It was his punishment for having attacked them so bitterly and venomously the day before. Niccoli accepted the task very gladly; and smilingly said that he hoped that his friends had understood that he was merely jesting the previous day. He had purposely spoken against the three great Florentines in order to goad the eloquent Salutati into taking their defense. He added that, since his friends insisted that he himself should speak in defense of the three great poets, he would eagerly do so. At this point the *Dialogi* deal with a long, eloquent, and even verbose defense by Niccoli of Dante, Petrarch, and Boccaccio, as immoderate in its praise of the three poets as it had been excessive in its attack of their works.

The *Dialogi* are projected against the background of fifteenth-century Florence. In them is beautifully evoked the figure of Luigi Marsili, a monk contemporary and friend of Petrarch, a man very learned in theology and a deep student of classicism, with whom Salutati enjoyed an intimate friendship. One also finds in the book a vivid presentation of the intellectual life of Florence in the last decades of the fourteenth century, when the Greek scholar, Emanuele Crisolora, taught there and attracted the attention of the very youths who now were discussing the culture of their time with the beloved and highly respected Coluccio Salutati. We are informed in the *Dialogi* that Crisolora did not possess the gift of eloquence. He owed it to Coluccio and his silver tongue if the beauty of Crisolora's thought had reached the intellectual men of Florence.[5]

The personal tone of the *Dialogi*, while it gives a literary character to the work, allows us to notice the close communion that bound these men together through their intense interest in classical culture.

The important critics [6] who have worked on this book have valiantly striven to determine to what extent Niccoli shared the ideas revealed in the *Dialogi*, especially those attacking the three great Italian poets. Kirner, Santini, and De Franco quote Bruni's invectives against Niccoli and the *Paradiso degli Alberti*, a novel written in the beginning of the fifteenth century by Giovanni Gherardi, in order to prove that Niccoli, in his ardent enthusiasm for classicism, actually spurned modern life and literature. These accusations fall of their own weight when one reads in the *Dialogi* the statement by Niccoli that he had learned the whole *Divine Comedy* by heart, that he had gone as far as Padua to copy from the original Petrarch's works, and that he had given money to the Augustinian convent of Santo Spirito in order to honor the memory of Boccaccio by having all his works collected there.[7]

There is no doubt that Niccolò Niccoli is presented in the *Dialogi* in the light of the historical reality of his impetuous and aggressive temperament, as well as of his boundless love for classicism. It is equally true, however, that he who lends him the ideas here expressed is Leonardo Bruni. If this be true, it seems logical for us to conclude that the Niccoli of the *Dialogi*, although he is the spokesman for Bruni, is a character that exercises a fictional function in the book and that the central figure of the *Dialogi* is Leonardo Bruni Aretino.

To this effect let us notice that Bruni indirectly confesses that Niccoli's ideas are also his own when he places on Coluccio's lips the paradoxical statement that he, Bruni, "prefers to err with Niccoli rather than to use his intellect with him [Coluccio]." [8]

It also seems useless for us to ask the question whether Niccoli revealed his real views when he attacked the great Florentine poets or whether he spoke truthfully when he defended them.[9] What value can Niccoli's invectives have against Dante, Petrarch, and Boccaccio if he retracted them, and then exalted the three poets to the point of placing them near and even above classical poets?

It seems to us that the essential part of the *Dialogi* on which we should focus our attention is that portion, and that portion only, containing the accusations which Niccoli did not retract on the following day, when the group resumed the discussion in the gardens of Roberto de' Rossi. In substance, these accusations can be reduced to one only: the grieving complaint, on the part of Bruni, expressed by Niccoli, concerning the low level of culture in the modern era. Bruni declared here, in an unequivocal form, that classical civilization was the measuring rod of the greatness of any civilization. In the light of the classical age, the modern age was low and barbarous. The state of mind reflected in the *Dialogi* is that of a person who feels ill at ease in the cultural conditions of his time and aspires to a new civilization that he wishes to create. The old world that Bruni rejected was that generally referred to as the medieval world. The new culture of which he dreamed was that of the Renaissance. More than in any other book, the Renaissance was already conceived in the *Dialogi* as a copy of classical civilization, thus anticipating Vasari's views by more than one century.

The book opens with the complaint, on the part of the author, that, while Florence, with its large population and its magnificent monuments, was economically and politically significant, the *studia humanitatis* and the arts were neglected.[10] This complaint on the part of Bruni became a violent and dramatic accusation on the lips of Niccoli as the *Dialogi* developed. When, at the very opening of the book, Coluccio grieved over the neglect of eloquence and the art of forensic disputes on the part of the young, Niccoli shouted dramatically and passionately that it was not possible to be eloquent when in the city there existed a lamentable want of books and that all the arts had sunk to a very low level, even to the point of having completely disappeared.[11] In this attack he stressed the sad conditions of philosophy, that from the height reached in the days of Cicero could only show the works of Cassiodorus and Alcidius.[12]

In attacking scholastic philosophy, Bruni departed very sharply from the attitude of Petrarch and Salutati because, while these illustrious men had lamented that scholasticism had degenerated from its primitive purity, Bruni attacked scholastic philosophy in itself, accusing his contemporaries of using incorrect texts in which Aristotle himself could not have recognized his own thought. Bruni even attacked his contemporaries on the ground of impeding every progress in the search for truth through their blind respect for the authority of Aristotle. We are informed by Bruni that his contemporaries had made an idol of the Greek philosopher and were constantly shouting: "Aristotle says so!" He added, on his part: "To contradict Aristotle is a crime against divine law. These people have identified truth with what Aristotle says."[13]

As to logic, if we follow what Niccoli said, we are led to believe that its status was not happier than that of philosophy in

general. Logic was in the hands of the barbarians beyond the
Alps: Farabich, Buser, Occam, whose harsh-sounding names suf-
ficed to fill one with horror.

We are also informed that the studies of grammar and rhetoric
had sunk to such a low level as to discourage Niccoli from discussing them. He put an end to his eloquent peroration by mourning the loss of the works of Varro, Livy, Sallust, Pliny, and Cicero.
Niccoli's contempt for the culture of his times gradually became
a sincere grief in the speaker as he revealed that he felt surrounded by deep darkness while he longed nostalgically for the
greatness of classical Rome.

It should be pointed out that some of these accusations were
withdrawn on the second day, and that Coluccio made little opposition to these attacks against the conditions of learning around
1400. Although he stated that, if one wished, one could acquire
learning even in their own days, he admitted that the arts had
lost the splendor which they had enjoyed in classical Rome. On
this score Salutati was in perfect agreement with Bruni or Niccoli.
Salutati and Niccoli were also in agreement on the question of
language for learned people, and concluded that Dante should
have written in Latin and not in the Italian vernacular.

The discussion on Dante, Petrarch, and Boccaccio is of the
utmost importance for us, but only in that, for Bruni, the greatness
of the three poets should be placed on a different basis, and
evaluated from the standpoint of doctrine, culture, and eloquence.[14]

On the first day Niccoli directed many accusations against
Dante. He took him to task for not having understood the verse of
Virgil

> Quid non mortalia pectora cogis,
> Auri sacra fames?

> To what extremes don't you urge the hearts of men,
> O unbridled hunger for gold?

and for having presented Cato as an old man while the latter had
died at the age of forty-eight, as well as for having placed Brutus

among the traitors while, in reality, he defended the liberty of Rome. These accusations have no value for us because, on the second day, they were retracted by Bruni. Dante, by way of example, was justified by him on the ground that poets are free to take whatever liberties they wish in dealing with history. But there is one accusation that Bruni did not retract, and this is of the utmost importance to us. Niccoli, on the second day, did not recant the accusation that Dante lacked *latinitas*, the sense of the Latin language and of the spirit of Latin literature and civilization. It is this fact that proves for us the erudite and aesthetic attitude of Bruni in the *Dialogi*.

Bruni, in the *Dialogi*, was fully conscious that his idea of civilization and culture was very far from that of Salutati. Salutati looked at life from a deeply religious and moral point of view. Like Petrarch, he had not been able to rid himself of the effects that the asceticism of previous centuries still exercised on men of the fourteenth century. Their life philosophy was very austere.[15] Simplicity was their ideal in all life forms.

Like Petrarch, Salutati placed Christian authors side by side with pagan writers. Neither Petrarch nor Salutati felt any contrast between the great Christian saints and the great pagans, nor did they conceive any clash between the pagan and Christian civilizations that these outstanding individuals represented. The fact that the figure of Luigi Marsili was recalled with admiration as a man versed in classical authors and the Fathers of the Church documents this important trait of Humanism in the fourteenth century.

This harmonious attitude toward the classical and Christian civilization crumbled definitely in Bruni at the writing of the *Dialogi*. Bruni entertained the deepest contempt for the authors of the Christian era because of the uncouth form of their writings. For Bruni, the greatness of Dante did not rest on the beauty of the poetry of the *Commedia*, but on the doctrine which the poem contained and on the rhetoric which embellished it. Petrarch and Boccaccio were also praised by Bruni in that they were men of doctrine and interested in rhetorical style. Bruni was, and felt himself to be, different from the grammarians of former centuries through his passionate love for the beauty of form and the harmony of beautifully constructed clauses. Both the grammarians of the past and Bruni were interested in Latin words, but Bruni's interest was closely associated with the aesthetic use of words and not with the words themselves.

For Bruni, men should not seek in the books of the classics the application of the *cursus*, the great goal of men of the Curia and the Church.[16] Bruni had set a higher goal for himself and for his contemporaries: that of revealing the thirst for beauty of form that he felt shone brightly in the pages of the classical authors. Bruni attacked vehemently especially the grammarians of his time and likened them to those who, in the days of Cicero, read Aristotle in search of words, unmindful of the thought conveyed by them.

The deep change documented by the *Dialogi* was not restricted to the field of letters, but it embraces every aspect of Italian life. If the stern moral sense of Dante and Salutati yielded place to the aestheticism of Bruni, the democratic life represented by the Communes was gradually and insensibly disappearing under the violence of the new rulers, the despots. It was not without reason that Caesar was defended by Niccoli from the accusation of having destroyed the liberty of Rome. The *Dialogi* appeared when the republican ideal was losing its power and Florence, once the bulwark of democracy, was beginning to realize the well-veiled designs of the ambitious Medici. Bruni, in the *Dialogi*, disdainfully refused to associate himself with the common people in their admiration for Dante, Petrarch, and Boccaccio.[17] This is implied by the statement that Dante lacked *latinitas*.

After reading this book, in spite of the fact that Niccoli was made to retract most of his accusations, the reader discovers in himself the impression that a great gap existed between the generation of Niccoli and Bruni and that of Coluccio Salutati: Salutati, the symbol of a severe and serene life; Bruni, the symbol of a new generation, restless, aggressive, passionate, conscious of the storms of history and life that the strong and plain countenance of

Salutati had been able to dominate or to ignore. One can even think of the strength and serenity of Salutati with the same nostalgic feeling with which Bruni longed for the splendor and grandeur of the classical civilization. Yet, the fact remains that Bruni is very close to us, children of the modern age, in his sensitivity and in many of his attitudes. Without his ardent desire for the beauty of form it would be difficult to understand that explosion of the arts that Italy gave to the world in the fifteenth and sixteenth centuries.

Realistic Elements in Tasso's
Aminta

IT MAY not be amiss for us to study Tasso's *Aminta* from a strictly aesthetic point of view, independently from the historical and cultural values that it possesses through its wide influence on the courtly literature of western Europe.

Critics have surrounded Tasso's work with an atmosphere of idyll and dream not warranted by a careful reading of the text. Giuseppe Toffanin in his *Cinquecento* states: "Tasso succeeded as a great poet in the *Aminta* (1573) only. The only theme in it is the indefiniteness of love, and contrast is destroyed between the core of poetry and the elaborateness of form. The central theme is not a love story. It is love itself that takes life in evanescent figures, lives on itself, suffuses everything as if it were a reflection of a nostalgic intimacy." [1] Very much in the same vein, Vittorio Rossi had already written in his *Storia della letteratura italiana:* "The idealization of pastoral customs, already realized by ancient authors of bucolic poetry, is here entirely suffused with a quite modern sentiment of exquisite and voluptuous melancholy, which constitutes one of the greatest attractions of this most singular jewel of our literature." He also speaks of "the passionate soul of the poet who, young and happy, loses himself in the dream of an ideal world, entirely characterized by courtly refinement, mysterious melodies, and soft and gentle tenderness." [2]

It is our purpose to prove that there are no evanescent characters in *Aminta*, and that its outstanding quality is that of an often crude realism that gives to the pastoral and intentionally Platonic theme the heaviness of a comedy.

The plot is extremely simple. It deals with the unrequited love of Aminta, a young Arcadian shepherd, for Silvia, one of Diana's nymphs, who is vowed to chastity and whose only delight is hunting wild beasts. At the suggestion of Daphne, a shrewd older nymph, Aminta is to attack Silvia as she bathes naked in a pool. When the lover nears the pool, he sees the object of his love threatened by a satyr who has tied beautiful Silvia to a tree with her own tresses and is about to attack her. Aminta drives the satyr away and frees Silvia who, overcome by shame, disappears into the deep woods. She seeks shelter in the abode of Nerina, another nymph, and later the two pursue a fearful wolf in a swift hunt. Soon Silvia outdistances Nerina. As the latter nears the spot where a pack of seven wolves is crunching some bones, she comes upon a veil drenched with blood which she recognizes as that which she had given to Silvia. Nerina concludes that her beautiful and dauntless friend has been devoured by the ferocious beasts, and brings the sad tidings to Aminta. Silvia's lover, upon hearing this, tries to commit suicide by throwing himself into a ravine. Some faggots break his fall and he escapes death. Silvia, meanwhile, has returned from the hunt unscathed. Upon being apprised of the tragedy, deeply moved by the greatness of Aminta's devotion, she breaks her vow and requites the love of the passionate shepherd.

It is evident that in its outer aspect *Aminta* suggests an idealistic love theme, as befitting a composition dealing with Diana's nymphs and with the unrequited love of Aminta. It suggests also a romantic aspiration toward primitive and exotic nature, such as the deep woods of Arcadia were originally meant to signify. However, in reality, the conventionally pastoral theme is developed through a love concept so definitely and openly sensual as to be incompatible with an idyll.

In an imaginary manner we are hiding ourselves among the joyous courtiers of Ferrara for whom the play was written in 1573 while the Este family was summering on the island of Belvedere in the Po River.[3] Laughter must have readily rippled over the audience as, in the Prologue, Love appeared under the guise of a child, a fugitive from his mother Venus, and promised

> o dolci baci o cosa altra più cara

> either sweet kisses or something else that is dearer

to anyone who would hide him in the pastoral abodes of Arcadia. The worldly courtiers of Ferrara did not miss, we are sure, the implications of that promise. Nor must they have missed the point as Love announced that his goal in going to Arcadia was to smite Silvia who was rebellious to Aminta's love. He will wound her with his dart

> in quel punto
> che fia più molle

> in that part
> that will be softer.

The tone of comedy is accentuated in the opening scene when Daphne, who speaks and acts very much like an ordinary go-between, tries to persuade Silvia to love Aminta. In deprecating the fact that Silvia spurns love and finds her joy in the

> cura de l'arco e de gli strali,
> Seguir le fere fugaci e le forti
> Atterrar combattendo;

> care of the bow and arrows,
> To pursue the fleeting wild beasts
> And to kill the strong ones in combat;

she comments:

> Insipidi diporti veramente
> Ed insipida vita: e, s'a te piace,
> È sol perchè non hai provata l'altra.

> Truly insipid amusements
> And an insipid life: if it pleases you,
> It is because you have not had a taste of the other.

She confides to her friend:

> Mostrommi l'ombra d'una breve notte
> Allora quel che 'l lungo corso e 'l lume
> Di mille giorni non m'avea mostrato.

> The shadow of a short night
> Showed me what the long passing and the light
> Of a thousand days had not shown me.

Daphne's long and eloquent speech to induce Silvia to love Aminta is far from being a "winged glorification of love" as the latest critic of *Aminta*, Professor Luigi Fassò,[4] wants us to believe. In his unbounded enthusiasm and admiration, Professor Fassò has failed to see the comical element in Daphne's argument when, upon learning that Silvia considers Aminta her enemy because he desires her, she queries whether Silvia would likewise consider the ram the enemy of the ewe and the bull the enemy of the heifer:

> Stimi dunque nimico
> Il monton de l'agnella?
> De la giovenca il toro?
> Stimi dunque nimico
> Il tortore a la fida tortorella?

> Do you deem then the ram
> An enemy of the ewe?
> The bull of the heifer?
> Do you deem the turtle an enemy of his spouse?

It is true that the poetic tone of Daphne's speech rises as she describes spring as the season of love, but the effect is destroyed by Silvia's mocking answer when she concludes:

> Orsù, quando i sospiri
> Udirò de le piante,
> Io son contenta allor d'essere amante.

> Well, when I shall hear
> The plants sighing, then
> I shall be satisfied to give myself to love.

Daphne's strange characterization (strange since she is one of Diana's nymphs) is more sharply brought out in the scene in which she and Tirsi plan to have Aminta attack Silvia, as the latter bathes in the shady Pool of Diana. It is somewhat surprising to hear a nymph say:

> È spacciato un amante rispettoso,
> Consiglia 'l pur che faccia altro mestiero,
> Poi ch' egli è tal. Chi imparar vuol d'amare,
> Disimpari il rispetto: osi, domandi,
> Solleciti, importuni, al fine involi.
> E se questo non basta, anco rapisca.

> A respectful lover is doomed to failure,
> He who wants to learn the art of love
> Must forget respect. Let him dare, ask,
> Solicit, insist, in the end, let him take,
> And if this is not enough, let him steal.

It is equally surprising to hear Daphne make this statement to Tirsi concerning women:

> Or non sai tu com' è fatta la donna?
> Fugge, e fuggendo vuol ch'altri la giunga;
> Niega, e niegando vuol ch'altri si toglia;
> Pugna, e pugnando vuol ch'altri la vinca.

> Don't you know how a woman is made?
> She flees, and in fleeing
> She desires to be pursued;
> She denies, and while denying she wants to be taken.

Daphne's language is befitting her characterization. In her conversation with Silvia she repeatedly uses such phrases as "pazzarella che sei" [5] and "or guata modi, guata che dispettosa giovinetta." [6]

She succeeds in being commonplace to such an extent that one is not surprised to hear Tirsi characterize her as

> Femina, cosa mobil per natura
> Più che fraschetta al vento e più che cima
> Di pieghevole spica.

> Female, something fickle by nature
> More than a twig in the wind
> And the flexible top of an ear of wheat.

Likewise, the reader is baffled by the contradiction between Aminta's characterization as a romantic lover and the role assigned to him of attacking Silvia. Aminta's attitude when he sees the beautiful nymph tied to a tree by the violent satyr is not that of the dreamy lover that he is supposed to be:

> Egli rivolse i cupidi occhi in quelle membra belle,
> Che come suole tremolare il latte
> Ne'giunchi, sì parean morbide e bianche.

> He turned his greedy eyes towards those beautiful limbs,
> That seemed soft and white
> As milk is wont to quiver in young white rushes.

Aminta's character is even more clearly brought out by the scene in which he relates how he stole the first kiss from lovely and innocent Silvia through a subterfuge. He pretended—so he painstakingly informs Tirsi and the audience—to have been stung by a bee on his lower lip. Moaning and whining, he begged Silvia to suck out the poison with her divine lips. In this manner he had the supreme happiness of being kissed by her, although Silvia refused even to speak to him from the day that his love became known to her. To us this situation is highly farcical in spite of its erudite origin,[7] and we do not doubt at all that the courtiers of the Este household found a great deal of social entertainment in it.

The episode bespeaks the realism of the love concept ever present in the play. To this effect is to be noted the insistence with

which Tasso refers to the fact that Silvia is *ignuda e sola* in the
pool and to the pre-eminence given to the sensual quality of the
nymph's beauty.

The keynote in the treatment of the love concept, however, is
most forcibly expressed by the chorus at the end of the first act
when it harks back to the Golden Age:

> o bell'età dell'oro.

> O happy Golden Age

In it Tasso glorifies the Golden Age, not because an eternal spring
blossomed on earth, not because honey flowed from the trees, not
because the harvest came without the toil of man, not because
wars were unknown, but because morality had not yet taught men
to resist sensuality. Throwing overboard pagan as well as Christian
ethics, the poet proclaimed that the supreme law of nature and of
life is pleasure:

> s' ei piace, ei lice.

> if it pleases you, it is licit for you to do.

One naturally thinks of Dante's stern rebuke to Semiramis:

> Che libito fe'licito in sua legge

> Who made what one likes the supreme guidance
>   in her laws.

and cannot help pondering over the change that the artificiality of
court life has produced in Tasso.

It is pertinent to ask at this point why Tasso should have chosen
a pastoral theme with implications of Platonic love as proven by
the presence of Diana's nymphs, only to steep it in sensuality.
Why did he not choose comedy as a medium of expression,

following in the footprints of Machiavelli, Aretino, Lasca, and Cecchi, who had established a definite tradition in this genre? There are two important facts to be considered in this connection. One is the existence of the pastoral tradition kept alive in previous centuries by Humanism, and revived by Agostino Beccari, whose pastoral play, *Il Sacrificio*, was performed in the court of Ferrara in 1554. For a poet as respectful of conventions as Tasso, this was of great importance. The other fact is that Tasso was to write a play for the pleasure-loving courtiers of the Este household. Because of both the setting and the public, a conventional Arcadian theme, with outward forms of idealism and Platonism, appeared most appropriate to him. But the play was to be presented before one of the most dastardly realistic groups of noblemen that history has ever known, if we believe the records of their immorality. Hence, the innuendos with which the play ripples and the risqué situations which it presents.

Tasso served a clearly pragmatic end in writing *Aminta*, and the court atmosphere had definite effects on his play. It is well known that several of Tasso's contemporaries are disguised under the characters in *Aminta*: Sperone Speroni in Mopso; Giovan Battista Pigna, secretary of Alfonso d'Este, in Elpino; Battista Guarini in Batto; Lucrezia Bendidio in Licori; the poet himself in Tirsi. The courtships to which reference is so repeatedly made are reflections of those of the members of the court. In short, the characters that Tasso took from the pastoral tradition were given the morals and tastes of the courtiers, and the pastoral world of Arcadia became the court of the Este family.

The contrast between the idealism of the theme and the realistic treatment accorded to it in the play creates, however, a sharp clash between the traditional nobility of the characters and the roles that are assigned to them. The result in the finished work is a definite lowering of tone which may be largely attributed to court life and to the need of stressing sensuality in order to gratify the hedonism of the courtiers.

Sensuality constituted the greatest obstacle with which Tasso was confronted in giving artistic expression to his pastoral theme.

In a lyrical play, sensuality makes heavy the wings of imagination and it directs them toward the earth away from the iridescent fields of poetry. This very element, so necessary to the poet for practical reasons, was responsible for the two fundamental weaknesses of the play: confusion in the use of the Platonic love concept, and psychological uncertainty in the characters.

As to the love concept, confusion is engendered in the play by the idealism of a theme that deals with Diana's nymphs and the realism of their words and deeds. If an inquisitive reader should ask the quite pertinent question why Silvia was offended by Aminta's love, he would find two answers in the play. One, very superficial but idealistic, is supplied by tradition: her vow, and her interest in hunting. But there is another answer, grossly sensual, supplied by Love in the Prologue, when he states that Silvia's resistance is due to

> Quel duro gelo che d'intorno al cuore
> Le ha ristretto il rigor de l'onestate
> E del virginal fasto.

> That hard coldness that around her heart
> Has gathered the rigor of modesty
> And of virginity.

Even more explicit is Daphne in her analysis of Silvia's refusal when Daphne attributes it to her ignorance of the joys of passionate love.

Unquestionably Tasso wanted to differentiate between brutal passion and Platonic love, as is proven by the presence of the two characters, the satyr and Aminta. But Aminta actually, though gradually, merges with the satyr since he is supposed to do precisely what the satyr does—attack Silvia. His exquisite words do not deny the fact that he agrees, be it reluctantly, to do so, and they stand in sharp contrast with his actions.

The theme of the powers of love that are capable of refining brutal nature had often been treated in the arts of the fifteenth and sixteenth centuries, and it may be looked upon as a continuation of the Platonic motif since the days of the poets of Provence who had ennobled courtly love by assigning to woman the power to guide man toward spiritual perfection. This motif appeared also in the poets of the *Dolce Stil Nuovo*, and it flowered beautifully into art in Botticelli's picture, "Pallas and the Centaur." Botticelli treated this theme allegorically. The concentrated power of his intuition is suspended in the luminous grace of his art. Tasso in writing a play needed a greater and more sustained psychological complexity than Botticelli in order to give full development to his theme. This complexity could be achieved only by intellectualizing the love experience of his characters, all the more that he dealt with Diana's nymphs and with Aminta who in his unrequited love has all the earmarks of a romantic lover. Instead, Tasso, concerned with the reaction of his audience, allowed sensuality to stifle the Platonic motif of the theme, thus offending the logical development of the play.

In analyzing the treatment of the love theme it is pertinent to wonder whether Tasso saw clearly the import of his statement that love inspires "nobil sensi a rozzi petti." There was a great deal of flimsy and confused thinking in relation to the nobility and dignity of man during the fifteenth and sixteenth centuries. As always, and as is logical to suppose, in those centuries there were truly "noble men," in attitudes, feelings, and deeds, just as there were those who merely "looked" their part. It is a question of being clear-headed, discriminating, and logical in studying them. If Tasso was interested in giving "nobility" to Aminta's love, he certainly could not do so by making his character attack Silvia. Another fundamental question is whether he saw in a clear light the import of "rozzi petti." He could not literally refer to the people of the lower classes because these were ignored in the courtly tradition, and anti-democratic utterances are repeatedly voiced in the play. Therefore, one must conclude that he referred to the falsely rustic inhabitants of Arcadia or to the courtiers for whom he wished a higher form of love. If the poet formulated such a promise for them, he did not succeed in expressing it in his play, as is clearly proven by the "happy ending" that he assigned to Aminta's love. Had not Tasso yielded to hedonism, he would have given full realization to Aminta's melancholy mood by sending his character to a tragic end. His melancholy would then have been an exquisite foreboding of his impending death. It should be noticed that the beautiful lines that stud the play like precious stones are not due to the realistic approach of the love theme. They are the expression of Aminta's sense of loneliness, which unquestionably mirrors that of the poet. When Aminta is led to follow the path of happiness, he loses significance. The faggots that break his fall and his ultimate fate in the arms of Silvia that

> Giunse viso a viso e bocca a bocca

> Joined face to face and lips to lips

and

> Sì come ne gli occhi avesse un fonte,
> Inaffiar cominciò col pianto suo
> Il colui freddo viso;

> As if he had a fountain in her eyes,
> Began to bathe with her tears
> The cold face of him.

are situations not becoming the lyrical quality that Tasso attributed to his main character.

An even greater weakness of the play is found in the psychological inconsistency of the characters. Aminta's utterances upon reaching Silvia, who is resisting the brutal satyr, bespeak an utter lack of emotional propriety. He makes a long speech full of conceits to the woman who has just escaped the danger of being raped by the satyr, just as Silvia is made to recite her role with a detachment that can be determined only by lack of depth in her psychology. At the end of the play she turns to love with the same readiness which she showed in the beginning in spurning it. Her words are erudite, but they fail to convey any genuine feeling. Likewise Tirsi's literal or social references do not add to the significance and depth of his personality. These characters are suspended between the ethereal quality of would-be inhabitants of Arcadia and the heaviness of grossly sensual beings. As such, they are evanescent symbols that the poet has failed to individualize as dramatic personalities. They are undefined, and the contour of their personalities is blurred.

The fact that, for practical reasons, the poet failed to go inwardly accounts for the presence of conceits and farfetched expressions, in which echo sentiments and feelings after the pattern of the imitators of Petrarch in the sixteenth century. The very central situation in which the naked Silvia is presented tied to a tree by her own blond tresses (blond like Laura's) partakes more of the nature of a fable or a fairy tale than of a play. But the external quality of the play is especially revealed by the conceits which fill it. The character that indulges in them most is Aminta, whether he describes his love for Silvia or expresses his sorrow at being spurned by her. In the above-mentioned scene of the kiss, the bee that stung Silvia's friend, Fillide, is made to do so by Aminta through mistaking her cheek for a flower:

> A le guance di Fillide volando,
> A le guance vermiglie come rosa,
> Le morse e le rimorse avidamente;
> Ch'a la similitudine ingannata
> Forse un fior le credette.

> Flying to the cheeks of Phyllis,
> To her cheeks as vermillion as a rose.
> Avidly bit them over and over again;
> Deceived by the similarity to a rose,
> Perhaps she believed them to be a flower.

The delicate quality of Aminta's sorrow gives place to an exaggeration of grief worthy of Gian Battista Marino:

> amor satollo è del mio pianto omai,
> E solo ha sete de 'l mio sangue: e tosto
> Voglio ch'egli e quest'empia il sangue mio
> Bevan con gli occhi.

> Love is surfeited by my tears,
> And is only thirsty for my blood.
> I want that Love and this pitiless woman
> Soon may drink my blood with their eyes.

Upon seeing Silvia tied to a tree he resents that its trunk should share the privilege of happy lovers, that of having her golden tresses intertwined around its rough bark, a privilege, alas! denied to him. To these excesses was Tasso led by his hedonistic preoccupations! These weaknesses explain, perhaps, why two great writers, Galilei [8] and Manzoni,[9] entertained a somewhat negative idea of Tasso's literary significance.

From the aforesaid it is very evident that *Aminta* moves on two distinct planes: conventional and Platonic on one side; sensual with implications and heaviness of comedy on the other. All considered, we feel justified in concluding that Tasso's *Aminta* is a delicately lyrical motif that when distempered in a play ends in comedy. An author assumes certain responsibilities when he chooses conventional themes and traditional characters. To have a noble king behave like the villain in a comic opera is a liberty that an author cannot take without the penalty of relinquishing the stately precincts of tragedy and entering the ludicrous ones of comedy.

Aminta is a typical fruit of what is generally called "Platonic literature of the Italian Renaissance." We are not referring to Platonism as a coefficient of culture. As such, Platonism belongs to a chapter of philosophy, and it constituted one of the channels that in the centuries of the Renaissance enriched the European thought through its renewed and direct contacts with the Greek philosopher. We are referring here to Platonism in poetry, that is, as a sincere expression of the love experience under the guidance of the Platonic idea.

Plato tried to eliminate dualism in love by reducing love to the intellectual affinity of the lovers. In search of universal unity, he covered the most disturbing element in it, passion. The same attitude was followed by Dante who, as far as Beatrice was concerned, was a truly Platonic lover. It is of paramount importance to notice what he states in the *Vita Nuova:* "And although her image, which continuously abided with me, took the form of the power of Love that overpowered me, yet, it was of such a noble force that it never allowed Love to hold me without the faithful counsel of reason in those matters in which it was useful to mind that counsel." [10] By his conscious elimination of passion Dante shows that he moves in the company of the true followers of the Platonic tradition. He was so completely steeped in it as to deem the representation of passion unworthy of true poetry. In the very beginning of the *Vita Nuova* he states: "And since to dwell on passions and on aches of such extreme youthfulness seems a manner of speech worthy of the *fabula,* I shall depart from them, and, leaving behind many events that could be taken from the memory whence these are taken, I shall come to those words which are written in my memory under more important headings." [11] We can see that Dante was placing the poetic tradition that he was establishing on a plane quite distinct from that of the *fabula* or popular art. He was driving a wedge between the two art modes by the means of a different ethical attitude toward passion, the same as the one pointed out by Plato. To what an extent Dante's Platonism was of the unadulterated kind may be judged by the fact that it flowered into the great art of the *Divine Comedy,* the stately monument of Dante's love for Beatrice, and the most significant blossom of the true Platonic tradition. Be it in a lesser degree, Petrarch may be said to be truly Platonic in his attitude toward Laura. Both he and Dante took the form and substance of true Platonism. But later, especially under the influence of court life, poets, while keeping the forms of the Platonic cult of the lady, tried to avoid dualism by reducing love to pure sensuality and by proclaiming pleasure the supreme law of life. This accounts for Tasso's statement: "s'ei piace, ei lice" and for the artificiality of a large part of courtly literature that bears the outward marks of Platonism. Giovanni Boccaccio may be called the forerunner of pseudo-Platonism in that he constantly sought classical and pastoral themes but treated them in the salacious manner to

which his temperament of a good Florentine bourgeois was at-
tuned. Few writers have been less steeped in classicism than the
author of *De Genealogia Deorum*. Few have treated classicism
and pastoral themes with a more crude and extreme naturalism.
A typical example may be found in his pastoral poem, *Il Ninfale
Fiesolano*, and particularly in the treatment of the love of Africo
and Mensola.[12]

The true Platonic attitude in its intrinsic nature was eminently
individualistic. It applied only to a few rare individuals who were
capable of rising above the carnal. When it was codified into a
system, it lost its fundamental characteristic and became pure
form. When it was incorporated into the social etiquette of court
life, it became a sham that hid an often basely sensual life. In this
respect we should not forget that, generally speaking, Platonism
in the sixteenth century was ordinarily a convention, and conventions, if allowed to affect our feelings, are likely to dry up the
source of poetic inspiration. When this happens we must speak
of pseudo-Platonism out of respect for the true Platonic tradition.
The American authority on Platonism, Paul Elmer More, writes:
"Half the enthusiasts and inspired maniacs of society have shielded
themselves under the aegis of the great Athenian. Not to mention
the detected mountebanks, the list is replete with the names of
accepted sages whose wisdom, if brought to the test, would prove
to be only a finer form of spiritual flattery." [13]

As to Tasso's *Aminta*, we do not hesitate to group it with the
pseudo-Platonic works of his age. Tasso followed the tradition of
Boccaccio and not that of Dante. He sacrificed to the hedonism of
the court the Platonic treatment of Aminta's unrequited love. Indeed he stressed those impulses that true Platonism repressed, thus
besetting the play with a deep contradiction. This contradiction
robbed his play of the temper of truly great creations and gave to
it a highly decorative character.

Giambattista Vico and Reality:
An Evaluation of De Nostri Temporis
Studiorum Ratione

THE opening exercises at the University of Naples in the year 1708 might have been as uneventful and commonplace as many other such ceremonies had not Giambattista Vico, then an obscure professor of rhetoric, pronounced an address that was to prove momentous in the history of ideas in modern Europe.[1]

What chiefly made that address memorable was the fact that for Vico learning was not a stereotyped activity, but a part and parcel of his daily life. The sad, even tragic, experience of his family life [2] forced him to notice the vast difference that existed between the abstract schemata through which the teachers of logic and philosophy presented life to their pupils and the picture of it that he had drawn from having a son whose mind was deranged and a wife who was illiterate. For this reason the theme of reality echoed with impelling force within the cold halls of the University of Naples, even if his listeners, in all probability, were not struck by the novelty of Vico's ideas and the earnestness of the appeal contained in his inaugural address.

Vico painted a sad picture of the conditions of learning and education in his time:

Today pupils are taught by being led at random in the field of logic by an Aristotelian instructor, in that of physics by an Epicurean, in that of metaphysics by a Cartesian. They learn medical theories from a follower of Galen, they study jurisprudence from a pupil of Accursius, the Pandects from a disciple of Favre, the books of the Code from a follower of Alciati.

What appeared calamitous to Vico was that "their instruction is without a basis and superficial, because teachers, although learned in single points, lack synthesis, the flower of real knowledge." These teachers were neither philosophers nor investigators. Vico resented that, in his day, each branch of learning had formulated its principles and rested supinely upon them, thus barring any further investigation into the realms of nature, whereas philosophy should hold together the various branches of knowledge, although allowing the latter to remain autonomous within their own precincts. He compared the methods of education of his day to a tyrant who, having conquered a flourishing and populous city, scatters its inhabitants to various parts of his kingdom lest the latter rise against him and recover their freedom. The eagerness with which Vico gazed on the ever-changing universe made him opposed to any form of intellectualism in which principles and methods had not been derived from contact with reality and experience.

From the context of his address, it seems evident that Vico gives to the term "perfect nature," which so often echoes in it, the meaning of reality in its constant flux, always new and rebellious to the systems of philosophers. If reality is constantly new, it is but natural that any schema that tries to reduce and fix it in its unchanging molds is destined to failure, since each schema is constantly antiquated in terms of the new forms that reality assumes. This conviction placed Vico against the existing systems and made him plead for a new system capable of adjusting itself to any new phase of reality, a system that each age must fashion for itself, commensurate to and resulting from actual experience.

The key point of Vico's address was his critique of the method used by his contemporaries for attaining truth. Since logic, that is, the art of correct thinking, was for Vico the basis of all knowledge, he especially stressed the inefficiency of the teaching of this branch of instruction. In his day, logic was imparted through the *Summulae* of Peter the Spaniard and of Paul the Venetian. Their deductive process forced life into arbitrary schemata, leaving out whatever did not fit into the prearranged molds of the logicians. Vico passionately asked of what value was a picture of life that was perfect without being true, a picture made up of geometrically straight lines, but the very negation of the patterns that one can establish in terms of one's actual experience.

The method against which Vico reacted so earnestly and so passionately was the Cartesian method universally accepted in his day. Referring to it, he declared, "Our critics have placed their fundamental truths before, outside, and above every bodily image of reality." The books of the logicians had covered the countenance of real life with a network of hypothetical and abstract principles in the light of which they rejected as untrue and unreal the strange situations that constantly arose before and around them. Vico was more interested in these strange situations that baffle the understanding of man than in the perfection of the systems offered by the logicians.

Equally significant was his critique of both the syllogism and sorites, the instruments used by Scholasticism and Cartesianism in the search of truth: "He who disputes through syllogism," stated Vico, "does not bring forth anything new since the conclusion is implicit in his major and minor premises. Likewise, he who maintains a proposition through a sorites only explains a second truth contained in the first." This realization led him to regard the Cartesian method as a "divinatory art, an activity to be placed next to witchcraft." Cartesianism was for him a new form of the deductive method that he wanted replaced by an inductive one in which conclusions would be the result of the examination of reality and of experimentation.

The clearest proof of the barrenness of the Cartesian method lay, as far as Vico was concerned, in the fact that its followers had discarded that section of logic called *topica*, that is, the part that taught how to find and arrange arguments. Such a procedure was to be expected of a method that merely superimposed an arbitrary construction of reality on the living one. But this deprived pupils of the inner conviction that binds together intellect and heart, reason and sentiment. Vico saw in the absence of *topica* in the teaching of logic both the proof of the artificiality of the system and the explanation of the lack of eloquence that characterized his own time. How could pupils or his contemporaries be eloquent when what they said was not born out of an inner conviction? Since their points of view were not supported by arguments, their eloquence was emotional and failed to persuade their listeners. The disappointment of Vico as a teacher of rhetoric became in this address a passionate pleading for an inner conviction that would make one eloquent. The keynote of the address was his concern for a personal truth, the same one that constantly echoed in the teaching of Socrates. This concern led Vico to state, somewhat paradoxically, that he preferred to have youths trained to plead "a case which actually happened, even if it did not have a semblance of verisimilitude, rather than a false one based on a logical situation."

That this concern must have occupied his mind with tormenting insistence is shown by the fact that he recalled the names of those who, in the history of eloquence, played only on the emotions of the hearers, and those who, in addressing an audience, tried to convince their listeners by molding their conviction in the light of the truth that they themselves felt most deeply. He contrasted the serene and quiet eloquence of Socrates with the charlatanlike efforts of the Stoics and of Carneades who, Vico disdainfully says, "one day maintained that there was justice and the next claimed that there was not, with greater wealth of words than force of argument." The convincing eloquence of Cicero was likewise stressed, in contrast with the emotionalism of an orator like Marcus Brutus. The parallel was continued by comparing the originality of Pico della Mirandola with Tommaso di Vio from Gaeta,[3] a great believer, according to Vico, in abstract syllogisms. The Cartesian thinkers of his time were the direct descendants of the type of verbose eloquence that was found in the history of oratory. He saw very clearly the reason for such attitudes and contrasts: "All this motley wealth of attitudes derives from the fact that truth is one, verisimilitudes are many, falsehood is infinite." Truth engenders the restraint of true eloquence; falsehood needs verbosity to appear convincing.

The pedagogical method of his day was also attacked by him on the ground that, by teaching reliance on abstract principles, imagination was killed in the young. In this the ancients were superior to the moderns in that they stressed the use of geometry in presenting images of reality to the young. Vico reminded his hearers that for the ancients "geometry was the logic of children." In fact, geometry is closer to reality than is logic in that the physical universe has a solidity that can be rendered better through geometrical forms than through the abstract principles of logic.

Another serious charge against the pedagogical method of the eighteenth century was that the deductive procedure "dulls in pupils that faculty, so proper to philosophers, that consists in discovering analogies between objects vastly different and diverse." At this point Vico remarks that "subtlety and acuteness are not identical, since subtlety possesses only one dimension while acuteness has two."

Having established the inadequacy of the critical and pedagogical method of his contemporaries, Vico analyzed the various aspects of the scientific and intellectual life of his time. He examined first physics and mechanics and rejected the *a priori* method of the scientists of his day on the ground that they had reduced the study of science to a mere application of rules. It was enough to shift and apply them in order to be a physicist, an activity similar to that of "those who, having inherited palaces that are perfect for magnificence and comfort, have only to rearrange and redecorate the furniture according to the style of the time." Rules are not enough, according to Vico, if we wish to discover new theories concerning the laws of nature or if we expect to be inventive in the field of mechanics. Rules are based on past discoveries, and they are actually a stumbling block in the progress of physics and in scientific discoveries, since they compel us to remain entrenched behind old positions. A true scientist is faced by a dilemma: "Either to repudiate such a science in order to focus his attention on the contemplation of perfect nature or, if he wishes to adhere to it, to arrange it according to a new method and explain the new phenomena as corollaries."

The scientists of his time claimed that their principles freed men "of the great trouble of contemplating nature any further," because their science, when "taught with their method, is nature itself." Vico felt the immensity of the universe fluctuating outside the narrow fetters of the laws of the Cartesians, and he rebelled against them, fully conscious of the smallness of human efforts before the boundless universe. He concluded: "We demonstrate geometrical forms in that we can make them. If we could demonstrate the physical world, we should be able to make it." In this conversion of truth and act, Vico's longing for a truth based on direct experience was clearly visible. The marvels of engineering, he insisted, were not made by the application of old rules. They were the creations of men of genius. The theorists of architecture denied the possibility of constructing domes in churches, and Brunelleschi built the dome of Santa Maria del Fiore amid the general incredulity of his contemporaries. Archimedes invented wondrous war machines without the rules accepted like dogmas by Vico's contemporaries. Modern artillery, sailing ships, the clock, church domes were constructed before these rules appeared. He recalled to his listeners the example of G. Perot, a French physicist and engineer, who "constructed a ship according to the accepted analytical rules and with all the required proportions, hoping that it would be the most swift of all vessels, but, when launched, it was as immovable as a rock."

Even more serious were the charges that Vico directed against the physicians of his time, since they, stated Vico, studied diseases through sorites and were not different from the followers of Galen who conjectured concerning diseases through syllogisms. To Vico, "diseases are always new and diverse in different individuals," a fact that was not recognized by his antagonists who, arguing that, since diseases refer to the genus, they include also those of all subordinate species, classified all diseases under one and the same category. Here again Vico stood for an inductive method and proclaimed the necessity of considering specific cases independently of one another. The source of this thought was clearly and beautifully revealed when he invited his hearers to consider the fact that he was not the same individual when he left his physician's office as when he had entered it a short time before. "Innumerable moments of my existence have elapsed," he stated, "numberless changes have intervened which urge me on toward my last night, death."

After examining the domain of science, Vico passed to the consideration of ethics as then studied, a branch that Vico regarded equally valueless. His contemporaries judged human actions according to universal principles based on "reason," unmindful that "since men are for the most part foolish, they are governed not by reason, but by instinct or chance." Of what value was a system of ethics abstractly based on the world as it should be, when it was to deal with unpredictable actions? Vico feared that someone might accuse him of an excessive pragmatism, and he retorted that he wanted men "to be concerned with truths as they appear in life and to seek an honesty that is universally accepted." He was opposed to the application of an "unbending intellectual gage that was unfit to measure the actions of man." He suggested that these be measured "with an elastic Lesbian gage that does not bend bodies to itself but, vice versa, bends itself to the bodies of men." He added:

Foolish men care neither for the highest nor for the lowest truths; shrewd though illiterate fellows concern themselves with unimportant ones, neglecting those which are basic; imprudent men of learning start from the highest truths in order to reach the most humble ones. Wise men, unlike all of these, ascend from the smallest to the highest and primary causes.

This method and process represented Vico's idea. He defended the consideration even of "appearance" in the evaluation of moral actions, quoting the famous maxim of Cardinal Ludovico Mandruzio: "Princes must not only seek a cause which is true and just, but they should also be concerned with that which appears such." He suggested that out of the consideration of all human actions, the most important as well as the most paltry ones, men should be able to reach the proper method for the study of the fundamental stimuli of human conduct.

The chapter concerning jurisprudence is very illuminating as to the spirit and condition of law in Vico's day. He traced its development from Greece to the modern age with a breadth and accuracy of vision possible only in one who, a few years later, was to write a treatise on law which is of fundamental importance: *De uno universi iuris principio et fine uno*.[4] He made a sharp distinction between jurisprudence, that constituted for him the philosophy of law, and the application of justice exercised by magistrates. The Greeks had not known jurisprudence, since in Greece jurisprudence was a part of philosophy. In Rome, however, it became a branch of law and the privilege of patricians who used it as their most potent weapon against the plebs. They surrounded it with a halo of religious mystery, and they left to the praetor its application, denying to any other class the right of studying and professing it. In time, Roman jurisprudence became the instrument by which emperors repressed the ambitions of the patricians. Vico distinguished the spirit of modern law from that of the past by pointing out that at present laws are bent to the individual case while in classical Rome individual interests were sacrificed to keep the inviolability of the law. In Rome, law safeguarded the state; modern laws safeguard the individual. He was aware that the absence of jurisprudence as a branch of modern law was responsible for the infinite number of laws that existed in the eighteenth century. In his subconscious relativism he was not opposed to this, inasmuch as the multiplicity of laws reflected the "infinite cases" that were brought before justice. It must be added that he conceded this somewhat reluctantly, since he felt that the majesty of law should be safeguarded as it was under the Roman system.

The chief contribution in his address was to the field of aesthetics. Believing that art is the result of an instinctive force, he declared himself against the theory of imitation evolved by the Humanists of the sixteenth century. He openly stated that he was opposed to the teaching of poetics to children because it "blinds their fancy and ruins their memory." He was definitely against the Humanists when he mockingly pointed at the current belief that: "There would not have been a Virgil without a Homer, nor in our literature a Tasso without a Virgil." Vico rejected this belief and declared that actually, strange as this may seem, "the best models are more a hindrance than a help in studies based on imagination." He even went so far as to say that "it would be necessary, in order to have excellent authors, to go to the extreme of destroying the best artistic models." Since, however, this would be barbaric and nefarious, he suggested that these models be left for mediocre minds. Those who are endowed with a superior intellect should keep away from them and focus their attention on the "living reality." To us, be it in a vague manner, Vico ushered in the Romantic movement, and it is not without significance that two distinguished men of the following century, Saverio Baldacchini and Cataldo Jannelli,[5] hailed him as the man who had brought a new light into Italian thought and art, especially through his *Principii d'una scienza nuova,* published in 1725.

As in the case of logic, pedagogy, science, and the law, Vico reached his concept of art as the product of imagination by viewing experience as the basis of all knowledge. He was aware that really great masters did not imitate other artists but took nature, that is, their experience of reality, as their guide and source of inspiration. Imitation appeared only after the passing of the great masters, when mediocre artists, through their lack of genius, accepted the traditions of the masters. For this reason Vico praised Titian for having sought and found a technique different from that of his two great contemporaries, Raphael and Michelangelo. Vico quoted Titian's words to Francesco Varga, ambassador of Charles V to the Venetian republic, to the effect that imitators are less than mediocre.

If we postulate that the moderns were those who felt the autonomous character of their age and culture, Vico was definitely a modern. As is often true of constructive minds, he did not repudiate the whole past and its traditions. He viewed them in the function of an integrating factor in the cultural life of the present, but postulated the original character of the latter. He suggested, be it in a veiled manner, that the main difference between culture and art is determined by the receptive character of the former and by the creative character of the latter.

These attitudes led him to assume positions toward Humanism that appear to us extremely constructive and new. In the consideration of the study of law, for instance, he suggested this problem: Accursius wrote the *glossae* to Roman law, which was a definite asset for culture. But what happened to the laws existing at that time which were stifled under the revival of Roman jurisprudence? Was not modern life hampered by the application of Roman law, the spirit of which was so different from the spirit of modern legislation? How could modern civilization accept mechanically those laws enacted in a civilization so different from ours? Vico also accused Accursius of having subjected Roman jurisprudence to the evil of trifling divisions. On the other hand, Vico expressed his admiration for Andrea Alciati for having restored the Roman code to its original splendor, looking at it from the perspective of his time. Alciati and his French followers, stated Vico, "restored their laws to the Romans rather than transmitting them to us adapted to our state." Is there not here implied, if not definitely expressed, a true evaluation of the function and meaning of Humanism that should be looked upon, not as a rebirth of classicism for the purpose of hindering the growth of modern life, but as the achievement of restoring the ancient world to its native purity and splendor? Vico's attitude toward Accursius was parallel to that assumed by him toward the followers of Galen and their negative contribution to medicine. In the light of this attitude, Vico allows us to divide the Humanists into two groups: those who proclaimed the canon of imitation and thereby hindered the creative process in art, and those who, conscious of the endogenic character of culture, studied the ancient world, restored its original purity, and gave us a definite and accurate knowledge of it that we might use it to enrich our modern age. In this constructive attitude Vico takes sides with such universal men as Erasmus,

Leonardo, Vivès, the Cardinal of Cusa, men who lived in too close touch with the present to lose sight of it, even when facing the grandeur of classical civilization.

Vico pleaded in his address for a new method of studying and of living. He envisaged it through the consideration of the question of the relative superiority of the ancients and the moderns. This question had already attracted the keen minds of Giordano Bruno [6] at the end of the sixteenth century and of Alessandro Tassoni [7] in the beginning of the seventeenth. Both had decided in favor of the moderns. Vico, more philosophical than either, reached a new conclusion after clearly distinguishing the relative merits of the two civilizations. These, according to him, could not be compared because they were two distinct entities. They had exercised their creativeness and had excelled in different fields. Their respective advantages and disadvantages in the history of art and culture were too diverse to be properly evaluated and compared. It was not possible to compare the works of art of the ancients and moderns because art is vertical, and each work is, in its essence, unrelated to the other. Science is cumulative, and we owe to the ancients many inventions, just as the modern age can claim many contributions to the history of science unknown to antiquity. Vico was fully aware of the achievements of the modern age and cited its glories in the scientific field: the solution of problems of geometry, the progress of chemistry applied to medicine, the development of mechanical engineering and anatomy, the invention of the telescope, the compass, the printing press, the founding of universities, and the evolution of modern law.

The chief aim of Vico's address was to offer a new method in seeking and attaining truth in the realm of reality. For this reason the author constantly referred to the necessity of basing one's conclusions on experience of the outer world as the sublimation of what one perceives, feels, and thinks. Feeling preceded thinking for Vico. Urged by this deeply-seated conviction, he enjoined the youths who were listening to him to fashion for themselves a new method, personal and original, along the lines that he had outlined. It was a vast undertaking, and it embraced problems of ethics, philosophy, and art, basing the new conclusions on the creative quality of man. This new method should constitute a departure from the conclusions of the ancients as well as from those generally accepted in their age. The chief contributing factor in molding it should be imagination, which would replace the abstract reasoning of the followers of Descartes. Vico intimated that order and harmony abide in the spirit of each man and not in the schemata of the logicians. Reality is constantly new, and it calls for constant revisions in the field of knowledge. These ideas, shared and developed by other thoughtful men, echoed with increasing force during the eighteenth and nineteenth centuries and constituted the living kernel of the age of Romanticism.

Benedetto Croce has shown what Vico contributed to aesthetics in his great *Scienza Nuova* through the theory of the autonomy of fancy and its superiority to reason in the field of creative art.[8] The present essay, delivered in 1708, allows us to go back a few years in marking the dawn of a new creed that was destined to change the forms of literary art in Italy and in Europe.

Giacomo *Leopardi's* L'Infinito

THE famous critic Francesco De Sanctis,[1] commenting upon this jewel of Leopardi's poetry, reaches the conclusion that the poet romantically loses himself in the sea of infinity evoked by his thought. To us, it seems that, through this interpretation, Leopardi's *L'Infinito* loses the continuity of thought which is its greatest asset.

De Sanctis's interpretation shows us a Leopardi who mystically rises toward infinite space, forgetful of the earth where he is dwelling and wavering between two quite different planes: earth and heaven, finite and infinite. We feel that *L'Infinito* rests on three different planes: the world of nature, the concept of the infinity, and between these two worlds, a third zone where Leopardi loves to dwell, for it is a creation of his own thought. In this discussion we hope to prove that our interpretation can be supported by reconstructing the psychological mood as projected in the poetry.

Giacomo Leopardi was the victim of tuberculosis of the spine, the dread disease that brought him to an early death. One of the few pleasures that he allowed himself in the studious life that he led in his father's house was to stroll up the Tabor Hill, near Recanati. He tells us:

> Sempre caro mi fu quest'ermo colle
> E questa siepe, che da tanta parte
> Dell'ultimo orizzonte il guardo esclude.

> Always dear to me was this bleak hill
> And this hedge, that from such a large part
> Of the faraway horizon excludes my gaze.

The higher he climbed the wider the horizon became. When he grew tired and sat beneath the tall trees to rest, no longer able to see the fields in the valley and the faraway horizon, he began to dream, wondering what there was above the blue arch of the sky. His mind found that there were only "endless spaces," "super-human silences," and "deepest quietude." The poet informs the reader that a sense of fear overcame him because he found himself face to face with nothingness.[2] He was awakened from this awe by the murmur of the leaves of the trees, which carried him back to the world of nature that was throbbing with life, buzzing with insects, the flights of birds, human toil, and joy. But even here, suffering flesh and poor tortured heart that he was, he could not find a haven of rest, and his thoughts entered into play. The poet created his own infinite, humanized and solidified, alive with the beauty that surrounded him and touched his heart. It was only then that the previous terror turned into infinite sweetness, as he concluded the last lines of his idyll.

The central point, on which a critic must focus his attention, is the passing of the poet from his awe to the feeling of joyous intimacy, conveyed by the last line:

> e naufragar m'è dolce in questo mare

> and to be shipwrecked in this sea is sweet to me.

Had Leopardi been a normal and healthy person, he would have lived in nature. He was excluded from it by the disease that crippled his body, turning his existence into slow agony. Neither could he accept the concept of the infinite, as does a religious-minded believer, who gives a religious overtone to his musing. He had suffered too much, and his mind was too objective and cold to fill the infinite sky with dreams and visions, turning the concept of the infinite into a religious fantasy. Rejected by earth and heaven, by nature and the infinite, his mind continued to ask whether the infinite could have any meaning whatsoever. All the strength of the poem is concentrated in this attempt that ends in harmony and intimate joy.

The *Infinito* is a short philosophical poem. It encompasses the brief drama lived within the solitude of Mount Tabor. It is philosophical poetry, like all great poetry, especially of the last century.

We have seen that, when the poet directed his gaze toward the sky, his mind turned to the infinite. He found there only silence, opacity, and a deadly quietude: only a white, shapeless desert, vanishing into nothingness. The rustling of the leaves of the trees brought him back to nature, sensuous and serene, as it spread all around its green cloak of beauty. How could the poet abandon himself to this life, which he saw tainted by the shadow of death? If yesterday's seasons fell into the pit of the infinite, the present one, too, carried within itself that certitude. The poet reveals this philosophical musing when he confided to us:

> io quello
> Infinito silenzio a questa voce
> Vo comparando.

> I that
> Infinite silence to this voice
> Go comparing.

Thus far he has revealed two moods only: that of awe and that of the awareness of the beauty of nature in its full bloom. But, then, why the ensuing joy of the poet, when he became aware that death urges everyone toward the abyss of nothingness? At this point a third mood appeared: his joy for having infused a human element into the cold and spectral concept of the infinite. It is this third mood that superinduces joy in his heart.

In the *Infinito* we see only the result or consequence of this creation: the poet's thought that loses itself in the feeling that envelops his mind before nature. The poet seems to confide to the reader: Yes, tomorrow this blooming beauty will wilt, but how very beautiful it is in this fleeting moment, how touching is the greenness that every year covers the earth. The "dead seasons" fall into the grave that surrounds the earth, but, before falling, they fill man's heart with joy. This is the certitude that illumines Leopardi's concept of the infinite. The emptiness has disappeared, and the abstract concept of the infinite has acquired a new reality: that given to it by the poet's mind. This reality cannot be found in nature, which is life destined to death, nor in the concept of the infinite, which is empty, since it has filled the poet with awe.

We have said that the artist has revealed only in part the process of philosophical elaboration through which he reached the meaning that he gave to the concept of the infinite. In fact, he has told us that the thought of eternity and of the dead seasons was followed by that of the present season with its sounds and hues. If one admits De Sanctis's interpretation, one is forced to admit that the concept of the infinite was the cause of Leopardi's joy. Nor can one admit that nature itself was its cause. The very title of the poem, *L'Infinito*, denies this and, if so, and we exclude that the concept of eternity could be the source of his enjoyment, we can only identify the source of his joy with the reality that his mind was able to weave upon two extreme terms: one, the concept of eternity; the other, nature, alive and beautiful, harmonizing and fusing these two concepts in the poet's own concept of beauty and goodness of life.

One could believe that this sweetness to which the poet abandoned himself was in contrast to the pessimism generally attributed to be the only chord of Leopardi's poetry. His pessimism, however, was not objective and categorical; it was not all of one color, uniformly and monotonously black. On the contrary, in all of his poetry there was a constant and painful yearning for beauty, love, and happiness. How could he have continued to yearn unless life would have, conceptually, looked beautiful to him? The poet confessed that sweet life, as enjoyed by everyone else, was denied to him. One should observe *Il Passero Solitario* (The Lonely Sparrow), where the unhappy destiny of the poor

bird who spread his sad, monotonous song through the countryside is opposed to the other birds' lot

> a gara insieme
> Per lo libero ciel fan milli giri
> Pur festeggiando il lor tempo migliore.

> vieing with one another
> Through the free sky they make a thousand turns
> Rejoicing in the happiest time of their existence.

With a sense of harmony and clarity of form typical of him,
Leopardi compared his own sadness with the happiness of healthy
people:

> La gioventù del loco
> Lascia le case, e per le vie si spande;
> E mira ed è mirata, e in cor s'allegra.

> The youth of the town
> Go out of their homes and spread through the streets;
> And they look and are looked at, and rejoice in their hearts.

The essence of Leopardi's poetry is exactly in this endless oscil-
lating between the conclusions reached by his mind, that forces
upon him the outlook that life is evil, and the voice of his heart,
that inexorably directs him toward nature and love.

> Primavera dintorno
> Brilla nell'aria, e per li campi esulta
> Sì ch'a mirarla intenerisce il core.

> Spring all around
> Shines in the air, and it spreads its joy in the field,
> So that, to look at it, it makes my heart grow tender.[3]

Thus the sweetness reached by the poet in L'Infinito finds parallels
in many other poems. This fact explains clearly the shift from awe
to the sweetness in which his mind loses itself.

Another point, too, can help us to understand this change. We find it especially in the brief lyric *Alla luna* and in *Canto notturno di un pastore errante dell'Asia*. The poet feels the limitations of his own tortured flesh, upon which death stretches its cold fingers. But he is also conscious of the strength of his painful condition. It is what only man can do, and which is denied to brute nature. The moon is regulated by the same inexorable laws as govern man, yet it is not conscious of its own condition. The sheep led by the philosopher-shepherd in Asia are subject to these same laws, but they cannot look detachedly at themselves and gaze at their own tragic destiny whose only end is death. But man can do so. Is this not a source of great and just pride? Is this not proof of man's nobility and of his superiority over animal nature? Does this not show the great wedge that separates man and brute nature? If this is so, then man finds in being conscious of his destiny and in his understanding of the infinite the reason for an inner satisfaction that consoles him for all the sadness inherent in life.

In *L'Infinito* the poet finds this joy in the consciousness of being able to infuse a human connotation into the empty and cold concept of eternity. Not only the joy of thinking, but the joy of having created his very own "immensity," which, being the fruit of his own mind, is indeed his very own. This is much more than the generic "living within his own thought," attributed to the romantic poets. Leopardi has in his lyric created a short drama in which, through the poet's feeling, abstract thought has become living reality.[4]

The Realistic Approach in the Evaluation of Romanticism in Modern Italian Criticism

ITALIAN critical works on romanticism constitute a sort of vast and leafy forest that includes old and stately oaks, dating back to the literary quarrels between classicists and romanticists, as well as new saplings, the works of years close to our time. In the vast forest which we must cross, we shall single out the works that best represent the variations of critical taste in Italy as reflected in the study of romanticism.

The father of critical evaluation of Italian romanticism is Francesco De Sanctis (1817–83). We place him outside of the romantic movement because he did not follow what Manzoni called the "historical system," a perfect description of the accomplishments as well as the limitations of the romantic movement. The romanticists claimed modern history, dating back to Christianity, as the sphere in which artists were to seek the material of their art. De Sanctis's sense of reality was definitely rooted in the world close at hand. He was the master of the new realism that veered directly toward the study of the social environment and was best represented by Giovanni Verga in all the characteristics that differentiated his art from that of Alessandro Manzoni, the exponent of "historical" realism.

De Sanctis specifically analyzed the romantic age in two courses which he gave at the University of Naples in 1872 and 1874. A distinguished pupil of his, Francesco Torraca, took down in writing the ideas of the master, and another not less illustrious disciple, Benedetto Croce, edited those notes under the title *Italian Literature in the XIXth Century*.[1] De Sanctis, who lived near enough to the romantic age to deal with his subject as a personal recollection of his youth, considered romanticism, not as a strictly literary expression but as a movement embracing every manifestation of Italian life in the first half of the nineteenth century. According to him, the history of the time was created by the clash of the two schools of thought: the "liberal" one headed by the serene and well-balanced Manzoni; and the "democratic" one headed by the revolutionary Mazzini. De Sanctis saw these schools "arrayed against one another in the fields of literature, philosophy, science, and even in the roar of battles and revolutions."[2] In the evaluation of the two modes of thought he departed from the strictly historical method and considered the events that crowded the first half of the nineteenth century as a chaotic whole to which he had to give order and form as well as sequence by correlating the literary activity of the various men that he studied. He established and followed a sort of poetic law in terms of which every movement is formed around a great literary figure and then gradually disintegrates owing to the fact that the increasingly mediocre members of the group, through lack of creativeness, imitate the works of the leader.[3] Accordingly, De Sanctis considered Manzoni who, as a point of fact, refused to have any official connection with romanticism, as the leader of the movement, and he presented Tommaso Grossi "as a degeneration of Manzoni and Carcano a degeneration of Grossi."[4] Around Manzoni, beside the above-named novelists, De Sanctis placed Vincenzo Gioberti and Antonio Rosmini as the philosophers of the movement, Massimo D'Azeglio as its political theorist, and Cesare Balbo as its historian. Around Mazzini De Sanctis gathered Gabriele Rossetti, Pietro Colletta, Giovanni Berchet, and Giambattista Niccolini. In spite of this external formalism, De Sanctis left a deep imprint on the criticism of the romantic age through the living portraits that he made of the leading men of the time and especially of Manzoni.

Parallel to De Sanctis there developed the conservative historical school, whose followers contributed greatly to a thorough knowledge of Italian literary texts, though they lacked the critical sense of De Sanctis. Romanticism was painstakingly investigated by them, but, on the whole, they looked upon it as an exotic plant imported through Germanic penetration of Italy. Specifically, it was the third invasion, the first being that of the barbaric tribes of the fifth and sixth centuries, and the second that of the Reformation in the sixteenth century. How could realistic Italians follow the fantastic dreams of northern peoples like the Germans and the English?

This is the theme that one finds in the critical approach of Giacomo Zanella [5] who sees in romanticism "the literature that emerged from the study of the centuries of the Middle Ages. More strictly speaking, the movement should be called Germanism, and the poetry derived from it deserves the name of Germanic poetry." [6]

Not different in its essence is the attitude of the great teacher and poet, Giosuè Carducci. [7] Carducci looked upon romanticism as a disease. He repudiated its ideals because the romanticists were Catholic, monarchical, and liberal, while he, Carducci, was, until old age overtook him, anti-Catholic, republican, and revolutionary.

In spite of the vast biographical and bibliographical material collected in the two volumes of his *Ottocento*, Guido Mazzoni does not cast a revealing light on romanticism. His general outlook is beclouded by the following thesis, that he so states: "he who examines the canons of romantic art, as expressed by the best who discuss them, will realize that we had already achieved in a glorious past all that these men hoped for the future." [8]

Croce's influence on criticism began to be felt around 1900. We mention Croce's name here because, for the last fifty years, he has educated two generations of scholars by attributing to the term "history" wider implications and a nobler meaning than the followers of the historical school had applied to it. Yet Croce's treatment of the romantic movement is, to a large extent, inadequate. He seems to have carried the lamp to illumine the way for those who followed him and not for himself. While his individual essays on authors of the time, especially those on Manzoni and Guerrazzi, are definite contributions to the ethical and artistic delineations of those men, the evaluation of the whole age leaves the reader perplexed and disillusioned. Perhaps the attitude of the philosopher of aesthetics who tried to reduce art to universal principles interfered with the task of the historian in him. I am referring in particular to the essay on romanticism in his *History of Europe*, published in 1932.[9] His study of the romantic movement was developed in the light of a sharp distinction between speculative and practical romanticism. By speculative, he meant the stress given, from Vico down, to fancy, spontaneity, sentiment, and enthusiasm as an integral part of the creative process in art, as well as the contribution that the romanticists made to the study of history. All this was to Croce a noteworthy conquest and on it rested the glory of the romantic age. But in the practical field, in the field of ethics, romanticism assumed, according to Croce, a morbid and pathological character that moved the great thinkers of the time to look upon it with contempt and condemnation. The reader feels compelled to ask Croce what value can a movement possess which is perfect in theory and wrong in practice. Apparently Croce has failed to bridge the inevitable gap between the ideal and the relative approaches to it that can be realized in actual experience. More than by the positive aspects of romanticism, he has been attracted by its extreme forms and exaggerations. How could these extremes, existing mostly on paper, have any validity when one considers, as Croce does so ably in his *History of Europe*, the accomplishments in every field of activity of the generation of the romanticists? All the more that Croce admits that there are other aspects in romanticism besides the perversions and exaggerations to which he has referred. Why then not conclude that there is a living and pure center in romanticism at the fringe of which one finds exaggerations and perversions? Is there not a concrete and living nucleus in naturalism or in any other movement? And are there not exaggerations at the fringe? The exaggerations of romanticism may have gone skyward, those of naturalism earthward, but neither destroys the noble center where the reality of the movements abides.

Croce's attitude toward romanticism as well as his aesthetics have exercised a great influence, both positive and negative, on many critics. G. A. Borgese's book, *The History of Criticism in Italy During the Romantic Period*,[10] written in 1903, bears evidence of Croce's teaching of aesthetics, although its author had been preceded in this field by Gina Marteggiani's doctoral discussion on romanticism with the title *Italian Romanticism Does Not Exist*.[11] (Rumor has it that the real author of the quixotic dissertation was Giovanni Papini to whom Gina Marteggiani was engaged.)

Borgese confessed in 1920 concerning his former attitude toward romanticism: "We were not free from a certain fanaticism and we used to excommunicate everything that appeared to us infected with romanticism." [12] To him, too, romanticism was a disease and a world of shadows that one tries in vain to seize. Educated in the aesthetic school of De Sanctis and Croce, he brought into his analysis of Italian literature in general and of romanticism in particular the belief, often voiced by him, that Italian literature like Italian art "seems constantly disposed to sacrifice any other result to the hope of the sublime." [13] According to Borgese, the real goal of romanticism was not a reaction against pseudo-classicism, but "an attempt to exploit the romantic revolution for the purpose, all our own and not at all romantic, of freeing classicism from the narrow fetters of academism, and to understand it in a more authentic manner.[14] To Borgese romantic criticism can be reduced to classical principles since "the war between romanticists and classicists lacked almost completely sharp distinctions between the two contending parties. Those who defended romantic ideas were often, even without realizing it, more classical than their opponents." [15] The opinions of the leading men of the romantic movement are acutely discussed, but only in order to find in them the eternal principles of perfect art that Western civilization has learned through the literatures of Greece and Rome. Manzoni teaches us not to argue for a specific point by using arguments based on universal terms. In his letter to Chauvet he refers to ideas that "are independent of any specific system, so in conformity are they with the nature of dramatic art and with its universally accepted principles." [16] We must not detach the aesthetic ideas of the group of the *Conciliatore* from the context of their time, lest the universal become vague and generic. The dialectical brilliancy of G. A. Borgese could be accepted by the reader only if the romanticists had failed to make a sharp distinction between real classicism, which they admired, and the pseudo-classicism of their days, which they held in contempt. But the romanticists used the greatness of genuine classicism to prove the negative character of its copies in their own time, and they insisted that what made it possible for the ancients to achieve greatness was the fact that mythology was part of their history and, hence, capable of arousing enthusiasm in them, an indispensable condition in the genesis of poetry. From this they concluded that men living in the nineteenth century should use themes derived from their own history in order to be moved and to create real poetry. Romanticists were fully conscious, in a new and original historical perspective, of the division that beset antiquity and their age. They did not reach, to be sure, the belief that medieval history and classical material stand on the same footing as actual reality before the creative spirit of the artist, needing only the spark of the poet's sentiment to be transformed into poetry. However, romanticists specifically rejected the fables of antiquity as art material and thus paved the way to modern realism. They did not invoke a muse existing outside of the poet. Their muse abided in the heart of the poet. They can also boast of other achievements. They proclaimed the independence of Italian literature from classicism, insisted on the necessity of knowing other literatures, and enjoined poets to direct their art toward the people, all attitudes unknown to the classicists of their own time. To conclude with the author that "no principle of classical criticism crumbled" [17] with the aesthetics and the art of the romanticists is to ignore the development of art and of aesthetics from the days of Manzoni on.

There are also two other recent works that likewise seem to have felt the influence of Croce's teaching. I refer to Mario Praz's *Flesh, Death, and the Devil in Romantic Literature* (1930)[18] and Francesco Flora's *From Romanticism to Futurism* (1925).[19] Croce, as a theorist of aesthetics, has taught that genres, literary epochs, schools, and movements are unreal distinctions, and he has insisted that what actually counts is poetry or the absence of it. In fact, one of his books, dealing precisely with nineteenth-century literature, bears the title *Poetry and Not Poetry* (1923).[20] Perhaps it was this broad point of view, justifiable in the aesthetic field but misleading in that of historical criticism, that led the two above-mentioned authors, as well as countless others, to extend the term "romantic" to all subjective literature that appeared before or after Manzoni. Mario Praz's book, more than a critical study of romanticism, is a stimulating and genial work that presents a vast panorama of new forms in modern literature. Likewise, Flora's book, though containing a keen analysis of the leading contemporary authors, offers no real contribution to the study of the romantic period.

On the whole, modern criticism has been increasingly "realistic" in that it has departed from the strictly literary interpretation of romanticism and has drifted toward the consideration of the new political, social, and literary patterns that history assumed at the beginning of the nineteenth century. It has looked on the age of romanticism as a complex whole, made up of different and clashing tendencies, but dominated by the thought and fervor of the men who called themselves romanticists. According to this point of view, the age of romanticism is presented as possessed of an infinitely vaster scope than the romantic movement, though the latter colored the main characteristics and achievements of the former. The outstanding contribution is that romanticism is no longer identified with dreamy and indefinite aspirations, with sylphs and fairies, but with the well-defined program of national regeneration in its political, social, ethical, as well as artistic aspects, for which the romanticists stood against their opponents, both domestic and foreign. Manzoni's unheeded voice has finally prevailed.[21]

This point of view has been made possible by the vast material discovered by recent research, especially on the eighteenth century. A comparison between the *Settecento* by Tullio Concari,[22] published in 1900, and the *Settecento* by Giulio Natali,[23] published in the same collection in 1929, is most illuminating on this score. Concari, naturally enough, does not know the works of Ettorri, Calepio, Conti, Montani, and Becelli, whose contributions to aesthetics are well known to Natali, thanks to the studies of Benedetto Croce,[24] Hugh Quigley,[25] J. P. Robertson,[26] and Giuseppe Toffanin,[27] to mention only a few. Modern critics view the eighteenth century, that used to be largely associated with the Arcadia movement, as the pre-romantic age. Natali dedicates a whole chapter to pre-romanticism in the eighteenth century,[28] and he intimates that the romantic school, when it took concrete form with the group of the *Conciliatore* at Milan, reduced to a system the ideas that had freely circulated in the eighteenth century. The rules of dramatic unities rejected by Manzoni in 1820 in his letter to Chauvet had already been attacked by Martello, Carli, Metastasio, and Baretti. The main tenet of the romantic creed, a content of art that is popular, national, ethical, and Christian, had been repeatedly advocated in the eighteenth century, and exemplified in the works of Parini and Alfieri.

A man of the older generation who has contributed to the proper evaluation of romanticism is Arturo Farinelli in his *Romanticism in the Latin World* (1927).[29] Farinelli definitely cast aside the distinction between northern and southern peoples that Madame de Staël bestowed on Europe, and saw in romanticism a human expression not peculiar to any people.

The book, however, that, to us, best reflects the progress of critical studies of romanticism is Citanna's work *Romanticism and Italian Poetry from Parini to Carducci* (1935).[30] Citanna dedicates a detailed study to two eighteenth-century men whom he considers part of the romantic age: Parini and Alfieri. He includes Leopardi in the romantic system, studying the unifying force of imagination in his poems. One finds in Citanna's book vague reflections of the attitudes discussed above, such as ranking Giusti and Carducci with the romanticists and the belief that classicists and romanticists were fighting their own shadows. Yet he clearly admits that the neo-classicism of the late eighteenth century possessed something new and that it "had a new content which was nothing else but the thought and feeling of romanticism." [31] He also believes "that Chénier, Guérin, Hölderlin, Keats, Foscolo, and Grillparzer are all romanticists in their souls, and, therefore, their classicism, in its essence, was nothing but a nostalgic aspiration toward the past of their dream, the fantastic island of their restless and unsatisfied longing. This was romanticism." [32] Citanna, more clearly than anyone else, has viewed romanticism as an endogenic movement and not as a superimposed tendency, though we do not subscribe to many opinions and conclusions about individual authors.

In dealing with modern contributions to the study of romanticism we have used the term "realistic" because it seems to us that no other term could describe more adequately the constructive trend of modern criticism. Romanticism possessed a core of genuine and positive thought that modern critics have recaptured and expressed.

Realism During the Romantic Age

THOSE who have followed the recent studies on romanticism know that most contributors have departed more and more from the strictly literary interpretation of the new political, social, and literary patterns that history assumed during the eighteenth century and in the beginning of the nineteenth. Modern criticism has, in fact, moved toward the consideration of the age of romanticism as a complete whole, made up of different and clashing tendencies but dominated by the thought and fervor of the men who called themselves members of the romantic group. According to this point of view, the "age of romanticism" has an infinitely vaster scope than the "romantic movement," although the latter colored the main characteristics and achievements of the former. As a result, Italian romanticism is no longer identified with dreamy and indefinite aspirations, with sylphs and fairies, but with the well-defined and pragmatic program of national regeneration for which the romanticists stood against their opponents both domestic and foreign.

The documents of the realistic tendency are most numerous in the pages of the *Conciliatore* (1818–19), in Berchet's *Lettera semiseria di Grisostomo* (1816), in Manzoni's *Lettera sul Romanticismo* (1823), and in Di Breme's *Polemiche*, gallantly waged through the *Conciliatore*. Ermes Visconti in his *Idee elementari sulla poesia romantica* informs us: "Those same reasons that condemn the use of mythology urge us also to renounce the imaginary adventures of paladins, fairies, and necromancers." [1] And again in the same work: "Romanticism does not consist of endlessly telling fables about witches, gnomes, and miracles worthy of the *Prato Fiorito* [Flowery Meadow], nor in moaning and shuddering in cemeteries." [2] This clear repudiation allows us to relegate fairies and gnomes to the fringe of romanticism, a case

parallel to the aberrations that accompany every literary movement. A deeply-rooted realistic tendency was at the very core of
Italian romanticism.

The term "realism" can be differently interpreted, since each of
us can place his sense of the real in a different category. Two
forms have generally prevailed in the history of Western civilization: a photographic one, largely found in popular art, that placed
reality in the observable world, and therefore limited itself to the
consideration of instinctive life; and a subjective one, usually
identified with Platonism and Humanism, that placed reality in
the image of the actual object. During the age of romanticism,
realism assumed a deeper philosophical character, and it reached
conclusions that have since become an integral part of our way
of thinking. In concrete terms, during the eighteenth and early
nineteenth centuries one observes more clearly than before the
passage from an agricultural to an industrial society, the aspiration
to and the creation of a free and democratic Italy, the stress on a
concept of art that enjoined authors to express emotions and
ideas understandable to their contemporaries, assigning to art a
social and humanizing aim. During that time Alessandro Manzoni
wrote *I promessi sposi*, Giacomo Leopardi the *Canti*, while the
intellectual speculation of the time rests on the works of Antonio
Rosmini, Vincenzo Gioberti, and Giuseppe Mazzini.

In reading the polemics that the paladins of the new art waged
against the defenders of pseudo-classicism one is constantly aware
of the wide program in which the former were interested. Di
Breme predicated a new artistic consciousness on a national education: "... until we shall have created an Italian civilization, a
national education, and we shall not be interested in those deep
factors that modify in their direction our thoughts and passions." [3]
Pecchio contrasted the modern education that youth received at
Bern and the backward methods pursued in Italy.[4] He likewise
stressed the need of a new prison system in which punishment
implied the possibility of social redemption of the culprit. He
warned that "society has set before itself the goal not so much
of punishing as of redeeming the guilty ones." [5]

If we ponder over the aspect of realism in the aesthetic field, we become aware that romanticists constantly attacked the theory of art as pure form, that only aimed at pleasing the reader. This seemed to them empty hedonism that weakened and destroyed national character at a time when Italy needed moral strength and courage. The influence of the political problem on Italian romanticism could not be overstressed. The generation of romanticism recaptured its faith in a new art through pragmatic, social, and political programs. Berchet wrote on the "necessity of addressing our poetry, not only to the understanding of a few men of erudition, but to that of the people." [6] He felt that the people and poets should counsel each other at a time when "the tyranny of pedants is about to disappear in Italy." [7] He advised the poets of his time: "Be contemporary to your own times and not to the dead centuries. Free yourselves from the mist which envelops your writings, from old liturgies and old fables. Search into the soul of your own people, give to it thought and not empty words." [8] De Cristoforis echoed these ideas in an article in the *Conciliatore* in which he reviewed Torti's book *Sulla Poesia*.[9] On the whole romanticism insisted that three main characteristics were essential to modern art: sincerity, in terms of the author; modern history, and hence, Christianity, as to the proper subject matter of art; and usefulness as for the effect on the reader.

These new attitudes toward art and such considerations as that of enthusiasm in the creative process, the use of mythology and the question of the three unities drifted into romanticism from the justly famous *Querelle des Anciens et des Modernes*. This famous dispute re-examined not only the relation of classical and modern art, but also involved two distinctly opposed attitudes in politics and economics. As a rule, the defenders of pseudo-classicism were the defenders of caste and privilege while the moderns stood for a new society long before the French Revolution brought it about. An issue of paramount importance was at stake in it: Was modern civilization an entity unto itself, independent of, though influenced by, classicism? Should Italy try to free herself from the tentacles of rhetoric or should she continue to live, feel, and create as people did in the days of Athens and Rome? When one reads Berchet, Borsieri, Pellico, Di Breme, one is gradually forced to the conclusion that these early nineteenth-century men codified and crystallized ideas and attitudes for which men of the eighteenth century had stood singlehanded. Modern criticism singles out Ettorri, Montani, Becelli, Calepio, Conti, Baretti, Cesarotti, and the Verris as the forerunners of romanticism. It is equally evident that these men continued a trend of former days, that of Pico, Gelli, Berni, Aretino, Lasca, Boccalini, and Bruno. This continuity shows that in the eighteenth century the hidden stream of realistic thinking, largely unknown until then to the official agencies of culture, was reaffirmed and deepened, merging with the interest aroused through the publication of Bouhours' book, *La Manière de bien penser*.

It must be stated that the progress toward our modern sense of life and art began not in opposition to classicism but through the realization that if classic poets had achieved greatness by singing of their own civilization and without imitating literary patterns, modern poets should take inspiration from the history of their own people and relinquish the canon of imitation. In this manner, while respecting true classicism, they repudiated emphatically the pseudo-humanistic concept of art as application of rules, as expression of generic truths made universal through the exclusion of the subjective and actual elements; of art as embellishment of classical myths.

The renewal of Italian culture during the eighteenth and early nineteenth centuries was greatly helped by Cartesian thought through the polemics aroused by the above-mentioned book by Bouhours. The conclusions of Montani (language is a product of the individual mind, and, therefore, there is no philosophical language, but only a philosophical mind that molds and expresses itself in a philosophical diction); of Becelli (Italian poetry has characteristics of its own, different and diverse from those of Greek and Latin poetry; therefore, the theory of imitation is false); of Cesarotti (the necessity of recapturing the original character of the Italian language through the study of Ossian and of the poetry of primitive peoples); of Baretti (the complete independence of Italian literature from classicism) could not be understood without the influence of the Cartesian concept of truth and of the empiricism of Hume and Locke.[10]

The process whereby Italian culture assumed forms that we call "modern" was also aided by the fact that a few open-minded men (Montani, Conti, and Baretti) traveled outside of Italy and saw how backward their country had remained in terms of the progress achieved by England and France in the economic and political, as well as the literary, fields. The most significant of the observations made by Conti and Baretti was that England and France could boast of such masters as Shakespeare, Racine, Corneille, and Molière, who had appeared outside the classical traditions of Arcadia, the fashion whereby at that time poetasters tried to hide the lack of poetic gift. Was it not time for Italy to seek inspiration elsewhere? This attitude paved the way for the attacks against "the Arcadian contests, the strictly grammatical disputes, finally literature of empty words" [11] directed by Borsieri against the pseudo-classic poets of his time in the opening article of the *Conciliatore*. Likewise, the question of mythology, so often and vigorously discussed by the romanticists of 1816–19, had been placed on a more philosophical basis than before by Montani and the moderns of the eighteenth century. The most thorough and original treatment of the use of mythology is found in Manzoni's *Lettera sul Romanticismo* of 1823.[12] In it one very clearly sees how directly and profoundly Manzoni was influenced by the thought of Descartes.[13] The essential point in the discussion of mythology lay in the fact that it was approached by inquiring whether a myth could arouse the enthusiasm of a modern poet, since it was no longer a part of the civilization in which the latter lived.[14] By answering in the negative, romanticism reached the positive conclusion that contemporary history is the proper subject matter of modern art. Hence came the use of medieval and Christian themes that were looked upon as a part of modern history, in contrast with mythology that was regarded as a part of classical civilization.

Many corollaries can be deduced from this conclusion. The most important is that the source of poetry is the enthusiasm that historical reality arouses in a poet. Ermes Visconti through his sense of historical perspective thought it natural for Homer and Sophocles to sing of classical myths. On the same basis, however, he assigned to modern poets the task of extolling George Washington and the members of the Spanish Cortes, thus stressing the theme of political freedom.[15]

It followed, likewise, that if art originates from contemporary history, the language to be used should be the living and spoken one and not that of the fourteenth century, as the purists wanted. On this score, too, Montani and Baretti were the forerunners of Di Breme in connection with what the latter wrote in his *Proposal* for corrections and additions to the dictionary of La Crusca.[16]

The age of romanticism added a significant page to that fundamental transformation of modern history that has consisted in shifting our interest from the consideration of the essence of things to the interest in and study of their tangible characteristics. If later in the nineteenth century the doctrine of naturalism was proclaimed, and if modern art has more and more advocated the study of actual and observable reality, we owe it to the men of the eighteenth century who have been mentioned above and to the later romanticists who developed their thought. Italian naturalism reaffirmed the Italian tradition of realism that intellectually honest men had constantly kept alive. Among the latter were those who represent the positive aspect of romanticism.

Alessandro Manzoni
and the Realistic Novel

THE critical writings of Alessandro Manzoni are very closely associated with the ideas of his Milanese friends expressed between 1818 and 1819 in the columns of the *Conciliatore*. The contributors of the "blue paper" launched a spirited appeal not only for a new art, but also for a new political and economic life for Italy, at the very dawn of the wars for the unification of the country. Manzoni, in his *Del Romanzo Storico* (Essay on the Historical Novel),[1] echoed many of the original ideas that one finds in the pages of the Milanese paper. He wrote his essay in 1849 at Lesa, where he moved with his second wife, Teresa Borri, after the Austrian government had returned to Milan. It appeared in the month of September 1850.[2]

The essay opens with one of those remarks, so frequent in Manzoni, that reveal his humor, acuteness of mind, and integrity of character. He states: "The author would find himself in a fine predicament if he were to claim that the ideas propounded in his essay are in complete agreement with the letter that preceded it [letter to Mr. Chauvet]. He can only say that if he changed his mind it is not to go in a backward direction. It is up to the reader to judge whether this moving forward has been a progress along the path of truth or a fall into the precipices of error. We hope that our readers will feel the subject matter discussed in the essay is worthy of an opinion, whatever it may be." [3]

The essay is an admirable work, owing particularly to the autocriticism that the author exercises over himself, as well as to the rigorously logical process that he displays and the style that lends clarity and beauty to the reasoning with which the author analyzes the realistic novel.

Manzoni, the author of *I Promessi Sposi* (The Betrothed, 1827), the historical novel that had made him famous in Italy and in all of Europe, demolished in this essay this genre by proving to himself and to his readers that, at the writing of the essay, the historical novel was moribund, if not exactly dead. He proclaimed it to be a false genre like all works in which history and fiction are woven together. The historical novel—he admonished—in reality promises to the reader different and contradictory elements: material based on historical certitude and on fancy. It is a false genre in both content and form; in content, in that in the blending of historical accuracy with fictional material it offends the dignity of true history; in form, in that it lacks unity, precisely because it blends two opposite elements, the historical true and what, since it is fictional, is false or unreal. One can also add that it is false in that it aims at producing two opposite reactions in the reader. It expects him to believe literally in the historical events therein narrated and, at the same time, to accept as true the fantastic elements.

Arguing with admirable skill and logic, Manzoni asks: How is it possible that such a contradictory art mode may continue to deserve the esteem of modern readers to the extent of being the art of tomorrow?

All those who have read Manzoni's essay have concluded that the author was interested only in announcing the end of the historical novel that had met with so much success in the first half of the nineteenth century. There is no doubt that this is the first impression that one receives, even upon a careful reading. Yet when one's impression deepens into a serious opinion, one discovers that there is much more therein than the funeral oration for the historical novel.

The reader must not forget that Manzoni, although concerned with the past, was keeping his eyes on the future of the literature of his day. In referring to the vogue of the historical novel in the early decades of the century, he wrote: "That something has happened in the past is not a sure guarantee that it will continue in the future." The first part of the essay closes humorously by imagining that the historical novel asks the reader: "Admire me, but do otherwise." Basically, Manzoni was passionately interested in the future of fiction. If the historical novel was destined to die, then a new type of novel was bound to appear in the fiction of the future.

The attentive reader must not believe that Manzoni had arrived at the point of experiencing hostility toward the historical novel, in spite of all the attacks that he directed toward it. Indeed, he was very far from entertaining such a feeling. After all, he confessed in the essay to loving that genre. And how could he help loving the child of his imagination and genius, *The Betrothed*, the novel that gave him renown and fame?

The essay has been considered the "artistic suicide" of Manzoni, a kind of new Oedipus Rex.[4] Manzoni would be similar to the hero of Sophocles' masterpiece who insisted upon wishing to know the truth, sadistically tormenting himself with pitiless cruelty. Manzoni was a man too well balanced to arrive at the plight of the tragic Oedipus. His predilection for a quiet existence saved him from meaning literally the violent attacks that he directed against the historical novel, just as it prevented his searching mind from torturing his soul or even disturbing its serenity in the religious and ethical fields.

If one considers this problem dispassionately, one must conclude that Manzoni did not sacrifice anything at all or, at least, very little indeed. At the most, he sacrificed the aesthetic formula of the historical novel in relation to the contradiction engendered by the two opposite kinds of reality that formed his content: the historical and fantastic realities. But Manzoni openly exalted the fiction of Walter Scott, and it would be hard to believe that he would not place his *Betrothed* side by side with the works of this famous author, whom he called the Homer of the historical novel.

In general, critics have preferred to take into account the negative attitude on the part of the author of the essay, an attitude that is unquestionably in it, rather than the positive one that, although less conspicuous, is most certainly to be found in the pages of the long essay. Croce in his *Estetica* (Aesthetics),[5] referring to the concept of the true entertained by Manzoni, concludes: "He always leaned (as one can see in his *Discussion on the Historical Novel*) toward the identification of truth with what is historically and scientifically real." Amado Alonso, in his penetrating essay on the historical novel,[6] also follows Croce's point of view.

It must be evident that, if Manzoni had restricted himself to announcing the death of the historical novel, the value of his essay would be very relative. He would have restricted himself to the task of entertaining the reader by presenting to him himself who, Don Quixote-like, used the lucid sword of his logic against the ghost of the historical novel. In fact, critics who have seen only the negative part of Manzoni's essay have made serious accusations against its author. It has been said that Manzoni did not possess a clear idea of reality in art,[7] for he did not understand that, in art, there is no difference between actual truth and fantastic truth, between actual and historical realities. Every element, whatever its nature may be, can be molded into a new reality by the creative mind of an artist. Manzoni has also been accused of placing art below the category of history.[8] Attilio Momigliano goes so far as to say that the essay on the historical novel is far from being an important work.[9]

The central point developed by Manzoni in his essay aimed at considering three forms of art content on three diverse and distinct planes: that of history, that of its ideal forms, and that of artistic reality. The essay was penned by a great master of narrative art, and not by a college professor thoroughly familiar with the history of aesthetics but with a very limited understanding of artistic capabilities and an imperfect understanding of art.

The idea that most persistently returned to Manzoni's mind was that of the relationship between reality and art. In his youth he was obsessed by the importance of the historical reality, even to the point that in the *Conte di Carmagnola* (The Count of Carmagnola), written between 1816 and 1820, he drew a sharp line of distinction between the sections that were taken from history and those that were strictly imaginative.[10] But already in the rough copy of his letter to Goethe, that bears the date of 1821, he declared himself cured of a similar aberration.[11]

Manzoni's mind was too acute to remain caught in the strait jacket of aesthetic casuistry. His letters show that since 1828 he was contemplating writing on the spurious character of the historical novel, as suggested to him by Goethe: [12] and, in fact, it was in 1830 that Manzoni informed a friend of his, Bianchetti, that he was engaged in writing an essay on the historical novel.

In his essay Manzoni reached a very clear idea of the difference that divides not only the historical from the fantastic truth, to which he attributes the quality of possessing verisimilitude, but also the difference between actual and real. For him "the actual" belongs to the world of phenomena and "the real" is the product of imagination. Through fancy, the actual becomes real and abides eternally in the world of art.

In considering the character of poetry as perfect illusion, Manzoni presents three moments of the concept of reality. First, he spoke of a "reality seen through our mind in eternal forms or, to speak more accurately, irrevocably" (the ideally beautiful). Then he considered this concept as fixed in marble by a sculptor under the form of a beautiful human figure. Lastly, he considered actual reality in contrast with reality in art, and he asked, "If one, looking from a distance or in an imperfect light, should see a man standing still on a building, in the midst of statues, and take him for one of these statues, would the perception of the man be the product of art?"

In the essay on the historical novel, Manzoni proclaimed repeatedly the liberty of a poet in the treatment of a historical subject. Inventing new situations and circumstances is not looked upon by him as poetic license, but as the logical consequence of the freedom of all artists. He called this activity the "actual activity of poetry." [13]

Manzoni has collected in his essays the objections of an aesthetic and ethical character that at various times persistently appeared in his mind. He imagined that these objections were addressed to him by his readers but in reality they are objections that he addressed to himself. In his career as a fiction writer, he realized that in the historical novel fantastic elements are side by side with historical data. The reader felt himself constantly lifted or lowered from one plane to the other. He was constantly tormented by doubt of the credibility of what he read, and thus he lost the possibility of abandoning himself to the illusion created by art.

The important concern of Manzoni at this point was the consideration of the effect of actual or literal and fantastic truth on art, and the announcement that, in his opinion, the genre that was contaminated was fiction and not history. He keenly observed that in classical tragedy and epic poetry "verisimilitude, losing the possibility of seeming literally true, could freely manifest itself and exercise its own and extraordinary power and action, for it could not find itself side by side with the actual truth." [14] In the classical age, history and poetry were not split as they are in the modern age.

For Manzoni, the primary function of art was that of permitting the reader contentedly to lose himself in the fantastic, a characteristic that Manzoni recognized in the epic poetry of Homer, and that was plainly absent from the historical novel.

Manzoni did not reject either the historical or the fantastic reality. He assigned one to history and the other to the novel. If the historical novel was formed by the juxtaposition of two kinds of truth, and historical reality belonged to history, one is forced to conclude either that Manzoni wanted the destruction of fantastic reality, which would be equivalent to the rejection of poetry, or that he wanted fantastic reality assigned to a new and specific genre that could be, as it turned out to be, the realistic novel. If the historical novel confused two genres, the historical and the fictional, one of which genres was history, what else could the other genre be but the novel freed of historical data and elements, that is to say, the realistic novel that flourished around 1850?

It is well to point out the very deep remark of Manzoni that, in human history, one notices an always growing desire for truth, as evidenced by the fact that modern authors had felt the need of adding historical introductions and notes to historical tragedies. He stated: "Literature woven on truth is natural for modern people, to the point that epic stands to modern fiction in the same relation as alchemy does to chemistry." [15] He thus announced the birth of fiction as understood and practiced in our contemporary age. He assigned to it the traits that we recognize in it: "to ask of actual facts that they be recognizable as such [in fiction], and to expect a tale to produce one effect only is to ask precisely what is required in modern fiction." [16]

The announcement of the basic traits of the realistic novel could not be more explicit. The new novel should address itself to men of today, in whom the study of history has engendered a living sentiment of and desire for truth. If the reader is to assent to the reality of the novels that he peruses in order to achieve a complete enjoyment, what reality could produce such an effect on him more fully than contemporary reality?

The reader must not be confused by the fact that Manzoni openly declared himself for the realistic novel only at the end of his long discourse. In this he followed his customary conduct. He never wanted to display too ostentatiously his ideas and feelings. The true Manzoni was always hidden behind the impenetrability of his serene countenance. Yet there is not even a shadow of a doubt that here he was referring to the realistic novel, be it in the guise of one who throws a stone and immediately hides the hand that threw it. In fact, he wrote: "The historical novel does not take the basic event that it presents from history in order to transform it into a poetical situation. It invents it, consistent, in this, with the term 'novel,' the genre whose name it took and of which it constitutes a new form. I am referring to the novel in which contemporary actions are imagined; a type of literature completely poetical since in it both facts and words are only verisimilar." [17] He adds, very cautiously, "The poetic quality of this new genre is, let us be explicit about it, of a very modest kind, such as can arise from the consideration of private and modern events and customs, and can be couched in prose." [18] After having treated so shabbily the realistic novel, as he was wont to do, as if in atonement for what he had written, Manzoni plunged into a great exaltation of the modern age, as could be expected of a man belonging to the romantic age and a friend of the romanticists of Milan.

We have attempted to justify the praises given to this essay by many illustrious critics.[19] We have documented and developed what De Sanctis and Tonelli had perceived in this essay.[20] If our conclusions are logical and plausible, one can look upon it as an early document in which Manzoni expressed his ideas concerning the inevitability of realistic art. It was a clear declaration of faith in modern fiction and an outline of its possibilities in the second half of the nineteenth century.

Italian Verismo

BY THE term *verismo*, critics refer to the art and life philosophy that predominated in Italy during the second half of the nineteenth century. At this time the rest of Europe was living in the epoch of naturalism. Both naturalism and *verismo* were characterized by a strong leaning toward science, often conceived in opposition to religious faith. Socially speaking, this age saw the passing of Europe from an agricultural to an industrial civilization, with the result that colonialism was intensified and wars of conquest were fought in the general search for raw materials and markets. Art, too, was influenced by these new trends, and the exploring of the realm of emotions that had characterized the age of romanticism was followed by interest in the more tangible zone of sensations and the study of the new social environment that appeared with urbanization and industrialism.

Modern criticism has usually directed grave and unfair charges against the age of *verismo*, from which no aspect of the life of this epoch has escaped. In the political sphere most historians have written with irony and contempt of the *politica del piede in casa* (political staying at home), referring to Italy's disinclination, under the liberal government, to risk war in order to acquire colonies in Africa at a time when England, France, Germany, Belgium, and Holland were quietly partitioning that continent among themselves. In the field of art the late nineteenth century has been called fiercely positivistic, pessimistic beyond measure, interested in filth, in short, "the century of the narrow-minded middle class."

Benedetto Croce, in two significant works, *Storia d'Italia dal 1871 al 1915* (History of Italy from 1871 to 1915) and *Storia d'Europa nel secolo XIX* (History of Europe during the XIXth Century), has vindicated the age of *verismo* by exalting the contributions that it gave in every sphere of civilization. The present brief study of *verismo* aims at being a development of Croce's conclusions.

Among the charges against *verismo* there stands out the accusation that the literature of this period was a copy of foreign literatures and particularly of the French literature of that time. Alfredo Galletti, in his *Novecento* (The Twentieth Century), published in 1939, wrote: "Theoretically speaking, our literary *verismo* derives from Zola, and not from such writers as Flaubert and the De Goncourt brothers, or the English realists" (p. 120). Benjamin Crémieux, in his *Panorama de la littérature italienne contemporaine* (1928), speaks of Italian *verismo* as a "copy of French naturalism" (p. 59). Karl Vossler, in his essay on contemporary Italian literature (1916), concurs completely with the above-mentioned critics, stating that Italian *verismo* "more than anything else is an imitation of French authors and especially Zola" (p. 81).

Zola is invoked as the god who presided at the birth of Italian *verismo* because of his *Le Roman expérimental* (The Experimental Novel) that was published as late as 1880 and which, according to the author, was not well received, even in France. The truth is that Zola's essay does not explain the genesis of French naturalism nor that of his own fiction, the significant part of which had already been published in 1880. It explains the genesis of Italian *verismo* even to a lesser degree.

The negative attitude that modern criticism has expressed about this age is in part due to the disdainful attacks that the great poet Giosuè Carducci (1835–1907) unleashed against the Italy of his time. He considered himself a civic poet and, in his lofty dream of a new and nobler Italy, he naturally, as most poets have done and still do, complained about the conditions of his day. It is not, most assuredly, his fault, if critics of later days have continued to give an absolute value to the sentiment that often became an ardent passion of the great poet and thinker.

It may not be amiss for us to re-examine the critical works of the time in order to vindicate, in both the theoretical and actual fields, the originality of Italian literature of the late Ottocento.

We refer, in a special way, to Alessandro Manzoni's *Del romanzo storico* (The Historical Novel), 1850; Giosuè Carducci's *Ceneri e faville* (Ashes and Sparks), 1859–1901; Francesco De Sanctis's *Saggi Critici* (Critical Essays), 1855–1872; Lorenzo Stecchetti's *Nuova Polemica* (New Polemic), 1878; Luigi Capuana's writings, such as *Ismi Contemporanei* (Isms of Our Time), 1898; Vittorio Betteloni's *Impressioni e ricordi* (Impressions and Recollections), published posthumously in 1912; Edoardo Scarfoglio's *Libro di Don Chisciotte* (Don Quixote's Book), 1885; and the long, documented *Prefazione alle Rozeno* (Preface to the Rozeno Sisters), 1892, by Camillo Antona-Traversi. These are some of the documents without which one cannot gain a thorough and accurate idea of the nature and forms of Italian *verismo*.

We have set out to study the age of *verismo* with the basic persuasion that if, in the artistic process, there is a consciously reflective and formal part due to literary contacts (cultural aspects of literature), there is also a deeper and more living part that reflects the man in the writer, and which almost always germinates from the problems that beset the historical moment in which literary works appear. Just as we believe that the Renaissance was an original age in France or England, in the same way we are convinced that Italian *verismo*, in the creative nucleus that formed it, was essentially original.

On this point it is precisely Luigi Capuana who illumines our way, the very Capuana who is generally presented to us as the man who introduced in Italian fiction Zola's scientific method. Capuana informs us: "The critical theories of Zola are very debatable on some points. His qualification of the modern novel as 'experimental' is not very felicitous. In his artistic theory there is a large predominant part accorded to science that undermines artistic form, which is the very essence of art" (in *Studi sulla letteratura contemporanea*, p. 188). In speaking of Verga's *Malavoglia*, he wrote: "Positivism and naturalism exercise a true and radical influence on contemporary fiction, but only in its form" (*ibid.*, p. 140).

We are very far from denying foreign influence on various

authors, but we do not wish to confuse culture and art in the artistic development. Culture is antecedent to art. It is presupposed in an author, though it does not alter the creative quality of his mind. The independence of the Italian movement from parallel European trends is proven by the fact that the term *verismo* has its peculiar meaning and use only in the Italian literature of the late nineteenth century. It is different from both naturalism and realism. Both naturalism and realism, in relation to *verismo*, have an aesthetic and not a historical value. Naturalism restricts the field of observation on the part of an artist only to the most elementary and primitive instincts of man. The classical example during the age of *verismo* was *La Lupa* (The She-Wolf) by Giovanni Verga. Realism in fiction has a wider resonance and takes into scrutiny vaster zones of the human mind, consciously excluded by naturalism from its field of observation. A typical example of realism in fiction is Verga's novel *I Malavoglia* (The Malavoglia Family), in which the elementary figures of the closely-knitted and tenacious Sicilian family of the Malavoglias are projected against the wide screen of the concept of progress entertained by Giovanni Verga. But both *La Lupa* and *I Malavoglia* are an integral part of Italian *verismo* to which they are tied from a historical point of view.

Life and art in the second half of the Ottocento may be divided into two very distinct zones: the one in which lived and wrote the masters of the older generation such as Niccolò Tommaseo, Paolo Ferrari, Giulio Carcano, Vincenzo Martini, Paolo Giacometti, Francesco De Sanctis, and Giosuè Carducci; and that of the then younger generation to which belonged Achille Torelli, Marco Praga, Camillo Antona-Traversi, Vittorio Betteloni, Gabriele D'Annunzio in his early attempts at fiction and poetry, Matilde Serao, Neera, Grazia Deledda, and many others.

We draw a sharp line of distinction between the writers who flourished soon after 1850 and those of the last two decades because the mental habits of the latter were substantially different from those of the men of the older generation. Italian life, too, had deeply changed after 1870, and the noble patriotism of the older generation was being substituted by nationalism with evident marks of imperialism. It is symptomatic that both De Sanctis and Carducci refused to identify themselves with the *veristi*, although the latter had imbibed their teaching and had applied the theoretical positions in art that these two great masters had formulated. In them was repeated the attitude of Giacomo Leopardi, who refused to associate himself with the romanticists of his day, though he is the greatest poet of the age.

The old generation of Ferrari, De Sanctis, and Carducci entertained a deep faith in life that it conceived as activity, work, joy, and serenity. The young followers of *verismo* had totally lost this calm and serenity. It may appear paradoxical, but it is essentially so, to state that the younger generation was more objective and at the same time more inclined to yield to dreams, more tenaciously attached than its older masters to the human existence that it observed at a closer range. Its field of observation was the society of its time, of which it revealed the sorrows, shames, and sores. But it is not true that those of the younger generation were cold observers. They were men whose heart was wrung before the spectacle of the social injustices of their time about which they wrote with a fervor and exaltation not visible in men such as Ferrari, De Sanctis, and Carducci. In the young *veristi* nerves took precedence over serenity of thought and objectivity. The result of their attitude was a mode of art basically different from that of writers of the previous generation. They worked on a narrower canvas whose colors were gloomier and in which black predominated over white.

It has been frequently stated that the literature of the *verismo* period was middle class (borghese). In reality, and especially in drama and fiction, one notices a violent reaction against the new society that came into being in Italy as a consequence of the Industrial Revolution which was especially a revolution dictated by the middle class and its pragmatic spirit. It has been generally said that Marco Praga, Camillo Antona-Traversi, Giuseppe Gia-

cosa, Roberto Bracco, and, in fiction, Girolamo Rovetta, Luigi
Pirandello, Luigi Capuana, and Giovanni Verga were pessimistic
and cynical. In their works one notices an individual who suffers
because of the cynicism and the wickedness of his fellow men.
The atmosphere of the new society, rendered in terms of unethical
equivocation, immorality, or unmorality, forms the background
of these works, but playwrights and novelists direct their attacks
against it. The immoral characters who move in it are the antagonists of the author who uses the vicissitudes of the victims of the
new society as the pivot of the action that unfolds in his work.
These victims are the children of the author's fancy and bear the
names of Paolina in *Le Vergini* (The Virgins) by Praga, Susanna
da Ponte in his *Il Bell'Apollo* (Handsome Apollo), Luciana Rovere
in his *La Morale della favola* (The Moral of the Fable); Lidia in
Le Rozeno (The Rozeno Sisters) by Camillo Antena-Traversi;
Paolina and Nunzio in *Sperduti nel buio* (Lost in Darkness) by
Bracco, Caterina Nemi in his *Tragedie dell'anima* (Tragedies of
the Soul); Giulia Artunni in *Fantasmi* (Ghosts), Anna in *I diritti
dell'anima* (The Rights of the Soul) by Giacosa, Giovanni and
Nennele in his *Come le foglie* (Like Leaves).

In the field of fiction one finds parallel characters in *I vinti*
(The Conquered) by Giovanni Verga, and in the novels of
Rovetta in which he condemns the gross materialism of the Milanese society of merchants and manufacturers, who acquire wealth
and wallow in gold and pleasure at the expense of the individuals
on whom they callously trample. In both drama and fiction to exclude the attitude of rebellion and condemnation of the middle-
class spirit on the part of the authors is to rob their works not only
of significance but also of the element of dramatic action. Without
the contrast between the individual and society, the literature of
the age of *verismo* is meaningless and dead. When one reads in the
best critics of this period that one finds in Marco Praga "a total
absence of compassion," and that he is "artistically indifferent to
the passions of his characters," accusing him of "not feeling
sympathy for those characters that he depicts often with great

power of expression," one often wonders whether critics are writing about the same author that one is reading.

In most of the histories of European drama (not excluding that of Guido Ruberti, published in 1921) one finds a very short section dedicated to the Italian drama of the age of *verismo*. In a work recently published in America (*History of the Theatre* by Friedly and Reeves, 1941), after the customary and baseless condemnation of Italian drama of the late nineteenth century, one reads these words: "Problems of social reform such as labor legislation, woman's place in the world, divorce, and the liberalizing of marriage laws never interested Italian writers because these problems were outside their habits of thought." It is difficult to imagine a more complete and unfair condemnation. The very existence of the drama of this time is not conceivable without the passionate consideration of the problems that stirred the minds of thinking men of this time. Italian drama of the age of *verismo* was prevalently social. Yet one must not marvel that this period is thus studied abroad when Silvio D'Amico, in his *Teatro italiano del Novecento* (Italian Theatre of the XXth Century), 1937, coldly annihilates its significance by writing: "Italian drama of the Ottocento is typically bourgeois." His book opens with these words.

In truth, *verismo* possessed a much greater significance and importance. It constituted a new chapter of artistic life that unfolded in the last decades of the century and made its influence felt on painting and literature. Both fields should be better known in the United States. The only artist slightly known in America is Antonio Mancini, and even of Mancini a very scant number of paintings is found in our great museums.

Verismo meant the proclamation of truth and sincerity in both life and art. The password among the young of that generation was "the true," and it echoed in every nook of Italy and in every heart. In an obscure novel of the Sardinian Enrico Costa, *Il muto di Gallura* (The Mute of Gallura), 1884, the author confesses: "Non ho scritto un romanzo. I fatti che io narro sono *veri, veri* fino nei dialoghi ch'io riporto" (I have not written a novel. The facts that I narrate are true, true even in the dialogue that I report). The illusion of reproducing the true and actual world close at hand went as far as this, even to the point of forgetting that reality in art is not reality in life. Yet, like all great and lofty illusions, this faith and this passion had deep and beneficial effects. *Verismo* radically changed Italian art and produced great works with Carducci and Verga, just as, during the age of romanticism, "historicity" was fruitful of greatness in the days of Manzoni.

In order to understand *verismo*, from both the theoretical and actual points of view, it is not at all necessary to hark back to the scientific method outlined by Zola at a time when the latter had already written his best novels. The theory invoked by *verismo* was not new, either in Italy or elsewhere. There echoed in *verismo* voices that one hears in some of the great artists of the Cinquecento, down to the eighteenth century with Carlo Goldoni, and later with Giovanni Berchet, in his *Lettera semiseria di Grisostomo* (The Semi-serious Letter of Grisostomo) and the contributors to the journal, *Il Conciliatore*. What was new in *verismo* was the conscious effort to give dignity and an official character to the study of the true (*il vero*). The effort to use the study of actual life conditions, not to provoke unbridled and vulgar laughter, as in the comedies of the sixteenth century, but with the avowed purpose of studying contemporary society was new. The difference that exists between "unbridled and vulgar laughter" and "studying contemporary society" measures the great difference that divides the popular literature of the sixteenth century, especially in drama, and the literature of the age of *verismo*.

If one takes into account the forms and the spirit of the literature of this period one cannot help detecting intimate connections between it and the literature that unobtrusively had been flowering in the various provinces of Italy. The fact remains that between 1860 and 1900, especially in the field of narrative literature, Italian fiction was characterized by a keen interest in the life of the province. The background of the fiction of Verga, Capuana, and Pirandello in his youth is afforded by a sympathetic presentation of Sicilian life. The early writings of D'Annunzio dealt with life in Abruzzi; the fiction of Antonio Fogazzaro displayed the beauty of the Valsolda Valley; Matilde Serao projected her novels against Neapolitan life; and Grazia Deledda against that of Sardinia. It is interesting to note that this tendency was preceded and paralleled by the work of Giuseppe Pitrè, Alessandro D'Ancona, Domenico Comparetti, Giuseppe Bernoni, Angelo de Gubernatis, and Idelfonso Nieri who, with variations of interest and method, collected the popular traditions of the various regions of Italy. It is also dutiful to add that the literature of the age of *verismo* was accompanied by the flowering of a vast literature in the various dialects of Italy.

The progress reached by that country during the second half of the nineteenth century was truly astounding. It was during those years that Italy fashioned for itself a new civilization that allowed it to re-enter the currents of European culture, to accept courageously the responsibilities of progress, to find faith and joy in work, to fashion for itself a religion without bigotry, a morality without hypocrisies, an art freed of rhetorical preciosity that took its inspiration from contemporary life. Such efforts and such realizations deserve a respect that will cast aside the ironical toleration and the superficiality with which critics are wont to refer to the life and art of the nineteenth century.

The Novecento

THIS syllabus is being written in the belief that the study of modern languages and literatures is an essential part of the university curriculum, contributing with other subjects to the development of the moral, cultural, and aesthetic sides of American students.

An instructor in contemporary Italian literature should feel that there is something inherently new in it which is derived from the changed economic conditions, from our ideas and even emotions which have somewhat deviated from the ideas and emotions of our forefathers. These changes have brought about several outstanding characteristics which are peculiar to contemporary literature and of which our instructors should be fully conscious. The artist of today stresses personal creation to a larger extent than the writer of the past when a greater role was assigned to imitation. Imitation often took the place of translation at a time when translations were not as numerous and accurate as they are today.

Likewise we distinguish, rather sharply, between culture and art. Cultural elements belong today to the history of culture and not, as for the poets of the Renaissance, to poetry. Historical events belong to the domain of history more closely than they did in the days of romanticism. We have done away with the division between literary and spoken languages as well as with the rigid division of literature into genres (lyric, pastoral, epic poetry; tragedy, comedy etc.) with clear-cut, set rules to be observed in the pursuit of each genre and with definite classic authors assigned as models. Today these divisions are looked upon as purely formal elements since the critic is supposed to focus his attention on the spiritual drama of the artist as reflected in his work.

Moreover, contemporary writers stress more than our ancestors the actual and observable aspects of life. These aspects were veiled by myth in the days of Greek classicism, by allegory during the Christian age, by the picturesqueness of history in the Romantic period, while today they rise unencumbered and unfettered in our contemporary literature. Research shows, on the other hand, that side by side with the idealized rendering of the actual reality we find in the past the direct and blunt transplanting of it in art. Two necessary corollaries are derived from the aforesaid: namely, that not every book was classical in classic Greece, not every poet was allegorical in the days of Dante, that not every writer followed the tenets of Humanism in the fifteenth century and that not every work bore the traits of romanticism in the days of Manzoni, Walter Scott, and Wordsworth. And there follows also another, even more important, corollary which is that the gap existing between the ideal and actual realities gradually narrows as we approach our own age. To this merging and leveling process there corresponds a parallel movement in our social environment that goes by the name of democracy, a state in which all social classes are leveled by equality of duties and rights before the law and merged into the privilege of work. Deny democracy because of its partial failures and you will lose one of the leading threads with which man has woven his history. Deny the new elements and forms of art, and the understanding of the progress and growth of our contemporary art will be perplexing and obscure. It appears to us most vital that the student and teacher of contemporary literature should possess an understanding of and faith in our own civilization and in the aesthetic expression of it: contemporary art. This much for the mental and spiritual outlook in our instructor.

He needs, moreover, a literary background that will provide him with the material on which he will exercise his criticism. The sources of contemporary literature are of infinitely easier access than those of the literature of the past. Even publishers' catalogues keep in close touch with the present literary output. Besides, we have excellent bibliographical journals, critical reviews which are easily obtained in this country and which enable us to follow the progress of our literature. We find references to Italian literature even in journals only indirectly interested in it. The New York *Times* and the London *Times* have frequent reviews of our books. Directly and indirectly, through the various departments of *Italica*, we are told of the best books of the year and of what goes on in the literary life of contemporary Italy. The *Romanic Review* publishes an "Italian Literary Quarterly" in which O. A. Bontempo critically reviews the most important books of the day. *Books Abroad*, edited by R. T. House, contains, likewise, reviews of Italian books. As to Italy, numerous periodicals offer penetrating analyses of contemporary trends in literature and art. Among them we mention: *L'Italia Letteraria*, edited by G. P. Angioletti; *Pègaso* by Ugo Ojetti; *Il Leonardo* by Federico Gentile. To these many more can be added which will help us in the study of the literature immediately past and that of our own days. We mention among others: *L'Italia che scrive, I Libri del Giorno, La Voce, Il Marzocco, La Nuova Antologia, La Ronda, Il Novecento, Riviera Ligure, Rete Mediterranea, Athaenum, La Cultura.*

For a more serious and critical understanding of the main currents in contemporary literature it is necessary to consult books that deal specifically with the subject. For the period closing with World War I, the best sources are: Benedetto Croce's *La Letteratura della Nuova Italia* (six volumes); G. A. Borgese's *La vita e il libro* (three volumes), *Il senso della letteratura italiana;* Paolo Orano's *I Moderni* (five volumes); Dino Mantovani's *Letteratura contemporanea; Guide Bibliografiche* (Fondazione Leonardo, Roma). Other eminent critics of this period are: A. Albertazzi, L. d'Ambra, A. Anile, P. Arcari, G. Boine, V. Betteloni, E. Cecchi, G. A. Cesareo, G. Lipparini, T. Martini, V. Morello, U. Ojetti, G. Papini, G. Prezzolini, M. Puccini, R. Serra, E. Thovez, and A. Tilgher.

For the literature published during and since the war we can turn also to a great many critics, among whom we shall mention: B. Crémieux, *Panorama de la littérature italienne;* G. A. Borgese, *Tempo di edificare;* G. Prezzolini, *La cultura contemporanea;* A. Leoncita, *Scrittori del tempo nostro;* G. Manacorda, *Verso una nuova mistica;* B. Migliore, *Scribi, scrittori e artisti* and *Bilanci e sbilanci del dopoguerra;* P. Pancrazi, *Ragguagli di Parnaso* and *Venti uomini, un satiro e un burattino;* G. Ravegnani, *I contemporanei;* V. Piccoli, *Le notti novecentesche.*

We wish also to mention three anthologies that afford a good bibliography and give selections from contemporary writers: Papini e Pancrazi, *Poeti d'oggi;* G. Titta-Rosa, *Narratori contemporanei;* and the most recent of the three: P. Gorgolini's *Italica* (four volumes).

These books and journals should supplement the most important part of our preparation which consists in *careful* and *sympathetic reading of the various authors.* This work done, the student of contemporary literature can serenely proceed to exercise his criticism, which does not consist in pointing out which author a certain writer imitates, nor how many times he uses this or that word, nor in showing where he places his adjectives, nor whether he is redolent of Virgil or Aristophanes (all of which are necessary but secondary considerations in criticism), but in seizing the salient traits of the artist's temperament, his sensitiveness, his ideas, his outlook on life, and finally his way of fashioning his style, his use of it, his cultural background, his relations with his times and with other writers. Criticism is a creative activity and a critic should show the growth and unfolding of a central idea which circulates in a given work and finally is expressed as a complete aesthetic unity in the work he analyzes. It is, above all, the consideration of the artist's experience as he passes through life, at times wounded and bruised, at times exultant and joyous in the contemplation of the eternally mysterious face of the universe.

Were we called on to present to a class the present-day intellectual and literary life of Italy, we should divide our presentation into four parts. The first would take into consideration the cultural movements that stirred a new life in Italy in the beginning of our century when such representative men as Croce and Gentile, Borgese and Papini proclaimed the backward state of Italian culture and urged the new generation to rebuild it on a modern basis. They wanted rhetoric banished; they called for an active economic life which was to be parallel to the moral and aesthetic activities of man, since all these activities are expressions of the same force: spirit. This is the very basis of the neo-idealistic thought of which Croce and Gentile are the greatest exponents. To conduct such a class successfully we should have perused most of their works, and assigned to our pupils one or two of the significant books which express best the side of their doctrine that we wish to emphasize. For Croce, one should read at least his *Estetica, Storia della Storiografia Italiana, Storia della Età Barocca in Italia*. For Gentile, one should be familiar with *Sommario di Pedagogia, Studi sul Rinascimento, La Riforma dell'Educazione, La Riforma della Scuola, Scuola e Filosofia, Gli Albori della Nuova Italia, Filosofia dell'Arte*. It would be of great advantage to peruse the critical works of Adriano Tilgher (*Voci del Tempo, Relativisti Contemporanei, Ricognizioni*), of Luigi Tonelli (*Alla Ricerca della Personalità*), and to make a thorough study of Arturo Farinelli's critical ideas that are opening a new field of approach to the human problem in literature. The reading of these works can be supplemented by the study of Borgese's, Serra's, and Prezzolini's writings. The desire for the renewal of Italian life took a less academic form with G. Papini, and his works (*Esperienza Futurista, Stroncature, Ventiquattro Cervelli, Testimonianze*) will be of great help. Papini is a sort of link between the Olympian and serene thought of Croce and the extreme, radical attitude of the futurists headed by F. T. Marinetti.

The remaining parts of our presentation would naturally fall into three categories: theater, novel, poetry; a division that we should adopt for the sake of clarity and method and not for any essential difference existing among the three genres.

For the theater, we should begin with Sem Benelli and Luigi Morselli. They continue the classic drama revived by Gabriele D'Annunzio, but they lend to their characters a torment that transcends the exasperations of primitive instincts which D'Annunzio had so skillfully veiled under the draperies of grandeur. Such is the torment that one finds in Sem Benelli (*La Cena delle Beffe*) and in Luigi Morselli (*Orione, Glauco*).

Our consideration would now turn to the "Grotteschi," a weird mixture of pathos and laughter, pictured against the problem of being and becoming, of essence and appearance; a strange play of light and darkness which has revealed new depths in human personality in the hands of the great dramatist, Luigi Pirandello, and of his followers: Luigi Chiarelli, Luigi Antonelli, Fausto Maria Martini, Enrico Cavacchioli. Adriano Tilgher offers a keen analysis of this movement in his *Studi sul Teatro Contemporaneo*.

Another group of dramatic works can be studied under the heading of "lyric drama." It includes the works of Massimo Bontempelli, Dario Niccodemi, and Alfredo Casella's *La Morte in Vacanze*. Marco Praga's *Cronache Teatrali* is one of the most important sources to be consulted in studying contemporary drama.

Passing to fiction, we should begin by contrasting the naturalistic treatment of the novel (Verga, D'Annunzio, Capuana, De Roberto, Serao) and the writers who have continued in an original form this tendency (Deledda, Tartùfari, Messina, Cinelli, Gadda). We should then consider two strains: one which shows a deep concern about psychological and moral problems (Pirandello, Puccini, Gotta) and another longingly musing over the distant childhood spent in a provincial nook suffused with a haze of idyll (Paolieri, Martini, Saponaro, Brocchi, Beltramelli).

As to poetry, we should first stress the significant appearance of the now dead futurism, considering it as a violent and extreme reaction against the prevailing forms of traditional literature. The outstanding futurists were: F. T. Marinetti, Paolo Buzzi, Aldo Palazzeschi, Corrado Govoni, Luciano Folgore. We should then turn our attention to the group of the "Crepuscolari" (Guido Gozzano, Sergio Corazzini, Guelfo Civinini, Marino Moretti, Arturo Onofri). Finally, we should consider the group referred to as "La Ronda" with its neo-classic tendency (Vincenzo Cardarelli, Antonio Baldini, Emilio Cecchi, Riccardo Bacchelli, Lorenzo

Montano). The neo-classic tendency, following the traditions of Leopardi and Carducci, is represented by many distinguished poets: G. A. Cesareo, A. De Bosis, C. Roccatagliata-Ceccardi, E. Romagnoli, L. Siciliani. We should insist on the fact that "futurism," "Crepuscolari," "Ronda" are merely historical connotations and should be entirely disregarded in our appreciation of what is significant in the poetry of the different individuals. Of the contemporary poets we should insist on the achievements of Aldo Palazzeschi, Corrado Govoni, Lionello Fiumi, Giuseppe Ungaretti, G. Titta Rosa, G. Villaroel and E. Montale, men who have with success attempted to give new forms, coupled to a genuine sensitiveness, to Italian poetry.

This presentation could be made either in a one-year course by a young instructor who needs to build his own firsthand background or could be divided into four or more courses as the instructor's knowledge grows, until he may take a single outstanding writer as the subject of a year or a semester course, affording the pupil the benefit of a wide background. The future of our teaching and, above all, of our schools rests on a more vigorous, human, and constructive teaching, toward which we must always strive for the betterment of our youth.

Modern Italian Drama

INTRODUCTION

THE present brief analysis of modern drama in Italy has been written on the assumption that the term "modern" refers especially to the works of playwrights in which our own age can mirror itself. We are aware that the tragedies of Alessandro Manzoni written during the romantic period are not so close to us as are the social plays of Paolo Ferrari and the introspective works of our contemporary, Luigi Pirandello. In content, as well as form, the latter two have given expression to feelings and presented situations in which we can recognize ourselves more readily than in the historical tragedies of the romantic age.

The term "realistic" can be applied to works of the modern age not only in reference to setting but also to the fundamental intuition of the concept of life therein expressed. Modern playwrights have gradually destroyed the traditional way of splitting life into two planes: the real and the ideal. They have constantly veered away from concepts of reality and have focused their attention on the actual aspects of it. Even works strictly imaginative reveal, under their symbolism, their concern with the actual world.

This type of modern realism should not be confused with the realism of the sixteenth-century comedy as represented by Aretino, Lasca, Cecchi, Machiavelli, and the unknown authors of the *Commedia dell' arte*. These playwrights used the social setting of their time in order to reach comic effects with the specific aim of producing laughter through the sordid situations which they portrayed. Modern realists have used the social setting with the clear and avowed purpose of studying it, injecting into the study a dignity, a purposefulness, and a philosophical vein unknown before.

The history of realism is closely associated with the growth of nineteenth-century democracy. As citizens acquired a greater role in national and economic life, bringing into being a new type of social organization, dramatic art assumed a new aspect both because it had to address itself to a wider and more practical public and because the playwright felt himself to be a part of the new society. In the fifteenth, sixteenth, and seventeenth centuries, theaters were the privilege of people of the court. Although the republic of Venice and of a few other cities had public theaters in the eighteenth century, the opening of playhouses to the general public was distinctly a contribution of the nineteenth century. Prizes to encourage dramatic activity were instituted for the first time in 1852 under Cavour, the founder of the liberal state in Italy.

The history of modern drama is here presented first in terms of nineteenth-century realism and then through the study of the works of contemporary authors. The basis of this distinction rests on the change in Italian political history and culture that makes of the nineteenth and the twentieth centuries two strikingly distinct epochs. The nineteenth century stressed a more objective study of reality, whereas our own age has granted a wider role to imagination. During the nineteenth century science predominated, whereas during the first years of our own century an idealistic reaction claimed first place. This background is substantially accurate provided we do not take it too categorically and picture the nineteenth century as monstrously scientific and the twentieth century as idealistic in a volatile manner. The term "predominance" of one current presupposes and testifies to the presence of the other.

We propose to reconstruct the history of Italian drama in terms of the acclaim or indifference with which contemporaries received the various plays, and then to evaluate them from the observation point of the present when taste and environment have substantially changed. Thus the history of drama becomes a revision of the reactions of the public of yesterday by the criticism of today.

THE FIRST GENERATION OF THE REALISTS

Toward the middle of the nineteenth century the level of the Italian theater was far from being very high. It was still weighed down by the old division of comedy and tragedy, and examples of the former were as drab as specimens of the latter were stilted and rhetorical. The drama written under the historical tenets of the romantic school had not produced anything significant. Even the two plays by Alessandro Manzoni, *Il Conte di Carmagnola* (1820) and *Adelchi* (1822), fall short of the height that the author of the *Promessi Sposi* (The Betrothed, 1827) attained in his novel. In general, the romantic drama moved the public more because of its political message than by its power of human appeal. Likewise, the tragedy of classical inspiration, rejuvenated by Alfieri in the eighteenth century and continued by Ugo Foscolo and Vincenzo Monti, produced works that today are historical relics and nothing more. But around 1850, closely allied to the traditional comedy, there developed a play with a definite stress on the social element to which we apply the qualification of modern. This type of dramatic art was the outgrowth of the new social order that gradually had been established in Italy.

Two important events influenced Italian life and art in the second half of the nineteenth century: the unification of the country and its gradual passing from an agricultural to an industrial civilization. The unification of Italy culminated with the establishment of Rome as the capital of the new state in 1870. The economic and social life of the country was strongly affected by the opening of the Suez Canal in 1869, whereby Italy was re-established in its traditional role of link between the East and the West. Economic life was greatly benefited and social conditions were vastly improved. The new direction assumed by

Italian life was, on the whole, resisted by the older generation and defended by the younger one. The conservatives presented themselves in the conventional pattern of being Catholic in religion, monarchical in politics, and capitalistic in economics. In art they still adhered to the tenets of pseudo-classicism or to those of the now old romantic school, and viewed with hostility all forms other than the traditional ones. The younger generation, reflecting a more pragmatic point of view, stood courageously for a modern form of progress based on work, on avowed adherence to "facts," and accepted the challenge of modern conditions and problems. The level of the theater was enormously raised, and dramatic literature was given a new content by the fact that men of high intellect, endowed by a keen sense of observation, assigned to their art the task of studying the society of their time in their search for new situations and effects. These men possessed a well-balanced outlook on life and society, and clung steadfastly to certain basic principles in which they had an absolute faith. They were *galantuomini*, men inherently honest, whose conservatism was alive because it had been reached after a period of doubt and trial. Among such men as these appeared the playwrights in whose works was reflected a social preoccupation which, after 1850, is to be noted with increasing frequency. While Luigi Suñer (1832-1909) and Giuseppe Vollo (1820-1905) are only of minor importance, Vincenzo Martini and Paolo Giacometti deserve greater consideration.

Vincenzo Martini (1803-62), who held various positions in the government of the Grand Duchy of Tuscany, wrote, among other comedies, three plays that deserve to be mentioned: *Una donna di quarant'anni* (1853), *Il cavaliere d'industria* (1854), and *Il marito e l'amante* (1855). In *Una donna di quarant'anni*, he presents the thesis that it is unwise for an older woman to marry a much younger man. For this reason, when the forty-year-old heroine, Malvina Vercelli, falls in love with the twenty-five-year-old Count of Altavilla, she is discreetly led to give up that love. *Il cavaliere d'industria*, written in 1845, but not performed until 1854, is a keen study of the Florentine society of Martini's time that was too prone to open its doors to adventurers of the type of the main character herein presented in Mario Newdork. In *Il marito e l'amante* is depicted with realistic technique the adulterous love of the Duchess Olimpia for a cynical and dishonest nobleman. The woman is made to realize the sad consequences of her romantic attachment. Although the situations herein presented are at times very amusing, the intent of the author goes far beyond humor. Martini was very interested in improving the theater of his day, and furthered his attempts by writing on dramatic art under the pen name of Anonimo Fiorentino.

Paolo Giacometti (1816–82), a professional playwright who earned his living by attaching himself to several dramatic companies and writing for them, deserves special attention, not so much for his *Il poeta e la ballerina* (1841) and *Le metamorfosi politiche* (1849) which, though mediocre from an artistic standpoint, testify to his interest in problems of contemporary society, as for *La morte civile* (1861). In it Giacometti daringly advocates the necessity of divorce in order to safeguard an innocent mother and child from the punishment meted out to the husband who had been sentenced to prison for life for homicide. This play was very well received and it remains even today in the repertoire of good companies. It is a strong play, and Corrado, the main character, is well drawn. The complexity of his psychology lifts the play above the documentary value that the thesis therein presented gives to it.

The outstanding representative of the social play is Paolo Ferrari (1822–89). Ferrari was a thoughtful man who set forth in his plays his reflections and perplexities before the confused pattern of the society of his time. He often took refuge in the idealism of the past, but more frequently offered his own vision of the dignity of life and of man. He was a stanch patriot and a liberal, a man religious without bigotry, moral without prudishness, who lived a very active life as a journalist, a professor of aesthetics at the University of Milan, and as a playwright. He fought the formula of art for art's sake and wanted art to be fired by the desire to correct the social evils of the time. Both historically, in that he dominated the theater of his day, and esthetically, in that he wrote plays that are still performed and admired, he deserves serious consideration.

In his long and fruitful career he wrote charming comedies of manners, historical dramas, and social plays. His art did not follow the rectilineal development imagined by those who state that Ferrari passed from the comedy of manners to the historical play, and from this to the social play. The chronology of his works disproves this contention. His development, like all true growth, was internal and not external, and was based on his sense of observation and artistic technique that deepened and improved with the passing of years. His less serious mood expressed itself in humorous comedies such as *La medicina d'una ragazza malata* (written 1859, performed 1862) and *Il codicillo dello zio Venanzio* (1865). Among the historical plays, his *Goldoni e le sue sedici commedie nuove* (1851) is noteworthy and is generally recognized as one of the best plays written in Italy during the nineteenth century. It is hardly necessary to say that this reconstruction of Goldoni's life at a critical moment of his career is not significant because of its historical accuracy. Ferrari reflected in it his own aspirations and struggles as a playwright and for this reason Goldoni becomes a new and a live character. Historical, in the same sense, but without achieving the same perfection, is *Parini e la satira* (1856), which places in sharp contrast the noble poetry of Parini and the servile one of his rival, the opportunist Degianni. What animates the play is the passion for true art that moved Ferrari in writing his own plays. Other historical dramas that he wrote do not add greatly to his fame.

What entitles Ferrari to a very important place in the history of drama is a clear strain of social analysis that is found in his plays: *Prosa* (1858), *Il duello* (1868), *Uomini Seri* (1869), *Cause ed effetti* (1871), *Ridicolo* (1872), *Il suicidio* (1875), *Due dame* (1877), and *Roberto Pregalli* (1880). The themes he has developed in these plays testify to his awareness of the social problems of his time. In *Prosa* he suggests that true art is not to be sought in exotic adventures. In *Ridicolo* he holds up to derision the prejudice, then very general, that all actresses are immoral. In *Uomini Seri* he points out the lack of honesty in the political and business life of his time. In *Cause ed effetti* are seen the sad consequences of marriage arranged by parents without the proper consideration of the qualities necessary for the happiness of the children involved. In *Due dame* the problem of the redemption and nobility of a fallen woman is treated. In *Roberto Pregalli* the author discusses the question whether predisposition to crime is a legitimate cause for acquittal. These problems interested Ferrari in a vital and sincere manner, and his passion communicates dramatic force to the events that unfold in his plays.

What is of greater importance is the fact that Ferrari often reflected in his characters a moment of his own perplexity before the mixture of good and evil that life seemed to him. In a letter to Vincenzo Martini, in reference to his play *Il duello*, he spoke of the "inevitable contradictions between absolute logic and practical logic." This attitude prevents his characters from being categorical imperatives or ethical mannequins, the accusation most frequently addressed against him. It prevents him also from presenting absolute pictures of evil. Critics have repeatedly stated that Ferrari had a bourgeois mentality and justified the ethics and even the prejudices and social conventions of his time. In reality, the idea that he entertained concerning morality was contrary to the general and current one. In *Due dame* he leads Rosalia, a fallen woman, to the pinnacle of womanly perfection. Rather than subscribing to the current prejudice, he argued against those who considered it impossible that a noble heart may still abide in such a woman. If, in the play, she forbids her son to marry Emma, an adventuress not different from what she had been in her youth, this shows Ferrari's sense of measure and lends to the play one of the best scenes in his theater: the scene where the two women are face to face and Rosalia proves the strength of her moral fiber by confessing her past to her son, yet keeping his esteem, admiration, and love. *Prosa* shows Ferrari taking a stand against the popular idea that a poet has a morality of his own.

In *Ridicolo* he rises against those who believe that an actress is destined to live an immoral life and the man who marries her is certain to become the butt of ridicule. In the play, Federico Braganza, believing himself above this prejudice, marries a celebrated singer. The main concern of the playwright is to show that Federico himself was not capable of rising above that prejudice. Being a man deprived of moral sense, he is the cause of their unhappiness and not the actress who appears in the play as a woman of noble character. In *Il duello* it is shown that there are often situations in life from which we cannot break loose without having recourse to the barbaric practice of dueling.

The importance of Ferrari rests especially upon the creation of his characters. In most of his plays, even in those that are somewhat cumbersome in their structure, are to be found complex and well-drawn characters. Beside Rosalia and Emma we find Anna in *Cause ed effetti*, Clotilde and Marcella in *Il suicidio*, women endowed with strong will and nobility of soul. Anna reflects Ferrari's critique of the life of the aristocracy when she is made to say to her friend:

> You can readily understand whether this life is made for me: to dress and go for a ride, to dress and go paying calls or receiving them, to dress and go to the theater or to a ball: a crushing toil from morning until night in order to be idle, to hear and see the things that I do not like. . . . For us women, diversion becomes the chief task and goal of our lives. Don't you wish to understand that we women, too, have in our nerves and in our blood a force, a desire to act, that calls for something better than to dance or engage in social gossip?

She proves in the play the sincerity of her words. She is idealistic, compassionate, and constructive. When she loses her little daughter, she finds solace in adopting the child that the former mistress of her husband had had by Anna's father. Another strongly etched character is Count Sirchi in *Il duello*. First a liberal, then a man who hands his friends to the police of the reactionary Bourbons, Count Sirchi bears traces of deep psychological study. He is not a spy for gain. He uses this weapon to avenge himself for the contempt with which he is treated. Yet he is dissatisfied and tortured by the fact that he has lost the love of his wife and by the remorse of his wrong-doing. He is the embodiment of a fundamentally good person wasted by circumstances. His words ring with the torment of his inability to break the vise-like hold that evil has on him. When, in his diabolical determination to hurt his rival, he challenges the fiancé of the latter's daughter to a duel, he allows himself to be killed by his opponent because he remembers the gentleness with which the girl, whose happiness he is about to destroy, had spoken to him. Thus the duel becomes for him a means of redemption. Sergio in *Uomini Seri* is not the usual romantic adventurer. He is a character possessed of a distorted sense of moral values, who tries to deceive others as well as himself. His reliance on words to mask with decency immoral attitudes and projects lends to him a complexity that places his creator well above the other dramatists of his time.

Italian critics, with the exception of Benedetto Croce, have strenuously tried to reduce Ferrari's art to a mere reflection of the French theater of Augier and the elder Dumas. No valid foundation for such criticism has been established. Being a painstaking worker, Ferrari read attentively past and contemporary French playwrights. He even translated Augier's *Les Fourchambault* and Pailleron's *Les Faux Ménages*. These contacts with the French theater helped his dramatic technique, but do not warrant any charge of plagiarism.

However, Ferrari's art as a whole offers some points for legitimate attack. His language is not so limpid and pliable as one would wish. He often introduces fantastic and involved situations that mar the plot. His characters engage at times in long speeches that, although revealing the thought of the author, weigh heavily on the smooth development of the action. Yet, in spite of these flaws, Ferrari remains an outstanding personality. Whatever hostile critics may say of him, they cannot deny the fact that he knows how to mold characters and that several of his plays are still very much alive today.

THE DRAMA OF THE YOUNGER REALISTS

Although the cultural background of the second half of the nineteenth century possesses a certain unity, there is a notable difference between the generation that lived before 1870, when Rome became the capital of the kingdom, and the one that lived after that event. The keynote of Italian life was no longer political but social, and the country was called upon to face internal problems: economic development, the right to vote, abolition of taxes which were very hard on the lower classes, public instruction made compulsory and gratuitous. Let us remember that in 1870 the Left Party went to power with Agostino de Pretis as prime minister. The struggle between conservatives and liberals became more acute than before, and reflected itself in literature, too. Olindo Guerrini, to quote one of the liberal school, in his *Nova polemica* stated that his opponents did not "understand for what social change the positive school in both science and art stands." The clamor of the young for "truth in art" presupposed a more enlightened view of progress and acceptance of the inevitability of change. The differences that separated the older and the younger generations on political as well as social problems warrant us to establish a distinction between the old liberals and the younger ones, a distinction that, in the field of letters, may be expressed by differentiating between the older realists, as represented by Paoli Ferrari, and the younger ones such as Marco Praga, Giuseppe Giacosa, and Roberto Bracco.

In many ways the generation of the younger realists reduced to a formula the concepts of life and art that in Ferrari existed in a freer and more natural form. They adhered to the aesthetic formula that enjoined the representation of life close at hand, painted life in bolder colors than did Ferrari, and were more articulate, passionate, and personal than the old master in denouncing the social evils of their time. Thus they produced a comedy on a narrower canvas, but more impressive in its concentrated pathos. They shunned intrigues and adventures and looked askance at any sentimentality. They were helped in their struggle for a new and better drama by acquainting themselves with the dramatic art of Ibsen and Henri Becque.

Modern critics (Tonelli, Pellizzi, D'Amico) have contemptuously called these playwrights bourgeois and at the same time cynical and unmoral. A moral preoccupation, resting on ethical principles that made them rebel against the morality of the average man who pays lip service to it and uses moral formulas to excuse his mediocrity, is ever present in their works. Ultimately they react against the false ethical standards of the society of their time; therefore, they cannot properly be called bourgeois and unmoral. Fundamentally, they sought dramatic contrasts in the contradiction of the human heart and in the absurdities of social conventions.

The realistic drama of this time has been confused with the naturalistic plays of Giovanni Verga (1840–1922). Naturalism is a more elementary form of art than is realism, which is essentially selective. It limits its observation to the world of instinct and it does not possess the intellectual scope of realism. For this reason the realism of playwrights such as Praga, Giacosa, and Bracco has very few points of contact with the art of Verga. Naturalism meant for the latter a return to the primitiveness of Sicilian life at the time that he lived in Milan and Florence away from his beloved island. Encouraged by the experiments of the contemporary French theater (let us remember that the *Théâtre Libre* was founded in 1887 by Antoine) and by his friend Luigi Capuana, he tried the technique of naturalism in order to rid himself of the rather fulsome style of his early writings. In *Cavalleria rusticana* (1889), *La Lupa* (1896), and *La caccia al lupo* (1901), he wrote three dramatic sketches, very vivid in their concentrated pathos, that stand out among the best of our modern theater. These plays express with elemental force the power of instinct, and render brutal facts soberly and passively. In *Cavalleria rusticana* Turiddu, in love with Lola, is killed in a duel with Alfio. In *La Lupa* Nenni splits open his mother-in-law's head with a hatchet as she advances, like a hungry she-wolf, to tempt him. In *La caccia al lupo* Mariangela is discovered entertaining her lover; the latter thinks only of how he can escape, which so enrages Mariangela that she shouts from an open window to her husband to kill the fleeing coward. These are the jewels of Italian naturalism that we owe to Verga. In *Portineria* (1895), the story of the unnoticed love of Malia, a girl suffering with tuberculosis, for handsome Carlini, who marries her sister, and in *Dal tuo al mio* (1903), in which a worker who previously had had no compunction in occupying the sulphur mines of his employer, stands ready to defend them with his gun when they become his through his marriage to the owner's daughter, Verga has applied the objectivity of the naturalistic method, but the subject is outside the precincts of strict naturalism.

The naturalistic theater continued to be represented in the early years of our century by Salvatore di Giacomo (1862–1934), one of the greatest contemporary playwrights. He wrote in Neapolitan dialect *'O voto* (The Vow, 1909), *'O mese mariano* (The Month of Mary, 1909), *Assunta Spina* (Assunta Spina, 1910), unforgettable sublimations of the Neapolitan people. Cristina da Capua, a prostitute in *'O voto*, Assunta Spina in the play that bears her name, and the mother in *'O mese mariano* are characters that in the elemental force of their passions reach the height of real tragedy.

The younger realists we are considering in this chapter, Marco Praga, Camillo Antona-Traversi, his brother Giannino, Girolamo Rovetta, Giuseppe Giacosa, Roberto Bracco, Achille Torelli, and Sabatino Lopez, have a wider range of motifs than had Verga, and their attitude and technique are quite different from those of the Sicilian playwright. Although they focus their attention on passion, they stress the moral aspect of this theme and lend to their characters a more complex psychology. Their activity culminated in the last twenty years of the nineteenth century and extended into our own time. The main centers where this new drama was produced were Milan, Turin, and Naples. In Milan,

Praga dominated; in Turin, most of Giacosa's plays were produced; and in Naples, Bracco lived and wrote his plays.

Milan contributed more than other cities in the development of realistic drama. In that center worked also Carlo Bertolazzi (1871–1916), Silvio Zambaldi (1870–1932), and Sabatino Lopez, although the latter was born at Livorno. Bertolazzi, among other works, wrote *L'egoista* (The Egoist, 1901), the study of the egotism of Franco Marteno as a child, a husband, and a father, and *La casa del sonno* (The House of Slumber, 1902), the consideration of the moral and economic ruin of Luciano, who left his ancestral home to engage in speculation. Zambaldi is best known for his *La moglie del dottore* (A Physician's Wife, 1908), a psychological study of the reactions of a physician who meets the man who seduced his wife when the latter was a young girl.

The most ardent advocate of the realistic drama in the Milanese group in the nineties was Marco Praga (1862–1929). He was the son of the poet Emilio Praga who, in the sixties, had likewise advocated "truth" as the basis of art. Marco Praga started his career as a bookkeeper in a banking house, but soon dedicated himself to the theater and lived in and for the theater till the day he committed suicide. He was president of the Society of Playwrights and dramatic critic of the *Corriere della Sera* of Milan. His reactions to the contemporary theater are to be found in his eight volumes of *Cronache teatrali* (1921–28).

Recognition as a dramatist of note was accorded to him when his *Le vergini* (1889) was performed in Milan. This is the most representative of Praga's plays. It epitomizes the material in which the artist is primarily interested and, in presenting the vicissitudes of the characters, reveals his attitude toward the moral problem therein contained. The play deals with a middle-class family where a mother is not unwilling to permit her three daughters to have well-to-do admirers who pay with gifts for the liberties the girls allow. Praga studies pitilessly the attitude of the mother in her concern to keep a mask of decency on her home, balancing herself with perfect ease on the borderline of morality and immorality. It is the only means at her disposal of having her daughters go among their friends, well dressed, displaying fine jewelry, and being happy. This applies, at least, to Ninì and Selene, two of the sisters who play the game with extreme confidence; but not to Paolina, another sister, who is very unhappy in that atmosphere. The drama begins precisely here, carried by Paolina, the individual whose nobility serves the purpose of stressing diversity, creating contrast, and determining the action of the play. When Dario, a spineless student, asks her to be his wife, she is so overjoyed and ennobled that, on the eve of their wedding, she feels it incumbent upon herself to reveal to him that when she was seventeen she was seduced by Vercellini, a friend of her mother's, the same individual who had been chosen to be best man at the wedding. Dario, incapable of perceiving the nobility of this confession, cools in his matrimonial enthusiasm and proposes to her to become his mistress. Paolina refuses with words that echo the indignation of the author and make her tower above Dario's moral obtuseness. The accusation of immorality, so often addressed to Praga, is especially based on this play. From the standpoint of formalistic ethics, the subject may be called immoral, but thoughtful men have never subscribed to such a moral code. Praga advocates here a morality of the soul that can cleanse even the offense rendered to the body. To him immorality lies around Paolina and not in her. She is redeemed by her confession to Dario.

What is said of this play is also applicable to the rest of Praga's dramatic works. He is a grieving sentimentalist moved to expose the pitiful spectacle that society offers him. He does so with great earnestness and with an eye for the dramatic effect that such situations hold for his art. *Il Bell'Apollo* (1894) is developed along the same lines as *Le vergini*. It is a study of masculine profligacy, embodied in Pietro Badia and projected against the real love of Susanna da Ponte, a woman who falls not for vice but because her love has suddenly revealed to her the meaning of her whole existence and has transformed her into a new being. Near her Praga has placed two other women, Enrichetta, a young shirtmaker, and Dolores Arneiro, wife of a jealous Spaniard, irresponsible beings for whom love is part of their trade, or merely a caprice.

It is evident from what has been said that Praga differentiates between people for whom love is vice and those for whom love is an all-absorbing experience that, when sincerely felt, lifts them to a higher plane. Ninì, Selene, and Pietro Badia were followed, in subsequent plays, by Giulia in *La moglie ideale* (1890) and Alessandro Fara's wife Elisa in *Alleluja* (1892), just as Paolina and Susanna da Ponte were embodied in other characters of the same psychological texture as theirs. Lucia Lovere, in *La morale della favola* (1894–1901), is so fundamentally honest that, upon realizing the enormity of her act in yielding to her lover, Augusto Campese, she feels that she cannot return to her husband and children. Conscious of her moral sensitiveness, her uncle, Don Raimondo, a high-minded priest, persuades her to go back to her home and atone for her sin through her consciousness of it. False morality is satirized in the attitude of Augusto Campese, who mentions the sanctity of the home in urging the woman to return to her husband.

Marco Praga has constantly analyzed the love motif as a source of variety in his artistic material. In *La crisi* (1901), the adultery of Nicoletta is studied through the anguish of her husband Pietro Donati, who knows that she betrays him but loves her too much to live without her. Hence his grieving silence. The crisis is brought about by the sudden return of Raimondo, Pietro Donati's brother and an army officer. He senses the truth of the situation and challenges Nicoletta's lover to a duel. The scene in which Pietro Donati openly admits his cowardice is a masterful study of human psychology. Conscious of the irreparable harm that he has unwittingly done to his brother, Raimondo begs Nicoletta to deny her unfaithfulness to Pietro. The play ends with a repentant Nicoletta who returns to the love of her husband.

With the passing of years Praga searched more and more deeply into the theme of passion and the fruit of his search was *La porta chiusa* (The Closed Door, 1913). Eleonora Duse interpreted it and brought out the anguish of the mother who is made to atone for her sin through the loss of her only son, whom she adored.

The seriousness and conservatism underlying Praga's art may be seen in his last play, *Il divorzio* (1915), in which he presents the thesis that divorce "is a grotesque thing when it is not a filthy thing." Emilia, Prince Alessio, her second husband, and Edmondo, her former husband, meet by chance at a watering resort. A great emotional conflict arises in Emilia upon seeing again her little son Alfredo, who is now eight years old. Her grief at parting from him is the penalty that Praga, the moralist, has meted out to her.

The artistic creed of Praga was clearly revealed in the words that he addressed to young Italian playwrights in 1919 when he stated that drama is to be found everywhere, in every factory, in every home, and in the conscience of every man. He assigned to playwrights the task not only of reflecting their own time, but also of foreshadowing new states of mind and new events. When so conceived, drama assumed a deeply social and religious character.

Dear friends of Praga were Camillo Antona-Traversi (1857–1934), a professor of Italian literature in a military college, first in Naples, then in Rome, and his brother Giannino. Camillo Antona-Traversi took an active part in journalism and wrote literary criticism. He is especially known for two social plays, *Le Rozeno* (1889) and *I parassiti* (1901). The preface to *Le Rozeno* documents very minutely the hostility with which this play was received by conservative elements, especially in church circles. It informs us also of the warm praise it received from liberal-minded persons.

Le Rozeno bears close resemblance to Praga's *Le vergini*. There is the same background of immorality against which is projected a very sensitive young woman, Lidia Rozeno. There is the same family, living on the borderline of indecency, frequented by men who pay for the luxuries of the three daughters of Clarissa Rozeno. At the opening of the play, the precarious economic situation of the family is about to be stabilized at the expense of Lidia. An old and wealthy prince, believing the child that Lidia is carrying is his, will leave his money to her and the baby. Lidia, however, refuses to be a part of this sordid game. She knows that her child is the fruit of her love for the student Enrico Valenti. To the playwright, Lidia stands redeemed by the sense of purity that motherhood brings into her life. The play centers about this awakened sense of motherhood that is offended by the cowardiness of Enrico, who offers her the status of mistress.

I parassiti embodies a bitter critique of human dishonesty as studied in Gaudenzi and his family, types of modern parasites. The son Alfredo exploits his wife Ida, just as Gaudenzi exploits his daughter Lina and the gullible public by forming charity committees whenever there is an earthquake or a flood. Gaudenzi, however, is not presented as a lifeless type. He is studied in his resourcefulness, his genius for intrigue, and his childish optimism. In the opening scenes of the play we find him in a difficult situation. No great catastrophe has taken place of late and, furthermore, he has too many rivals in organizing charity committees. The sudden news of an earthquake helps him to face his creditors by organizing a new committee. But the committee dissolves because the shock has not been so serious as had been believed. Even now his resourcefulness helps him to overcome his plight, and he goes as manager to a Polish violinist on a tour of South America in which his daughter will be the accompanist.

It is evident that Gaudenzi is not the projection of Antona-Traversi's idea of honesty. The pivot around which the play revolves is the grieving amusement of the author before such phenomena of modern life as are seen in the parasitical Gaudenzi.

Giannino Antona-Traversi (1868–1939) was especially successful with one-act plays in which, with a lighter touch and more subtle irony, but with less dramatic power than Praga or his brother Camillo, he studied the society life of Milan in which he was a conspicuous figure. He seems bent on inquiring what becomes of the noble human passion of love in the heart, or rather, in the cold brain, of society people. In his opinion, flirting and gossiping are their all-absorbing occupations, as he informs us in

La carità mondana (1906), and deception is the trait that stands out before anyone who watches this playing with love. In *Il braccialetto* (1897), *La civetta* (1904), *Per vanità* (1902), and *La prima volta* (1910), we witness various aspects of the empty and pleasure-loving life of society people. Traversi dissects their flirting and finds base intrigues and degrading intentions in their acts.

In these plays the author is definitely ironical, although with a smile that tempers his attitude. More compassionately he treats the characters of *I giorni più lieti* (1903) and *I martiri del lavoro* (1909) in which he develops the theme that the moments of intimacy and happiness that should accompany the days before the wedding or those following it are disturbed and destroyed by the social obligations to which the two fiancés or the two newlyweds are condemned. Although the corruption of society can become conventionalized, Giannino is resourceful enough to produce interesting sketches in the above-mentioned plays, though he definitely fails when he attempts drama on vaster proportions.

La Madre (1909), a drama in four acts, is developed along very conventional lines in presenting the nobility of the old aristocracy and the depravity of a family of the lower class into which has married Fabrizio, the scion of Prince Redona. The mother is the victim of the situation, caught between the unbending principles of her husband and the weakness of her son. She is, however, a cold symbol of perfection rather than a character with strong human traits.

Giannino Antona-Traversi's contribution to the theater is not of great significance although his plays enjoyed great popularity in the days before World War I.

To the Milanese group belonged also Girolamo Rovetta (1853–1910). Although he was never very articulate concerning problems of dramatic art, he worked earnestly at his plays and novels. His plays usually have industrial Milan as their background. He was a gentleman of independent means and dedicated his entire life to works of fiction and the theater. What he thinks of the new Milan with the bustle of its intense economic life can be seen in the plays in which the triumph of dishonesty is portrayed with an insistence that, at times, engenders monotony. *La città di Roma* (1888) informs us that Andrea Borsieri refrains from revealing the adultery of his wife for fear that the latter, an able milliner, may, out of spite, open a shop at the next corner from his own establishment, and ruin his business. The author has reduced the moral sensitivity of the main character to this paltry proportion. We find the same atmosphere in *I Barbarò* (1890) and *La baraonda* (1894), plays that were first written in the form of novels.

Rovetta's best comedy is *La trilogia di Dorina* (1889), woven about the paradoxical stupidity of the Marquis Niccolino who asks his maid, a charming girl, to become his mistress and then marries her when she has become a famous singer and a corrupted woman. It is a delightful comedy presenting Dorina first as an innocent girl, who refuses Niccolino's advances and pleads with him to marry her if he loves her, and later as a coquette, expert in the use of her guiles. A motley crowd of characters surrounds her: bankers, industrialists, social climbers of all kinds, side by side with the humorous figure of her singing teacher. The simplicity and goodness of the girl stand out as an indictment of society and also of the vulgar temperament of the young marquis for whom Rovetta reserves the role of falling prey to his own sensuality.

I disonesti (1892) and *La realtà* (1895) also reflect a disconsolate outlook on life. In the former play, Rovetta ponders over the case of Carlo Moretti, a paragon of honesty as a treasurer whose moral sense is badly shaken when he discovers that the luxury of his home is being paid for by the head of his firm in return for the favors of his wife. When the death of the employer ends this unsuspected income, he goes to the point of stealing from the firm in order to keep up the impression of prosperity. In *La realtà*, an upright and progressive industrialist commits suicide when, through his wife's perfidy, he faces economic ruin and the destruction of his home. Even the workers, for whose benefit he had introduced cooperatives, abandon him when the financial collapse comes.

In Rovetta's somewhat conventional philosophy a strain of idealism is clearly visible. In *Papà Eccellenza* (1907) we are permitted to see, better than in other plays, the positive aspects of his idealism, since in it he depicts a character who, behind the occupation and successes of a political life, has as his only reality his love for his daughter.

Rovetta also wrote four historical plays with the clear intent of reducing historical figures to the humble proportions of men seen at close range. It cannot be said that he reached the human element in them. This is true even of *Romanticismo* (1901), which had a distinct success because of its patriotic appeal.

On the whole, Rovetta's attitude is that of a defeatist. He paints with two contrasting colors: the white of honesty and the black of dishonesty, with the black predominating over the white.

Giuseppe Giacosa (1847-1906) was a man endowed with a more positive and constructive mind than his friends of the Milanese group with whom he lived in intimate contact. The picture of the sadness and even tragedy of life is fringed in his work by a halo of faith and hope in man. He studied law, but from his early youth began to write short plays along the lines of the comedy of manners or historical scenes with a romantic turn: *Una partita a scacchi* (1873), *Il marito amante della moglie* (1879), *Il Conte Rosso* (1880).

The success of *Una partita a scacchi* encouraged him to abandon the law and dedicate himself to the theater. As Giacosa matured, he reflected his deepened sense of experience in *Tristi amori* (1888). This play that has been attributed to French and Scandinavian influences gives the measure of Giacosa's creative power. The author is ever present in it through his perplexity before Emma's action in betraying Giulio, her husband, for a worthless individual like Fabrizio, her husband's assistant in the practice of law. The assistant is the son of a penniless count who is dishonest to the point of forging Giulio's signature on a note. Home life, even in its most prosaic details, is made to loom beautiful and desirable before Emma, tormented by fears and anxiety. Giacosa paints her more as a weak than a vulgar person. Even in her tryst with Fabrizio, she longs for affection, as her own words indicate. When the tryst is discovered through the forged signature of Fabrizio's father, Emma is ready to leave her home, but she is touched by the sight of her child's doll and cannot tear herself away from it. Giulio returns and tells her that he is willing to have her live under his roof for their child's sake, though he will never forgive her. This solution is in keeping with Giulio's sense of right and wrong which, though not extreme, is unbending where decency is concerned. A new drama of broken love and destroyed happiness is envisaged in that solution, a silent drama that Giacosa exquisitely intimates in his restrained technique.

La Contessa di Challant appeared in 1891. Here is to be found the tragedy and complexity of the love theme in a historical setting. The plot is based on one of Bandello's stories, which Giacosa has molded with absolute independence, lending a new soul to the main character. He wrote the play for the great actress Sarah Bernhardt at her request. Bianca of Challant is portrayed as the victim of an unfortunate marriage. She had been thirsty for love and was married to a gouty count. If she passed from one lover to another, she did so because she sought a real love that she never found. She had loved Gaiazzo and had found him stupid. She had loved Ardizzino and found him vulgar. In the end she met real love in a Spanish youth who exposed himself to death for her. A different woman, no longer whimsical and changeable, was revealed in her. She sealed that love by offering her life for her young lover.

The thoughtful strain of Giacosa's mind is even better revealed by I diritti dell' anima (1889), the motivation of which is based on the question whether a husband has the right to search into his wife's soul when he knows that she has remained faithful to him. Paolo is shown tormenting Anna with his maddening inquisition concerning her feelings toward a distant relative who had fallen in love with her and, upon being rejected, had committed suicide. Goaded by his incessant questioning, Anna tells him that she loved Luciano and regrets now that she remained faithful to her husband by silencing the voices of her heart. Giacosa daringly brings his theme to a logical conclusion, and Anna leaves Paolo's home. The solution reflects Giacosa's desire for the new status of woman in the home and bespeaks his open and high mind.

The dramatic success of 1900 was *Come le foglie*, which presents to us the sad existence of Giovanni. He has worked "like an ox" all his life, and all his hopes that he had placed in the members of his family have vanished like autumn leaves. His wife, to whom he was devoted, has died. Giulia, his second wife, is superficial and vacuous, interested in studying painting with a Swedish artist who makes love to her. Tommy, his son, spends his youth gambling and flirting. Nennele, his daughter, with her inefficient goodness, withers in the silence of his home. Giovanni is tied to his work, the only tangible but crushing reality of his life. In this gloom and sadness there is a character that brings a positive and healthy note—Massimo, a cousin, healthy of body and of mind, who embodies and expresses Giacosa's constructive views on work, nature, art, and life in general. To him is assigned the task of saving Nennele as well as Giovanni's home. When the girl, unable to stand any longer the burden of her existence, has decided to take her life, Massimo appears and tells her of his love for her.

The social element is quite evident in Giacosa's work, and it plays a paramount part in *Il più forte* (The Stronger of the Two, 1904), which depicts the crisis that arises between Cesare Nalli, a banker, and his son Silvio, an artist. The crisis is determined by the clash of two opposite views of honesty. Silvio, the spokesman of Giacosa, feels that his father, one of those bankers who, with the control of huge capital, holds in his hand the destiny of millions, cannot be called honest according to his meaning of the term. It is true that, according to the letter of the law, he is honest, but is it honest to evade the spirit of the law? Cesare Nalli, the man of iron in his business transactions, who loves his family tenderly, is hurt to the quick by the decision of his son to leave his home and earn a living by his art. The artist stands in the play as the stronger of the two.

Giacosa is a significant figure in the history of the modern theater. He also wrote librettos for Giacomo Puccini's operas *Madame Butterfly*, *Bohême*, and *Tosca* in collaboration with Luigi Illica. The adverse criticism that he has usually received seems to us totally unjust. His dialogue flows smoothly. His characters are human, complex, and alive. His outlook on life is that of a broad-minded man whose optimism bears traits of having been tested in the school of life.

Roberto Bracco (1861–1943) enlivens his observation of contemporary life with a wide vein of human compassion. The characters that most frequently appear in his plays are victims of society or women who give to love a sincerity that is unknown to men.

This typical attitude of Bracco can be clearly seen in *Pietro Caruso* (1895), the sketch of a shadowy figure of the Neapolitan world, a man without honor in his life of "jack-of-all-trades," which includes that of working for political candidates. But he has one redeeming feature: absolute faith in the honesty of his only daughter. When she becomes the mistress of the wealthy man whose political aspirations he serves, Caruso kills himself. A similar drama develops in the poor quarters of Naples in *Sperduti nel buio* (1901). It is the drama of Nunzio and Paolina, a blind boy and a girl, daughter of a prostitute, who meet in a cheap café where Nunzio plays the piano. The short idyl is broken by a man who courts and takes Paolina away from Nunzio. She is, perhaps, the daughter of the Duke of Valenza whose dying moments, embittered by remorse for having abandoned an illegitimate child, are portrayed in the third act. *Nellina* (1908) deals with the same atmosphere of social degradation in which the mother, a prostitute, cannot reveal her identity to Nellina, herself a prostitute. However, in Bracco's mind society has not been able to wipe out the maternal instinct on which the play is based.

When Bracco relinquished themes set forth by means of local color and sought his material in higher social circles and more complex figures, his attitude did not change. In *Tragedie del-l'anima* (1899) and *Maternità* (1903) we find the same faith of Bracco in the fundamental goodness of woman, crushed by the irresponsibility of man to whom love is merely sensuality or a pastime. Psychological treatment and social concern remain the poles around which his drama revolves. In these two plays he has created his drama out of the contrast between the indestructible instinct of motherhood and the sensuous considerations of the two husbands presented in them. The action of the plays assumes a symbolic character that does not jar against the realism that distinguishes it.

The theme of those who live like shadows or are crushed by insensitive persons is also treated in *La piccola fonte* (1905) in which Teresa, in her humility and self-effacement, stands as a sublime figure before the vagaries of her husband who is made to realize what a large part Teresa has played in his success as a poet.

As time went on, the art of Bracco veered constantly toward the psychological. *Fantasmi* (1906) and *Il piccolo santo* (1912) are beautiful examples of the height he reached in his development. *Fantasmi* presents the case of the masculine acquisitive instinct that goes even beyond death. Professor Artunni extorted from his wife Giulia the promise that after his death she would not marry Luciano Marnieri, one of his pupils. From the dark regions of death he was able to continue to stifle the existence of the woman. In *Il piccolo santo* Bracco shows how tragedy passes like a destructive storm over the refuge sought by a young priest, Don Fiorenzo, in the peace of a country parsonage. When Anita, the daughter of a woman he once dearly loved, comes to seek help from him, the old love is rekindled without his realizing it in the interest that he feels in the young girl. Giulio, his brother, returns from America and falls in love with Anita. On the day of their wedding, Barbarello, a half-wit who worships Don Fiorenzo, sensing the hidden tragedy of his master, kills Giulio.

Bracco used, with independence and originality, both the conclusions of the realistic school and his cultural contacts with Ibsen and the French playwrights of his day. Truly great authors, however, have always gone outside the precincts of schools and have not been enslaved by literary contacts. Bracco belongs to this group.

A Neapolitan like Bracco was Achille Torelli (1844–1922). Torelli was librarian of the Royal Library St. Giacomo at Naples, and he wrote extensively while attending to his duties. Benedetto Croce has pointed out that the theme of true love is the main chord in Torelli's dramatic work. His plays are, in fact, variations on this theme. It should be added that the author is led to envisage wider problems through it: art in *La scuola degli artisti* (1885) and *Scrollina* (1885); marriage in *I mariti* (1867) and *La moglie* (1868); women in modern society in *Donne moderne* (1886).

He became famous at the age of twenty-three when *I mariti* was performed at Florence in 1867. This comedy is a sort of modern version of *The Taming of the Shrew*, brilliantly conceived and perfectly worked out. Fabio, the husband, is made to succeed in acquiring, through tact and intellectual superiority, the love of his wife Emma, a daughter of the illustrious Herrera family, who had married him only to obey her parents. The play was enthusiastically received and critics (Ferrini, Capuana, Franchetti) spoke of a new era for the Italian theater.

The subsequent attempts at drama by the sensitive and penetrating author were, however, coldly received. He was unspeakably hurt and, as a result, condemned himself to a life of retirement, though he continued to write plays that met with increasing indifference. Yet the plays written after *I mariti* are an exemplification of the fact that Torelli tended toward a more subtle and psychological art in his tormenting study of love and passion. From the observation point of his lonely existence, Torelli was dismayed by the tragic power of passion and expressed his musings through attitudes and conclusions so idealistic and subjective that the public of the time refused to accept them. In *La moglie*, Maria, knowing of the blind passion that Malvina, her sister-in-law, has conceived for her husband, instead of dramatizing her jealousy and creating a catastrophe, shows to her brother the tryst of her husband with another woman and makes him see the tragedy of her situation that he may find strength to bear his own. She is a sublime victim who offers her shame and grief in sacrifice for the good of those she loves, including the husband whom she forgives. In *L'israelita* (1883) Bracco presents the case of a woman who is goaded into adultery, not by love or passion for her mate, but by her desire to have a child. So genuine is this longing in her and so consistent is the author in bringing his theme to its last conclusions that she refuses to marry the father of her child when her husband dies. The same subjective treatment is accorded to the theme of unfaithfulness in *L'ultimo convegno* (The Last Meeting, 1898), in which Patrizio, an invalid who is betrayed by his wife, tells her that he is aware of her infidelity, but begs her to face her guilt and acknowledge it in a spirit of humility that she may find atonement in her remorse. Likewise, in *Triste realtà* (1886), Rio, knowing that he is destined to die in youth, silences the voice of jealousy and the acquisitive instinct to the point of providing that his wife should remarry after his death.

In many ways Torelli, in his tormented individualism, seems to be the forerunner of contemporary playwrights. Thus, while he was close to the generation of Ferrari in *I mariti*, in his later works he went beyond the taste and comprehension of his contemporaries, who were accustomed to the more solid realism that prevailed at that time.

Sabatino Lopez (1867–1951) lived in Milan during a long career in the course of which he wrote an impressive number of plays. He was a teacher of Italian literature in the secondary schools of various cities until he relinquished that career to become president of the Italian Society of Playwrights and to dedicate himself to the writing of plays.

His first dramatic sketches were written in 1888: *Oriana* and *Di notte*. In these as well as in other attempts at drama Lopez was hampered rather than helped by the dictates of naturalism that he followed. In *Di notte*, which received the government prize in 1890, a husband kills his wife because he has seen a man flee from his home at night. The man proves to be the lover of his daughter.

The drama ends where it could begin since the consequences of the blunder are left to the imagination of the public.

Quite different in technique and content are *Ninetta* (1895) and *La buona figliuola* (1909) in which the author combined humor with realistic themes. Ninetta, D'Arcole's mistress, proves to be, in her genuine devotion to him, a better woman than the wife for whom he has abandoned her. When his wife betrays him, D'Arcole appreciates Ninetta better and returns to her.

In *La buona figliuola* Cesarina, a girl who ran away from home and became the mistress of a member of the Italian Parliament, has lost none of her attachment for her family nor any of the qualities of an affectionate daughter. She contributes in every possible way to the well-being of her sister Giulia, to whom she gives as wise advice as a mother would give her daughter. Is this irony? Is it sentiment? It is both, and these two traits are very much in evidence in Lopez's works. This benevolent irony is also found in *La morale che corre* (1904), in which he informs us that Giugiù, a man by no means noted for morality, is very severe upon learning that Giuditta, his housekeeper, though unmarried, is with child, and dismisses her. But later, on meeting her again, as a fashionable harlot, he has no compunction in courting her. Perhaps the best example of the humorous treatment of a realistic theme is found in *La nostra pelle* (1912), which places in sharp contrast the hardships that fall to the lot of Elsa, a modest schoolteacher, when she offers a piece of her skin to be grafted on the body of one of her pupils who has been badly burned, and the good fortune that comes to Fioravanti for having killed a man who terrorized the whole village. Elsa, after her heroic sacrifice, marries the mayor of the town only to become the nurse of his invalid and irascible mother, and the slave of the household. She is also exploited by the father of the child whose life she saved. Her husband sums up well Lopez's point of view: "Some are tied to virtue as others to vice; virtue is an iron ball tied to your feet." *L'ultimo romanzo* (1920), *Fatica* (1920), *La Zia Lu* (1921) are all developments of the author's mood that oscillates between humor and pathos, and they are very effective.

Bufere (1907) shows a different aspect of Lopez's art. It is serious drama. In it he sounds the love of Sabina and Antoniccu, who love each other with the exclusive love of the silent and repressed persons of Sardinia. Their quiet and happy life is broken, however, when Cora Parnell, a circus acrobat, steals Antoniccu's love. Sabina leaves him and returns to her home in Sardinia. The play centers in the conviction of the playwright that Sabina's place is near her husband in his days of trial. (The theme that forgiveness is the only solution in the case of adultery is developed by Lopez in *Il viluppo*, 1913.) But Sabina, true to the ethics of her native island, returns, not to forgive, but to kill Cora with a surgical instrument belonging to her husband. Of Lopez's attempts at serious drama, *Bufere* is the best.

Lopez has continued to entertain the Italian public during and after World War I. Even as late as 1937 he produced a new play, *Luce*. He has remained untouched by the experiments in technique and content that have characterized our epoch, clinging steadfastly to the forms and substance enjoined by the theory of realism that was formulated during his youth.

To have a clear idea of the condition of Italian drama at the end of the past century we should keep in mind that other literary currents coexisted with that represented by the younger realists. The historical play was represented at that time by Felice Cavallotti (1842-98), a republican member of parliament; Giovanni Bovio (1841–1903); and Pietro Cossa (1830–81). Cossa is still remembered for his *Nerone* (1871) in which he applied the procedures of the realistic school to historical drama and presented a Nero quite different from the bloodthirsty tyrant of the popular conception of that historical figure. In Cossa's drama Nero is a fickle individual, not deprived of impulses for goodness, suddenly overpowered by cruelty and cowardice. The play is enlivened by the presence of an exquisite Greek dancer, Egloge by name, who gives her love to Nero and dies for it.

To the same generation also belonged Enrico Annibale Butti (1868-1912). He was a solitary man of letters, very much detached from the problems of his age. In his plays *Vortice* (1893), *La corsa al piacere* (1900), and *Il castello del sogno* (1910), he expressed vaguely mystic and religious aspirations portrayed against the background of the materialism of his age. His plays are brutally realistic when the author looks at modern life, and dreamy and romantic when he reflects his own idealism, to which, however, he was never capable of giving concrete form. He deserves mention for his play *Fiamme nell' ombra* (Flames in the Shadow, 1905), in which the drama of a young priest is effectively portrayed. The flames are the world, the blood that tingles in his veins, the possibility of advancement in his ecclesiastic career, the moral fall of his sister; the shadow is the life of silence and prayer to which he condemns himself in the hope of redeeming his sister.

In Butti, nerves begin to be in greater evidence than muscle, to use an expression that Benedetto Croce aptly employs in pointing out the difference between the last century and our own.

THE NEW REALISTIC DRAMA

From the first years of our century to the present day, Italian culture has formed a compact though varied zone, dominated by the desire of having Italy not only re-enter the current of European history but also to contribute something new to it. In political life, as well as in art, there has been a break with tradition. The hazy ideologies of fascism obliterated the clear-cut pattern of the philosophy of government by the liberals and the social democrats of former days. In art, too, the same departure from tradition was represented by futurism and *La Voce* before the days of World War I; the former extreme, erratic, irrational, plebeian, and theatrical, the latter very constructive and sane as the expression of the vision of the best minds of the time: Prezzolini, Papini, Salvemini, Amendola, and Soffici. Numerous movements appeared at that time which aimed at directing Italian life toward new goals: in religion, modernism; in politics, nationalism; in art, futurism; in sociology, syndicalism.

During this period drama assumed a great variety of forms that reflected in a varied measure a harrowing desire for novelty. The descriptive captions of contemporary works bear witness to this trend. Contemporary playwrights have discarded the old terminology of tragedy and comedy and called their works "parables," "grotesque" (used as a noun), "adventures in color." Pirandello even called his *Sei personaggi in cerca d'autore* (Six Characters in Search of an Author), "comedy yet to be made." Nevertheless, whatever technical changes have been introduced, the fundamental qualities of a drama that presents living personalities in situations fraught with tragedy and humor have not been changed, and the works we are to review are to be judged in the light of the effectiveness of the finished product. For clarity's sake, we have divided the copious production of the contemporary drama into several sections: comedy, historical drama, lyrical drama, and the drama of the mind.

Variations of taste and culture are reflected in the drama. The strong anti-bourgeois tendency of the early years of our century was followed by the anarchy that characterized Italian art during and after World War I. A moment of spiritual reconstruction could be observed around 1925, which was disturbed and eventually destroyed when Mussolini inaugurated his warlike foreign policy and then led Italy to its present tragedy. Gabriele D'Annunzio was the most famous and even notorious playwright in the years preceding 1914. During the war, the authors of the "grotesque" enjoyed great popularity. Luigi Pirandello, together with Dario Niccodemi, dominated the postwar years.

On the whole, dramatic art assumed during this time a greater psychological complexity which led serious authors to fathom nooks of the human heart unknown to the writers of the previous generation. The art of Luigi Pirandello, Sem Benelli, Luigi Morselli, Cesare Vico Ludovici, and Luigi Chiarelli gained in depth through this analysis. Others produced only ephemeral works in which the study of human personality ended in empty symbolism or in experiments in technique and form.

Among the cultural factors that influenced the contemporary playwrights were Croce's theory of art as a subjective intuition of reality, as well as contacts with foreign authors such as Ibsen, Maeterlinck, Rostand, Hauptmann, Gide, Bernstein, and the Russian authors: Tolstoi, Turgenev, Dostoevski, and Chekhov. Theatrical technique, aided by the innovations of Max Reinhardt, became more subtle and effective, just as language was made richer and more flexible in expressing a more complex psychology.

On the whole, the last thirty years have been a period of experimentation with themes and techniques. There have been more than two thousand small and large dramatic societies and centers where authors have been allowed to present the results of their efforts.

REALISTIC COMEDY

Under the heading of comedy we are including not only the plays in which, though differently treated, appear themes once dear to the traditional comedy, but also those that reflect a concern for political as well as social problems.

In the early part of our century the theater reverberated with the political struggle that was being waged between social democracy and the resurgent nationalism represented by Enrico Corradini (1865–1931). The works of Corradini (*Le vie del-l'oceano*, 1913), Vincenzo Morello (*La flotta degli emigranti*, 1907), and Tommaso Monicelli (*L'esodo*, 1908, *La terra promessa*, 1910) are closely connected with the new concept of nationalism which they sponsored. Questions involving the sanctity of the hearth, emigration, the beauty of agricultural life, the destructive power of commercialism are no longer here envisaged in the light of a humanitarian ideal as in the works of the nineteenth-century realist, but in their relationship with the future of the Italian nation.

The question of emigration, for instance, is reflected in the works of these three men, although their plays are developed around events in which emotions have a large part. In *Le vie dell'oceano* by Corradini we view a clash between an old emigrant to Argentina, who has remained attached to the little Italian village whence he came, and his children who know only the country where they were born and have lived. Likewise, in *La flotta degli emigranti* by Vincenzo Morello (1860–1933), the corruption of a deputy of the old liberal school, Lantosca, is combined with the theme of emigration and his scheme to defraud the shipping companies that carry Italian emigrants to the Americas. It should be noted that in his plays Morello often insisted on the need of an enlightened dictatorship, as in *I condottieri* (1921). *L'esodo* by Monicelli (1883–1946) as well as *La terra promessa* and *Il viandante* (1907) are works that, dictated by political considerations, serve to make us understand the subsequent changes that have intervened in Italian political life.

Such themes, when treated at a later date by younger authors, show a more thoughtful attitude toward international as well as national problems. Thus, in *Il calzolaio di Messina* (1935) by Alessandro de Stefani (1879–1944) are studied the nature and role of justice in organized society. A young and well-intentioned man of the lower class, who takes it upon himself to mete out justice, is made to realize that his blunders are different from the possible errors of duly-appointed judges, because he is not strengthened by the authority vested in him by society. He stands in his own eyes as a murderer and not as a judge, through the remorse that tortures him. A similar motivation is found in *La padrona del mondo* (1934) by Giuseppe Bevilacqua (1891–   ). Our materialistic age is symbolized by a queen who assigns to herself the task of giving happiness to suffering humanity through her discovery of a scientific process whereby she can make gold. The thoughtful and idealistic author concludes in his play that she failed even as our commercial age has failed.

Another trend observed in the best examples of comedy is the psychological trend found in the plays of Lucio D'Ambra, Renato

Simoni, and Giuseppe Adami, a trend already noticed in Giacosa, Bracco, and Lopez. Lucio D'Ambra (1880–1939), dramatic critic of the *Tribuna* and *Il Corriere della Sera*, treated various themes, comical, sentimental, historical, and psychological. His best comedy is *Via Basento, Lanterna Rossa* (Basento Street, Red Light, 1926) in which the psychological element is used to achieve a dramatic effect through the unexpected reaction of a physician who finds in a brothel, where he goes for professional reasons, the peace and tranquillity that he has vainly sought in his home. The author is interested in the elusive play of the character's mind, in a manner dear to Luigi Pirandello.

Renato Simoni (1875–1952), also a dramatic critic, is especially well known for *La vedova* (1902). It deals with a young woman who, upon the death of her husband, is forced to go to live with her in-laws. She brings into the old and musty home a breath of youth, charm, and beauty that wins the love of her father- and mother-in-law, of their friends, to the point where they accept with joy the announcement that she is going to marry again. It is an excellent work of contrast: beauty and widowhood on the one hand, the old home and the spirit of youth on the other.

Close to traditional comedy is the work of Giuseppe Adami (1878–1946), who succeeds best in representing life in minor tones: the joy of a quiet love in *Provincia* (1936), the poetry of old age in *Capelli bianchi* (1915). His main characters are often middle-class and virile women, as in *Felicita Colombo* (1935) and *Nonna Felicita* (1936).

It is interesting to notice what contemporary authors have done with a clever rehandling of old themes. In Aldo de Benedetti's *Lohengrin* (1933) we see a once-gay and romantic youth who, after many years, returns to the scene of his gallantries and adventures. Comedy arises especially out of the dismay and amusement of the matured women of the town in seeing again the Don Juan of their youth, now sedate and rotund. A more subtle and psychological treatment is found in the works of Cesare Giulio Viola (1887–   ), who presents in a new fashion the theme of the philandering husband in *Fine del protagonista*

(1930). It shows one such husband in Riccardo who returns home after many years and finds it impossible to remain, when he is received without much ado by his family. The modern play-wright stresses the point that the husband finds himself unspeakably humiliated when his return home does not provoke the recriminations that he expected. He is about to resume his odyssey when an old aunt, the stout defender of the home, the clear-headed analyst of his tortuous way of feeling and reasoning, uncovers to him the boundless pride that hides under his false humility. Riccardo remains and re-enters the peaceful home life to which he belongs.

The traditional theme of the relationship between parents and children appears centered in the loneliness of children of today in Stefano Landi's *La casa a due piani* (1923). In this play the author, whose real name is Stefano Pirandello (1895–   ), considers the all-absorbing love of the husband for his wife as the cause of the disintegration of the home and the ruination of the children, one of whom commits suicide. The same theme is given humorous treatment by him in *Un padre ci vuole* (1936). He develops his comedy by reversing the characters of father and son, the former presented as gay and reckless, and the latter sedate and preoccupied. The son assumes the role that his father has relinquished.

Those in this field who stood out among their contemporaries during and after World War I were Dario Niccodemi and Cesare Vico Ludovici. Niccodemi (1875–1934) lived in and for the theater. He was a dramatic critic in Argentina, secretary of the famous actress Réjane in Paris, and head of a dramatic company that he formed after his return to Italy from France in 1914. He has written plays in Spanish, French, and Italian. In his early plays, written in French, he relied to a great extent on the technique used by Henry Bernstein: sudden and striking contrasts capable of casting a revealing light on a situation and of determining a new direction in the action of the play. This is especially true of *Il rifugio* (1912), which was first written in French. In it he does not go beyond rehandling the old triangle theme by utilizing clever technical means. His interest lies exclusively in the sparkling dialogue in which words are used like polished swords by Gerardo and Saint-Airain for the possession of young Dora.

After his return to Italy, Niccodemi, sobered and saddened by the spectacle of war, produced two plays in which two traits that are fundamental and enduring in his theater affirm themselves: intimacy and sensitiveness. His characters under a worldly appearance that is used by the playwright for love of contrast are condemned to a grieving existence. In *L'ombra* (1915) a young wife, an invalid, finds that during her illness her husband has created for himself a new family and that a child has been born to him. What else can she do, according to Niccodemi, but re-enter the nook where her existence withers in silent sadness and loneliness? *Scampolo*, written in the same year and beautifully interpreted by Dina Galli, possesses a romantic vein in the touching and amusing story of a poor girl lost in the noise and confusion of Rome. In her elemental simplicity there abides a distinct personality that is revealed first by her interest in a Bohemian student, whom she happens to meet, and then in her devotion to him. This devotion gradually grows into a love that completely transforms her and rids the student of a profligate woman who had taken hold of him.

That Niccodemi was capable of thoughtful works became more apparent in the plays that followed. They deal with problems arising from the war: *La nemica* (1917), *Il titano* (1917), *Prete nero* (1917), and *La Volata* (1920). *La nemica*, the best of these plays, presents the tragic conflict in the heart of a mother placed by the war in the situation of having to make a choice as to whom she would desire to have die—the legitimate son or the illegitimate. She worships the former and hates the latter, for she sees in him a constant reminder of her guilt. She desires in her heart that the legitimate son be spared. As her eyes are riveted on the prelate who has come to break the news of the death of one of her children, the illegitimate son appears in the doorway.

In *Acidalia* (1922) Niccodemi seems to have abandoned himself to that moment of intellectual bewilderment that was reflected by many authors of the turbulent years that followed the war. The play is a comedy on infidelity seen through the eyes of a pseudo-sociologist who wants to prove that men must be betrayed by their wives in order to attain complete happiness. Yet all his women—a wife, then two mistresses—have apparently been faithful to him, much to his scientific distress. In the end the author, with satirical laughter, shows that all have betrayed him, without happiness as his reward.

A higher tone and a return to a situation heavy with pathos and sacrifice are observable in *La casa segreta* (1923) in which the strange conduct of Claudio Varchi toward youthful Anna is characterized by an extraordinary nobility. It is the drama of Claudio who stifles his love for Anna when he realizes that he is doomed to blindness. He goes to live in a solitary villa where he dictates to his secretary the dreams of his poetic mind.

Niccodemi is a master of dialogue and dramatic technique. His plays and his other efforts on behalf of a dignified theater in Italy deserve greater praise than has yet been accorded to him.

Cesare Vico Ludovici (1887–   ) is especially well known for *La donna di nessuno* (1919), a work that enjoyed wide and lasting success. Rather than focusing his attention on the daily existence of his characters, he aims at giving expression to emotions and feelings that fringe their lives like a crown of thorns. In his intellectual form of drama Ludovici considers actual conditions only as the data on which his play is based. Since he is primarily interested in the contrasts and unforeseen situations that beset and torment his characters, actual reality is of secondary importance to him. His art seeks constantly to avoid customary situations. Love for a child had always been a simple means of unraveling a plot. Ludovici, in *La donna di nessuno*, strips the heart of his main character even of this fundamental instinct, making of the woman an automaton. Nevertheless, the effect is truly striking. Viera, in *La buona novella* (1923), finds in herself no moral element that prevents her from experiencing happiness in the fact that she is going to bear an illegitimate child. In *La ruota* (1933) the heroine commits suicide by hurling herself under the wheel of a mill. How exasperating was its constant turning and whirling that marked every moment of her harrowing existence! The life of the woman is soberly presented as an unbearable torment, torn as she is, in the role of a wife, between love as a burning passion of the senses and a romantic aspiration toward the purest form of love. Her husband finds it impossible to understand her and she has no other solution than to yield to the voice of the mill wheel. Earlier dramatists, as a rule, have turned to exotic situations to express such a contrast. Ludovici transports it in the ordinary setting of married life, and paints the torment of the woman so powerfully as to make her suicide plausible.

The greatest tribute that can be paid to the art of Ludovici is that, in spite of presenting such tortured and unusual figures, he knows how to hold the attention of large audiences. The truth is that in his plays he touches the fundamental urges of man. The case of Viera in *La buona novella* is particularly illuminating, for in her rebellion against man she stands as the symbol of motherhood untrammeled by social laws and conventions. Unlike similar heroines in the plays of Praga or Antona-Traversi, she embodies the modern woman who is not so dependent on man as the woman of the past had been.

THE DRAMA OF THE GROTESQUE

It is customary to single out the theater of the grotesque and accord to it a separate treatment. The grotesque theater was an aftergrowth of futurism which had proclaimed in one of its famous *programmi* (1915) the need of the regeneration of the theater, and in its antagonism to tradition had urged authors to be different at any cost. In reality, if we go beyond the subtleties, forms, and technical experiments of the theater of the grotesque, we find in it a variety of comedy with a strong leaning toward social satire. Such are the works of Luigi Chiarelli, Luigi Antonelli, and Enrico Cavacchioli, produced during the period of intellectual and artistic chaos of World War I. They felt the influence of Luigi Pirandello's idea of human personality, but seldom in a positive way.

The genesis of the theater of the grotesque has been linked to the farcical interpretation that Virgilio Talli gave to *La maschera e il volto* (The Mask and the Face, 1916) by Chiarelli, a work said to have been written as serious drama by the author. But this is a legend and nothing more. The grotesque was the sublimation and projection of the mental distress that tormented the generation of Chiarelli, living as it did through the agony, physical and mental, of World War I. It is interesting to note that the mania for revealing the interplay of reality and dream has been humorously satirized by Arnoldo Fraccaroli (1880–   ) and Luigi Barzini (1874–1947) in their comedy *Quello che non t'aspetti* (1921). The protagonist, in search of escape from the monotony of reality, finds a superreality, created by a troupe of cinema actors, anything but profitable when real thieves ransack and rob his home. This is indicative of the reception that serious-minded people gave to the idiosyncrasies of the theater of the grotesque. Nevertheless, the effect that this group of young playwrights had on the Italian theater was highly beneficial and, from their midst, came many comedies of note.

The most distinguished representative of the theater of the grotesque was Luigi Chiarelli (1880–1947). A depraved and corrupted society forms the warp on which he has woven his comedy, *La maschera e il volto*, the dramatic triumph of 1916. It presents the case of a man who, having said that he would kill his wife if she were unfaithful to him, has not the courage to do so when he finds himself in that predicament. He sends his wife, Savina, abroad, and announces that he has murdered her by drowning her. He is acquitted and becomes a hero to all the ladies of the city, who offer themselves to him. Upon the sudden return of Savina, however, on the day of her planned funeral (the corpse of a woman has been found in the river in a state of putrefaction and all believe it to be that of Savina), Paolo runs the risk of going to prison for having declared himself guilty of a crime he had not committed. Hence his rebellion against the law and society, and the happy denouement of the play in the reunion of Savina and Paolo. Seldom has the banality of social convention been expressed in grimmer tones. Chiarelli has created truly dramatic situations in making Paolo witness the funeral of a living Savina amid the insincerity of tears and hollowness of ceremony. He has placed Savina face to face with Luciano Spina, her lover, who had succeeded in having Paolo acquitted by proclaiming the profligacy of his wife. The importance of the play rests on the force of contrasts therein created: the contrast between the reality of Paolo's feelings and the falseness of the mask he wears, between the reality of what has happened and the absurdity of his alleged crime, between Paolo who, when believed guilty of having killed his wife, is freed by the court and lionized by society and Paolo who, innocent, runs the risk of going to prison. This play was staged with great success in London, but failed twice in New York. It is nevertheless intriguing, strong, and impressive drama.

The plays subsequently written by Chiarelli reveal even more clearly, but with infinitely less art, the satirical strain of his temperament. *La scala di seta* (The Silken Ladder, 1917) is a satire on political life, viewed through the successful career of Desiré, a dancer, who ends by becoming prime minister. *Chimere* (1919) shows how weak moral principles are when selfish interest is at stake. *La morte degli amanti* (1921) is a satire on romantic love, whereas *Fuochi d'artificio* (1923) shows the vacuity of social position in modern society. But *La maschera* is a first-class play. Biting satire is not confined to one aspect only of life. It is directed against life itself, and definite characters move in striking situations.

Another playwright, usually connected with this movement, is Luigi Antonelli (1882–1942). He tried to renew the old comedy by inserting fancy into his plays as a new *deus ex machina*. One usually finds in his works a logical proposition from which he departs into boundless distances, where he leads his characters through extraordinary experiences. In *L'uomo che incontrò se stesso* (1918), the logical proposition from which the author starts is that it is not true that man profits by experience. According to this philosophy, if we could live our lives over again, we would do precisely what we did in our youth. The fantastic adventure in this play is that of unsuspecting Luciano who, after being betrayed by his wife Sonia, goes to a strange island where a magic Dr. Schmidt has the power of transforming the dreams of man into reality. Luciano is thus given the chance of living his life over again. He again falls in love with Sonia, exactly as he had done in his youth. In spite of the abstractness of the motivation, *L'uomo che incontrò se stesso* is an amusing and interesting play.

In *La fiaba dei tre maghi* (1919) Antonelli presents, in each of the three acts of his comedy, three magicians, embodying Truth, Justice, and Poetry. We witness amusing situations through the effects of the exalted virtues of Truth and Justice. In the first act, for instance, through a magic potion, the characters are made to speak the truth with results that can be well imagined. The critique of Justice is not less devastating since we are made to witness the cruelties due this stern force. The only salvation is in poetry, which offers man an escape through illusion. It is evident that the real core of Antonelli's theater is a satire of man and society. In *Bernardo l'eremita* (1920), Luciano, posing as the fiancé of Nora, whom she has never met, succeeds in making her fall in love with him and in marrying him. In this manner, the "real" fiancé is eliminated by the fictitious one. The author may have meant to embody in the two men actual reality and the fictitious one, but this intellectual motivation is not realized in the play, which remains a weak comedy and nothing more. In *L'isola delle scimmie* (1922) the author projects his idea of the superiority of animal life over human society, in which morality is an aphrodisiac. In one of his latest plays, *Il maestro* (The Master, 1934), the author deals with the genuine interest that a famous actor has in the daughter of a woman he once loved. He finds joy in that transference of affection until his quiet dream is shattered by the girl, who falls in love with the actor's youthful son. The everyday reality which in former plays was hidden behind the externals of the grotesque theater has, with this play, come out in clear evidence.

Another much-discussed playwright of this group is Enrico Cavacchioli (1884–1954). Fundamentally, in Cavacchioli there is a typical romantic intuition of man, though carried on the plane of everyday life and exemplified through ordinary mortals. He uses technical contrivances of many kinds: marionettes, wheels that replace human eyes to express their mobility in persons overly excited and under a highly nervous tension, green hair, and the like. But ultimately Cavacchioli looks at man in terms of the split between intellect and the senses. This contrast is expressed by him in *L'uccello del paradiso* (1919) through Lui, a character in the guise of a skeleton dressed in tails and a white tie, who stands as the complementary part of the paltry and negative self of the characters who are swayed by the power of instinct. In the comedy there develops the old contrast between mother and daughter who are in love with the same man, the vacuous Mimotte, lover of the mother. The presence of Lui, who mercilessly dissects their emotions, gives wider range to the play than was encompassed by the old comedy. In *Quella che t'assomiglia* (1919) the place of Lui is taken by marionettes which allow the characters to see in a fixed form the value of their acts in all their vulgarity when stripped of the romantic fringe that they lend to them. The plot is afforded by a war story: a wife who is unfaithful while her husband is at the front. Gabriella is "young, green hair, voluble, sensual, sentimental to the nth degree, and finds her humanity only in sentiment." She falls in love with a charlatan, bald and fat, who knows how to use honeyed and beautiful words. The husband returns. He is blind, a wreck of a man. When, sensing the truth of the situation, he tells Gabriella to go with Leonardo if she wishes, the woman, for the first time, feels herself bound to him by the heroic unselfishness that he has shown her. He has touched the human being in one who had been only a puppet. The same dualism is found in the ludicrous events of *La danza del ventre* (1921), which presents Pupa, unmoral and irrational, a queer mixture of sensuality and idealism, between Nadir, pure spirit, and Arlecchino, pure sensuality. When Pupa chooses as her lover the servant Arlecchino, Nadir commits suicide; but when love is reduced to pure sensuality, Arlecchino, too, is doomed to be abandoned by Pupa.

That under the dazzling technique of Cavacchioli was hidden a sense of the comical has been proved by his later works. In *L'oasi* (The Oasis, 1935) Donatella, placed between the love of an old and celebrated painter and that of a young physician, proves what comedy has always proved: that youth wins over old age.

In spite of many eccentricities, Cavacchioli's works are essentially comedies enlivened by the author's belief that man is split between the little self that obeys the voice of nature and a deeper self that in the past was called conscience.

THE HISTORICAL DRAMA

In studying the historical drama we find ourselves in an atmosphere that is dominated by literary considerations more strongly than is comedy. For the most part, historical dramas are written in verse. Our analysis of such plays can be based only on the consideration of the temperament reflected by each playwright in his interpretation of historical figures and situations.

Gabriele D'Annunzio and Sem Benelli acquired fame in this field before and during World War I. Less striking personalities have represented the historical play in later years.

Though the fame of Gabriele D'Annunzio (1863–1938) was very great and spread even abroad, it must be said that real critics and the Italian public in general never accorded this writer of historical drama serious recognition. The testimony of Mario Puccini is very illuminating. He informs us that: "As for the stage, the characters of Giacosa and Bracco seemed the exponents, though acceptable, of an art of the third or fourth rank when compared with those of D'Annunzio, who spoke in a winged and hyperbolic language." But he adds: "As for me, the world of D'Annunzio was completely false." The pseudo-intellectual followers of D'Annunzio, as well as D'Annunzio himself, must be looked upon as the product of the industrial civilization that afforded to a large section of the middle class leisure and comforts that previously had been the privilege of the nobility. As was to be expected, these upstarts began to show contempt for their class and to mimic the mannerisms and poses of the aristocracy. D'Annunzio was a classic exemplification of this phenomenon. It is hard to understand the enthusiasm with which such plays as *Gioconda* and *La città morta* were received in democratic and realistic America.

It is generally conceded that the theater represents the weakest portion of D'Annunzio's literary activity. He turned to the theater in 1897 when his fundamental intuition, the reduction of life to pure lust, had become worn out through constant use and fruitless attempts to renew or deepen this inspiration. When a youth in his teens, he had well succeeded in expressing his joyous naturalism through the presentation of peasant men and women observed in the primitive life of his native Abruzzi. His early works in verse and prose are beautiful examples of poetry and storytelling. But when, in 1881, D'Annunzio went to Rome and came in contact with a complex civilization, he failed to realize that his joyous materialism could only be an artificial oversimplification of life when applied to that environment. His novels, written in subsequent years in the midst of and for the decadent Roman social world, are documents that prove to what complicated pattern he reduced the elementary character of instinct. His dramatic works show the ultimate form that this theme assumed in the man who, in 1892, had said that it was a question "of renewing one's self or of dying." That he had been unable to renew himself is proven by the monotonous repetition of the theme of instinct viewed, both in his novels and in his plays, through the concept of the superman. It is well known that he borrowed that concept from the works of Friedrich Nietzsche. That he did not understand Nietzsche is beside the point. He took from him what he needed in the illusion of reaching the height of tragedy through the exploits of his heroes.

The presence of the superman in D'Annunzio's plays indicated that he had failed to reach, understand, and express the complex and baffling entity called man. The presence of incest, as well as the superman, is indicative also of the effort on the part of the playwright to complicate the theme of instinct upon becoming aware that he had exhausted the artistic presentation of that theme.

An understanding of D'Annunzio's dramatic works becomes clear if we consider them as revolving around the hollow intuition of the superman who is not bound by the laws of average morality. In *La città morta* (The Dead City, 1898) the play centers around Leonardo, an archaeologist who goes to Mycenae to excavate the tombs of the Atrides. Written soon after D'Annunzio's trip to Greece, it is projected against the background of Greek civilization viewed in terms of fabulous riches and magnificence. From the tombs of the Atrides there emanates the fatal power that leads the hero to love incestuously his sister Bianca Maria and to kill her when his friend Alessandro, a great poet, falls in love with her. The words of Leonardo, announcing that he has done for her what nobody else would have been able to do, can only be understood if considered as the reflection of an individual not subject to normal passions and ordinary rules of human conduct. In reality, he expresses a hollow concept of man, and his actions are those of a degenerate, even if they are covered with high-sounding phrases. In *Gioconda* (Gioconda, 1899) we have the superman projected through the theme of art. A sculptor, Lucio Settala, needs the adulterous love of Gioconda to create his statues. He sacrifices the devotion of his wife Silvia for her. In *La gloria* (Glory, 1899), the superman is observed in political life. Ruggero Flamma, an imperialist and a nationalist, becomes the lover of an old harlot, Anna Commena, once the mistress of Cesare Bronte, the embodiment of the old liberal party. Tragedy is artificially introduced through the assassination of Flamma by Commena when the former, having established a dictatorship in Rome, realizes his dream of Latin imperialism and of an aristocratic government against which the people rebel. In *Più che l'amore* (Beyond Love, 1906) the superman is embodied in Corrado Branda, an explorer in Italian Africa, who bases his claims to a superhumanity on the fact that he once killed a lioness, and, on another occasion, led a company of native soldiers in an attack against the enemy. Actually, he is a vulgar viveur who in the end cheats at cards after seducing the sister of his best friend. The same concept of morality is applied to Marco Gradico in *La nave* (The Ship, 1908), and to the title character in the tragedy that bears her name, *Fedra* (Fedra, 1909).

The fundamental defect of these plays is that the serious motif that was intended by the author to assert itself is destroyed by lust—destroyed and not opposed. If D'Annunzio had been able to create a clash between the two forces, he would have remained within the boundaries of the human, and a dramatic contrast might have been obtained. By allowing lust to stifle the main theme, D'Annunzio placed himself outside the "boundaries of good and evil" as well as outside the boundaries of true art. *La nave* was meant to glorify the nationalistic aspiration to make the Adriatic an Italian sea, but the love of Marco Gradico for Basiliola occupies the foreground of the play and gradually eliminates the main motif. Love is presented as the supreme justification of the hero's life.

The theme of lust became such an essential and integral part of D'Annunzio's mode of writing as to force its way even into the religious theme dealing with the death of San Sebastian. The play *Le martyre de Saint Sébastien* (1910) was written in French while D'Annunzio lived in France in voluntary exile as a protest against the lack of appreciation of his art on the part of the Italians. It is not difficult to imagine how an artist can mix religion and lust, since even the lives of the saints exemplify this combination, though from a different angle. What offends real art is the lack of human feelings that prompts the author to imagine and painstakingly describe the erotic convulsions of the Christian women before the physical beauty of the handsome captain of the imperial guards who was awaiting his death with them.

D'Annunzio's tragedies are static. His characters thunder their greatness from the very beginning, so that there is no possibility of psychological development for them nor any unfolding of the action except toward the climax of a love affair. His characters speak of "the ego that transforms itself in infinite ways." The spectator waits in vain to see these transformations. The infinite ways in which the ego transforms itself are always reduced to a rhetorical exaltation of the power of lust. The spectator asks in vain why D'Annunzio's characters lay claim to the title of supermen. Their deeds are confined to erotic exploits with the result that their greatness remains a vacuous assumption.

Being subjective to an inordinate degree, D'Annunzio reflects himself constantly in his characters, so that his plays offer little or no variety. His tragedies are gaudy tapestries in which the gifted decorator has immobilized figures that are gigantic in bodily proportions and dwarfed in psychological depth. His characters remind one of Bernini's statues and of the rococo style.

It has often been said that D'Annunzio wanted to show that man, in the fullness of civilization, remains a prey to instinct as in the days of the cave man. This is precisely what he has failed to do through his literary and academic presentation of instinct. Compare the power of the treatment of this theme in Verga's *La lupa* or Di Giacomo's *Assunta Spina* with the verbose rendering of it in D'Annunzio's plays, and the emptiness of his pompous naturalism will be seen in all its weakness.

There are, however, three plays by D'Annunzio in which he can lay claim to exquisite beauty: *Francesca da Rimini* (Francesca of Rimini, 1902), *La figlia di Iorio* (The Daughter of Iorio, 1904), and *La fiaccola sotto il moggio* (The Light under the Bushel, 1905). *Francesca da Rimini* is a dramatization of the celebrated thirteenth-century love story that Dante presented in the immortal fifth canto of his *Inferno*. The play is important not only because beautiful pages are to be found in it, but also because D'Annunzio has introduced new characters, such as the youthful and fiendish Malatestino and Francesca's exquisite sister. Francesca is endowed in her heroic role with a sensitive soul in which love sings with a new voice. The reconstruction of the historical background of the thirteenth century is one of D'Annunzio's literary achievements.

The other two plays possess a note of intimacy in that they are the sublimation of the poet's fond memory of his native Abruzzi. His longing for the place where he spent his youth has taken life in figures and events that are dominated by primitive passions befitting their background. Instinct leads to real tragedy here. D'Annunzio treats his theme lyrically in *La Figlia di Iorio* in presenting Aligi's love, and more realistically in *La fiaccola sotto il moggio* in which we view the decadence of the Sangro family. For lyric beauty, both plays rank among the best that are to be found in Italian literature.

On the whole, D'Annunzio as a dramatist remains a creator of beautiful fragments in an art that is characterized by lack of content. The life that he lived and portrayed made it inevitable that he should be unable to impart to his plays a proper unity, though his native talent made it possible for him to write here and there pages of great beauty. He belongs in the company of exquisite decorators, and not in that of the strong creators.

Sem Benelli (1877–1949) also sought in history the basic material of his plays, though he often used realistic themes as a medium of expression. Benelli succeeded best when he reflected himself in characters who are goaded into action by a tormenting consciousness of their own weakness.

His first important play was *Tignola* (The Bookworm, 1908), a comedy of modern times. The chief character is Giuliano Innocenti, a wan employee in a bookstore, who enjoys a short-lived exaltation by presenting himself as a man of the world and full of ideas. For a while he succeeds in his pseudo-heroic role and even wins a mistress in a society woman, Adelaide. The husband challenges him to a duel, wounds him, and forces him to re-enter the musty air of the bookstore to which he is destined. In a vivid scene, the author places face to face Adelaide, who visits the bookstore as a dilettante of literature, and the poor bookworm who stands revealed in his pitiful insignificance.

After the success of *Tignola* Benelli tried the historical drama, and to this period we owe three plays that quite properly made him famous: *La maschera di Bruto* (The Mask of Brutus, 1908), *La cena delle beffe* (The Jest, 1909), and *L'amore dei tre re* (The Love of the Three Kings, 1910). The almost subliminal psychology of Giuliano in *Tignola* reflects itself, though in new form, in characters that fundamentally bear the same traits. Lorenzino de' Medici appears in *La maschera* not in his traditional role as a great lover of liberty but as a sly plotter who is tormented by his love for Caterina Ginori. It is for this love that he kills his cousin Alessandro. He is portrayed wandering away from Florence in anguish and despair until the dagger of his assassins, to which he offers himself, brings him liberation from an existence that had become unbearable.

The motif of a tortured mind found a more perfect expression in Giannetto, in *La cena delle beffe*, which was twice played with success in New York with distinguished casts that included first the Barrymores and then Basil Sidney. Benelli imagines him as a physically weak youth who has grown up with Neri and Gabriello, the two violent and powerful Chiaramontesi brothers. Giannetto stands out vividly in the humiliations to which he is constantly subjected by them. In the resignation forced on him his mind has become sharp as a sword. With this terrible weapon he engages in a deadly duel with his stronger rivals, planning a jest in the intricate net of which he catches his enemies. He, the weakling, succeeds in taking away from the gigantic Neri his mistress, languid Ginevra, once his own lady love. In the diabolic power of his mind he succeeds also in creating a situation in which Neri is driven to kill his brother Gabriello. The madness attributed to Neri in jest becomes madness in reality.

L'amore dei tre re is not, to such an extent as the other plays, mentioned as a drama of striking personalities since in it Benelli wanted to symbolize the effect that Italian civilization had on the medieval barbarians who invaded the beautiful plains of Italy from the north, but were conquered by its more advanced culture. Archibaldo, the old warrior, symbolizes the untamed barbarian who relies only on violence. Manfredo, his son, has, on the contrary, been changed by Christian civilization into a sensitive being, who loves beautiful Flora and marries her. She, however, loves Avito, an Italian prince, for whom she betrays Manfredo. The drama unfolds in a gloomy medieval castle and tragedy stalks into it when Archibaldo strangles unfaithful Flora. Her death is followed by that of her lover, who takes the poison that the old barbarian has placed on her lips, confident that Avito would go to kiss her as she lay in her coffin. Avito dies, but his fate is shared also by Manfredo in the same manner. Although the symbolic motivation of the play transcends that of the action in which the characters engage, the play possesses a rich vein of poetry that flows undisturbed through the love story of Flora and Avito. Its lyrical beauty inspired Montemezzi to write his well-known opera, *The Love of the Three Kings*.

This is not the case with the later historical plays in which symbolism assumed a predominant role and stifled the meager action that unfolded in them. *Il Mantellaccio* (The Mantellaccio Society of Poets, 1911) aimed at presenting the rivalry of various currents of poetry in the sixteenth century: poetry as pure and useless erudition; popular poetry, unadorned and vulgar; and finally poetry as expression of the soul. This aesthetic intuition is given expression through the love story of Silvia and Novizio, the latter a member of the Mantellaccio Society. The play wavers between the banal realism of the action and the larger but ineffective meaning that the playwright intended to convey. Like this reconstruction of the sixteenth century, an age to which Benelli was very much attracted, *Rosmunda* (Rosmunda, Queen of the Lombards, 1911), *La gorgona* (The Gorgon, 1913), *Le nozze dei centauri* (The Wedding of the Centaurs, 1915), *Fiorenza* (Florence, 1930), and *Caterina Sforza* (Caterina Sforza, 1934) do not go beyond an emphatic rendering of historical subjects with a strong stress on the note of patriotism. Although they possess interesting passages, they are ineffectual.

After World War I, Sem Benelli assumed in his plays the role of a self-appointed national poet. He proclaimed the necessity of overcoming materialism and sensuality, and insisted on the peaceful mission of Italy in the world and on the brotherhood of men. In the plays published after six years of silence (1915–21) Benelli, although keeping his original intuition of a character embodied in an individual torn by the contrast of what he is and what he would like to be, lent to the aspiration of his historical figures a hazy idealism that was not at all consonant with his cynical temperament. Through this orientation he sank into the rut of the old romantic dualism of spirit and matter, without producing any striking personalities in his work. *Ali* (Wings, 1921), *La santa primavera* (Holy Spring, 1923), and *L'amorosa tragedia* (Love and Tragedy, 1925) are very weak plays in their vaporous idealism. In *Ali* there is the aspiration toward a life of purity not offended by sensuality, but the drama of Luca and Marta is very blurred. The public found it difficult to understand a play in which Luca claims to need chastity in order to achieve his ideal life and is killed by the disappointed heroine.

In writing *La santa primavera* the author stated that he wanted to produce "a vast lyrical poem, freely conceived on a universal theme, not cramped by the narrow limits of acts and scenes." The work is, in fact, a dramatic poem, a hymn to goodness, to the brotherhood of man, to progress, as well as to the greatness of the Italian race.

A didactic purpose is also visible in *L'amorosa tragedia*, which had a tremendous success because it was performed in 1925 when Italy was on the verge of a civil war. In it Benelli stressed the need of peace by using a thirteenth-century episode in which figure the feuds between the Black and White factions in the city of Pistoia.

Benelli succeeded better in *L'arzigogolo* (The Enigma, 1922), a historical play with a thirteenth-century background. The figure of the jester bears resemblance to Giannetto in *The Jest* in his role of conquering beautiful and enigmatic Violante for his master. When Violante awakens his manhood by giving herself to him, Benelli expresses his drama with a force that reminds one of *The Jest*.

At a later date Benelli tried to recast his Giannetto in two characters presented in a realistic environment, but Fabrizio di Poggialto in *Il ragno* (The Spider, 1935) and Sergio in *L'elefante* (The Elephant, 1937) succeed in being no more than rather distorted character studies.

Sem Benelli, in the essential traits of his intuition of human personality, was the negation of D'Annunzio's superman. D'Annunzio placed on his inwardly weak heroes the mask of the superman; Benelli tears from his characters the mask of grandeur to reveal a pathetically human face that reflects the traits of a pitiful humanity.

Among Benelli's contemporaries who distinguished themselves in the historical drama were Ettore Moschino (1887-   ) and Domenico Tumiati (1874-1943). Moschino, a journalist in his youth who dedicated himself to the theater, is remembered for his *Cesare Borgia* (1913) in which he presents the tenacious and restless sixteenth-century prince as he meditates over his plans for creating a kingdom for himself in Italy. The play, centering upon the murder of his brother Giovanni, is regarded as a good dramatic poem. Tumiati, well known as an actor, took up the art of playwriting and explored and reconstructed the Risorgimento period. He wrote a cyclical work of vast proportions, preceded by a prologue and followed by five plays that illustrate the Italian struggle for unity through the activities of Mazzini, King Charles Albert, Cavour, and Garibaldi. These plays are better adapted to reading than to production on a stage.

More important is Federico Valerio Ratti (1877-   ). His work is characterized by a symbolic interpretation of the historical events with which he deals. *Il solco quadrato* (The Square Furrow) was written in 1911 but was not performed until 1922. Romulus represents in it the collective spirit of social order whereas Remus stands for a romantic individualism that aims at subverting that order. When the latter jumps over the square furrow that Romulus had plowed as the boundary line that was to enclose the future Rome, he is killed because his gesture meant rebellion and chaos. In *Giuda* (Judas, 1923) the betrayer of Christ is ennobled by the author who makes him a sort of Prometheus. In the play Judas does not sell Christ for greed of money. He is after the revelation of the mystery that surrounds life and which, according to him, Christ would reveal to man before His death. Judas is shown inquiring constantly after this mystery that disturbs him. In betraying Christ, he carries out the mission that he has assigned to himself: to lead Christ to death that the veils may be rent and the light of truth may shine on the world. Judas's quest is presented through the reasoning of a passionate dialectician. The play was well received.

Another play that met with success was *Il beffardo* (The Scoffer, 1919) by Nino Berrini (1879–   ). The scoffer is Cecco Angiolieri, a satirical poet of the time of Dante, who, in his collection of sonnets, related his unhappy life embittered by the unrequited love he bore for a wanton wench by the name of Becchina. The life of Angiolieri was dramatic enough in itself and the task of Berrini was not very difficult in transferring it into his play. The jeering and mocking spirit of the work was well suited to the political and social chaos that prevailed in Italy in 1919.

Criticism of today has justly appraised as negative the work of Gioacchino Forzano (1884–   ) who but yesterday enjoyed a great popularity in fascist Italy. His art bespeaks commercialism to the *n*th degree. He succeeded in dazzling the paying public through spectacular staging, but he lacks dramatic power. In his career he passed from one style to another, from the historical—*Lorenzino* (Lorenzino, 1922), *Ginevra degli Almieri* (Ginevra of the Almieri, 1926) to trite comedy—*Un colpo di vento* (A Gust of Wind, 1930); from the cyclical presentation of the French Revolution to that of the Italian Risorgimento.

The play in which he has succeeded best is *Gianni Schicchi* (Gianni Schicchi, 1918) the plot of which is taken from a well-known episode of Dante's *Inferno*. As is the case with men lacking in inventiveness but gifted in form, Forzano has succeeded well in presenting the roguish character of Gianni Schicchi that tradition offered him already molded.

Several original interpretations of historical characters and myths have appeared in recent years. The myth of Penelope has been cleverly rehandled by Raffaele Calzini (1885–1953) in *La Tela di Penelope* (Penelope's Weaving, 1923). Like Gerhardt Hauptmann, the Italian playwright casts a shadow of doubt on the optimism of old father Homer who presented Penelope patiently and faithfully waiting for the return of her wandering husband. In Calzini's version, Penelope is not endowed with any kind of traditional Greek beauty. She appears as a good house-wife, plump after twenty years of "widowhood," and greedy for good food. Telemachus is described as a prosaic and ineffectual youth. The royal palace is grimy and nothing remains of the splendid court life of old. Saddened by the contrast between the past grandeur and the present sordidness, Ulysses leaves the island without revealing his identity. After twenty years Penelope forgets for the first time to unravel her web when she contracts a love affair with Iro, a cheap comedian and one of Ulysses' companions.

The myth of Lucretia is also presented in a new interpretation by Giovanni Cavicchioli (1897–   ). In the traditional version, Sextus, who attacked the noble matron, is placed in a hostile light, cast on him by the many artists who have treated this dramatic episode. In Cavicchioli's *Lucrezia* (Lucretia, 1925) the real culprit is her husband, Collatinus, who had proudly boasted of the virtue of his wife, and, in his vanity, had paved the way by his famous test for the rape by Sextus.

Very keen and thoughtful is the psychological interpretation of the resurrection of Lazarus by Giuseppe Antonio Borgese (1882–1956). His *Lazzaro* (Lazarus, 1925) presents that biblical character as a noble youth, greedy for life, who lay for four days in a tomb on the eve of his marriage to beautiful Agar. As Christ calls him back to life, a terrible drama unfolds in him. While his mind and soul urge him to acknowledge the miracle, his natural self rebels at seeing himself as a corpse, a rebellion shared by Agar, who shudders at the idea of marrying a man who for four days was a cold cadaver. The climax of the play centers in Lazarus's unconditional acknowledgment of the miracle. As a kneeling multitude witnesses the ascension of Christ to Heaven, Lazarus, who is still struggling within and against himself, is gradually overcome by that vision; and a new resurrection, that of faith in Christ, takes place in him. G. A. Borgese has also written another historical play, *L'Arciduca* (The Archduke, 1924), that ascribes the tragedy of Mayerling not to the romantic passion of Rudolph of Austria for Maria Vetsera, but to the struggle which he, an enlightened prince, waged against the reactionary forces of his father's court.

Another interpretation of a traditional theme that attracts our interest is developed by Alberto Spaini (1894–   ), who retold the story of Delilah's betrayal of Samson in *La cattura di Sansone* (1923). Spaini views the betrayal as the effect of Samson's revelation to Delilah of the secret of his strength. By so doing he destroyed the halo of romance that surrounded the hero in the mind of the woman.

From what has been written here it can be seen how large the number of historical plays has been in our time. These plays show with what eagerness modern playwrights seek diversity and novelty.

THE SYMBOLICAL DRAMA

We have included in this section plays in which everyday reality loses its clear-cut contour, not because of lack of power of expression on the part of the artist, but because the latter aims at giving the value of a symbol to his subject. In such a case, characters whose countenances are intentionally blurred engage in actions that transcend those of the individual.

We find this lyrical afflatus beautifully realized in the works of Ercole Luigi Morselli (1882–1921). Morselli, who died of

tuberculosis, traveled a great deal on the sea in the hope of re-
gaining his health. His plays are variations on the theme of the
meaning of life and happiness, questions that poignantly turned
over in his mind during his existence as a wanderer. His works
give a first impression of pessimism, yet there runs through them
a note of faith in the power of the individual imagination. The
author went through the hubbub of the ports of the great markets
of the world, among surly men who were too intent on trafficking
to look skyward, but he kept his eyes fastened on the high masts
of the anchored ships as they gently swayed their tops toward the
sky and told him that ultimately only what we dream is true and
human material activities avail nothing. This is the message that
rings through Morselli's works.

The symbolism and faith of Morselli are revealed in three plays:
Orione (Orion, 1910), *Glauco* (Glaucus, 1919), and *Belfagor*
(Belfagor, published posthumously in 1930). Morselli was a
careful and patient artist who loved the pure contours of classical
art and the imaginative quality of myths. Both *Orione* and *Glauco*
are classical myths recast in modern form. Orione is viewed as a
great hunter, an embodiment of instinctive life, gigantic, powerful,
happy, given to love and indulging in orgies, who, one day, after
being bitten by a small scorpion, suddenly dies. The play seems to
be a critique of the vacuity of sensuous life and especially of the
age in which we live.

The positive part of Morselli's thought is intimately rendered
in *Glauco*. The hero, who seeks adventures far from his native
island and becomes unmindful of the great love offered him by
Scilla, symbolizes the vain wanderings of the poet when he sought
health and peace on the sea and in foreign lands. That peace was
not to be reached in the outside world, but closer by, where he
could mirror himself in the heart of his Scilla. Glauco returns
home after his wanderings and only then discovers how great
and beautiful was Scilla's love. But Scilla, an evanescent dream
and a diaphanous embodiment of feminine perfection, is dead.
The motivation of Glauco was strictly personal: Morselli's wife
died while he was on one of his cruises.

Belfagor treats in quite an original manner the motif of the well-known short story by Machiavelli, *Belfagor arcidiavolo* (The Arch-Devil Belfagor). Departing from Machiavelli, who directed his vitriolic satire against society and marriage, Morselli reinterprets the legend in order to reach a positive and constructive end. The devil comes on earth to experience married life, but the love of Candida for her poor Baldo triumphs over him.

The same thoughtfulness, expressed in a language that at times betrays excessive concern for poetic style, is found in Fausto Maria Martini (1886–1931). Martini lived in intimate communion with a small group of men of letters (Sergio Corrazini, Guido Gozzano, Marino Moretti) who have been qualified by the term *Crepuscolari* (twilight writers). Their art reflected a moment of disillusionment after a life given to sensuality and pleasure. They sang in minor chords the melancholy and mortification of a humble present. Two of them, Corrazini and Gozzano, died of tuberculosis when very young. Martini was badly maimed in World War I. The leitmotiv of his art is the idea that in order to reach happiness we must not evade the humble reality of our daily life.

In *Il fiore sotto gli occhi* (A Flower under One's Very Eyes, 1921) he presents Silvio, a husband, and his wife Giovanna, who, tired of the monotony of married life, decide to look upon one another as lover and mistress. The reality created by their fancy threatens to overpower Giovanna through the attentions of a suitor, so Silvio takes her away from the worldly atmosphere of Sorrento, and they both return to the modest existence which is theirs. The comedy is not a critique of bourgeois family life, as critics have asserted. On the contrary, it is a critique of the attitude of the two protagonists in their aspiration toward a worldly life. In *L'altra Nanetta* (The Other Nanetta, 1923) Martini presents a psychological study of the influence that the dead past can exercise on the living present. After a turbulent youth, Elena has settled down to a peaceful life with her husband Giacomo, a poet. When Giacomo uses her past in a poem, the heroine of which bears the name of Nanetta, Elena is so overwhelmed by its reality that she commits suicide. The same theme is continued in *La sera del trenta* (On the Evening of the Thirtieth, 1926), called by the author "the drama of what is insignificant." Husband and wife attend a club dance, the last of the season, and are treated in such a way by the snobbish people of the town that their usually peaceful existence is very much embittered. Martini is primarily interested in the psychological effect of the dance on the chief characters, for although the play is developed along realistic lines, the environment does not interest him.

His dreamy mood is revealed in his volume *Teatro breve* (Dramatic Sketches, 1929). In *Un cortile* (A Courtyard) the realistic rendering of the background ends in the touching episode of a blind player of a hurdy-gurdy and a blond prostitute, who takes pity on him.

Among the works of Martini there stands out as an anachronism a satirical play, *Ridi, Pagliaccio* (Laugh, Clown, Laugh, 1919), staged by Belasco in the United States in the early twenties with great success. It is another document of the tragic conditions that existed in Italy in 1919 as an aftermath of the war. That play marked a momentary eclipse of the positive attitude Martini usually reflected in his works. In Martini, too, the analysis of the human mind constitutes the pivot of his plays.

Ugo Betti (1892–1956) was one of contemporary Italy's best poets. In his poems published under the title of *Re pensieroso* (The Thoughtful King) he displays the tenuous grace of fables and legends reinterpreted by his exquisite fancy. His plays give the impression of being the negation of the imaginative world described in his poetry. In them he uses crudely sketched primitive men of the laboring class, but the main goal of Betti is to dramatize states of mind that assume a tragic and powerful resonance in the elementary consciousness of those men. This is especially true in *Un albergo sul porto* (An Inn Near the Harbor, 1934) and *Frana allo scalo nord* (The Landslide Near the North Wharf, 1937). The lyrical essence of these plays has been noted by another playwright, Alberto Cecchi, who points out that the dramatic power of *Un albergo sul porto* is not restricted to the lurid atmosphere that is there presented, but to the longing for fatherhood viewed as a cosmic force. Likewise, in *Frana allo scalo nord* the mob of ragged workers is not used by the author in order to reveal realistic elements in their outward appearance, but to make us aware of a fatal human law, atonement for the wrong we do. It is this feeling that gradually awakens in the consciousness of those men as they wearily walk away from the landslide they have caused. There is a great deal in Betti's plays which is "unexplained and unexpressed," but the absence of these elements is part of the technique consciously used by the poet Betti to render the impalpable atmosphere which surrounds men, their actions, and their emotions.

Alberto Casella (1883–1947) is mentioned here as the author of one of the best plays of the postwar period, *La morte in vacanze* (Death Takes a Holiday, 1924). It was performed in that year in Italy and received very coolly. In America, however, it met with an enthusiastic reception. Many Italian critics, including the keen-minded Silvio D'Amico, have looked upon it as if it marked the ultimate degeneration of the grotesque theater. There is nothing of the grotesque theater in it. Rather, in its essence it touches a human note in the old theme of love and death; life and death, so opposed to each other, and yet so near. The motivation of the play rests on the temperament of Grazia, a young girl, ill at ease in the worldly atmosphere of the aristocratic home of the Cattolica family. Grazia is an exquisite creature, who says of herself: "I enjoy everything that gives me a sensation, a vibration, but I enjoy it with melancholy." Melancholy bears within itself the seedling of death in Grazia. She is the only one for whom death under the guise of Prince Sirchi carries no fear. It is natural for her to abandon herself to her love for the stranger who fascinates her. He has revealed to her what Corrado, her young fiancé, never awoke in her heart. Grazia's love for Prince Sirchi is so strong that she follows him even when he tells her that he is Death.

This fantasy has offered Casella the opportunity of creating beautiful situations: nature, which during the holiday of Death knows no decay; the happiness of life when the black circle that fringes it has been removed; the anguish of Grazia's mother; Sirchi's attachment to life now that Grazia's love has made it so beautiful for him.

Casella has also written other important plays. It is significant that the Russian actress, Tatiana Pavlova, who lived in Italy in the twenties and formed a company of her own, should have noticed the art of Casella, and should have written a play in collaboration with him: *L'imperatrice si diverte* (The Empress Amuses Herself, 1934). It is a strong historical and psychological portrayal of Catherine of Russia who, from a humble servant, at last became an empress. The playwright singles out the episode of her love for Mons, chamberlain of Peter the Great, and the efforts of the Czar to discover whether she really loved him. A very dramatic situation is presented when the empress laughs convulsively and dances as Mons is tortured and even when his head is brought before her at the order of the jealous husband.

Rosso di San Secondo (1887–   ), whose real name is Pier Maria Rosso, seems to fit into this section through the central intuition that governs his dramatic output as well as the poetic language with which he describes the stage settings of his plays. For Rosso, humanity lives in exile from a land of purity and is constantly tormented by memories of it. The closest approximation to this mythical place is found by him in the lands that fringe the Mediterranean and in the people that inhabit them. The negation of it is in the north of Europe with its cold climate and its puritanical inhabitants. This intuition was given to Rosso, in its main traits, by Luigi Pirandello. Rosso elaborated on it through the contrast between the north and the south. From this background, with a logic that is far from flawless, emerge the figures that gave Rosso a great popularity after World War I. They embody persons who walk on this earth like automatons, restless, unhappy, unmindful of social ties and laws. If they abandon themselves to sensual adventures, they do so only to appease their inner torment.

Marionette, che passione! (Marionettes of Passion, 1918) is, in our opinion, the best play Rosso has produced. He has succeeded in projecting into it in living form the exasperation and restlessness of the time in which it was written. There appear in it three main characters that give the play a concentrated development which constitutes one of its chief merits. One afternoon "the lady with the blue fox fur," "the gentleman in gray," and "the gentleman in mourning" meet in a telegraph office, each with his passion and torment. They cannot resist the urge to speak and confide to each other their anguish. The events that follow are of no importance. Both men feel attracted to the woman and go with her to dine in a restaurant, where the woman's lover appears to take her back to her existence of passion and degradation. The two men remain alone, passive and bewildered. The "gentleman in gray" slowly puts poison pills in a glass of water, drinks it, leaves the restaurant. The "gentleman in black" throws himself on the table and breaks into desperate sobs. There are no names given to the characters. They are designated by colors or, for characters that represent ordinary humanity, by their professions: "Guard of the Telegraph Office," "First Worker," "Second Worker," "First Waiter," "Second Waiter." Only a featureless humanity can portray the tormented modern soul, "marionettes who are guided by the thread of passion," as the author states. The power of the play derives from the lyrical motif therein contained. The rest is technique, effective and unforgettable. Here we find the real Rosso, Rosso at his best.

In later plays, such as *La bella addormentata* (The Sleeping Beauty, 1919), he failed to reach the height of *Marionette*. Lyricism is here centered in the title and in the automaton-like existence of the Bella, a prostitute, pastime of the males of the town, who was seduced by a stingy and sordid notary. When she is with child, Il Nero della Zolfara, a sort of daring and violent Robin Hood, forces the notary to marry the Bella whom he has taken under his protection. The play offers many technical contrivances but, in effect, it deals with a theme that had often appeared in the traditional comedy of the sixteenth century and is also found in Luigi Pirandello's *Liolà*. In *La roccia e i monumenti* (Stone and Monuments, 1923) Rosso no longer relied on exotic technique. This is a serious drama embodying the idea that life is the raw material out of which each person has to fashion himself or herself. This thesis is developed in the study of Brunetto, a hero of World War I, who finds himself ill at ease in the prose of the daily life to which he has returned. He meets again Isabella, a woman who once loved him but who now is married to a blind man to whom she is devoted. The clash of Brunetto, life in the raw, and Isabella, life constructed into a moral scheme, is inevitable, but the woman resists, as stone monuments resist the storms that lash them.

L'avventura terrestre (Adventure on This Earth, 1924) is also serious drama. The bewilderment of Alessandra, a Russian woman living in Paris, is rendered with vividness and pathos. When she follows Ruggiero to Sicily and finds herself among peasants and miners, though still distressed by the loneliness that oppresses her, she finds relative tranquillity, and in the end decides to cease her wandering life and remain with the philosophical Ruggiero.

In most of Rosso's plays, however, the spectator passes from the intellectual plane to that of the irrational. This is especially true when the dramatist writes more to supply the market with new works than to obey his artistic instinct. In such a case it is difficult to understand what he means. One remains perplexed before such plays as *Lazzarina fra i coltelli* (Lazzarina among Knives, 1923), *La danza su un piede* (Dancing on One Foot, 1923), *Una cosa di carne* (Something Made of Flesh, 1924), *Il delirio dell' oste Bassà* (The Delirium of the Innkeeper Bassà, 1925), *Tra vestiti che ballano* (Among Clothes That Dance, 1927), and *Canicola* (Dog Days, 1929). We imagine that there must be a poetic nucleus in these plays, but it is evident that the author has failed to express it. Art is primarily an original intuition of reality but it needs also expression and clarity.

Rosso, after the success of *Marionette*, relied too much on technique, so much so that his plays became technical experiments and nothing more. Where Rosso failed, he produced plays that border on idiocy. In *Marionette* he created a modern form of tragedy.

THE PHILOSOPHICAL DRAMA

One of the most truly representative currents of the contemporary theater has been determined by a consideration of the
query: What is reality? The nineteenth century spoke of reality
in absolute terms and restricted it, on the whole, to the observable
aspects of life close at hand. Many contemporary dramatists have
asked whether reality does not also encompass the workings of
the intellect and the subconscious self; whether the latter, though
more elusive, is not as impelling as the angular reality of the
tangible world; whether actual reality may not be influenced by
the fantastic one to the point of being changed and molded at will.
These are the intellectual positions from which many contemporary authors have looked at life. Psychoanalysis, as well as the
cinema with its sudden shifting of backgrounds, and the quickened
tempo of modern life have influenced this new aspect of dramatic
art.

This attitude toward reality is not strictly confined to the
playwrights with whom we deal in this chapter. Indeed, it is more
or less diffused in the work of most contemporary authors.

In the treatment of characters this group deviated greatly from
the naturalistic tenet of modeling them on actually observed
human beings projected on a carefully reconstructed background.
The clear-cut contour of characters and the detailed rendering
of the background are of little concern to the playwright, who
is interested in the drama of the mind. In Pirandello the name of
the modern gentleman who, through madness, believed himself
to be Henry IV, is not given. Nor does the main character in
Quando si è qualcuno (When One is Somebody, 1933) bear a
name. He is presented as *Qualcuno* (Somebody). We have already
seen how Rosso di San Secondo and Cavacchioli have resorted to
various devices in order to express the impersonal quality of their
characters.

In the drama determined by intellectual motivation the author participates in the action in a more direct manner than did the playwrights of the past. The psychological element in such works plays a much greater role than it did in the realistic plays of the nineteenth century. Rather than in material gathered through the observation of matters current and lying near at hand, the contemporary playwright is interested in the modifying influence that reflection exerts on the instinctive impulse to act. His field of observation is to be found in the intellectual and reflective moments of the human mind and imagination.

This type of play was developed to an extraordinary degree during and after World War I by Luigi Pirandello, who for a long time had been agitating in his novels the problems of human personality conceived as an aggregate of conflicting and shifting selves. We are here considering the treatment of the drama of the mind through his work, not only because he has been the most significant figure of the modern Italian theater, but also because he exercised a deep and lasting influence on the playwrights of our generation.

The art of Luigi Pirandello (1867–1936) projects itself from a philosophical and religious background, though a vast crowd of characters, tragic and ludicrous at the same time, occupies the foreground of his dramatic work. They gesticulate, shout like persons under great nervous tension; they sneer, but all have a sad story to tell.

For Pirandello life is a cosmic and universal entity that roars, boundless and unfettered, at the fringe of the finite world. Fundamentally, his intuition is not different from the concept that philosophers and religious men have evolved upon looking at the universe and at man. Unlike them, however, Pirandello ponders over what happens to cosmic life when it becomes caught and immobilized in individual forms, be it a tree, an animal, or a man. Ciampa, in *Il berretto a sonagli* (Cap and Bells, 1916), informs us that the "divine spirit enters into us and becomes dwarfed into a puppet."

Pirandello has painstakingly dwelt upon the contrast between the cosmic and the individual in life. Man, unlike other beings that crowd the universe, is capable of formulating concepts of his existence and of his very self. Rather than deriving exaltation from this fact, as did the idealists of old, Pirandello reaches bitterly pessimistic conclusions. Through an infernal machine called logic man reduces himself, his fellow men, and the whole of reality into an abstract concept, thus losing touch with life. Ciampa declares: "It should be enough to be born puppets through divine will. No, we all add another puppet to that one: the puppet that each of us can be or believes himself to be." This idea is more fully developed in *Il piacere dell' onestà* (The Pleasure of Honesty, 1917) in which Baldovino, an outcast of society, is humorously made to serve honesty with the enthusiasm of an old paladin. Baldovino insists on the process that Pirandello calls *costruirsi* (to build up oneself), a process thus described by Baldovino as he talks to his rival: "When I enter this house, I present myself to you in a form adapted to the relation that I must assume with you. You, in receiving me, must do the same. But ultimately behind our minds, which are facing each other, behind the Venetian blinds and curtains of hypocrisy, are hidden our most secret thoughts, our most intimate sentiments, all that we really are for ourselves, aside from the relations we wish to establish with one another." What we really are is, for Pirandello, the cosmic that abides in man, painfully imprisoned in the individual self. By his artificial construction of himself, man, instead of obeying the warm flow of life, sees himself live as if from the outside, as if he were another person.

As to our attitudes toward our fellow men, we crystallize them likewise into cold and unchanging entities. We look at them and say: this man is honest, that one dishonest; this one is serious, that one comical. Here is a poet, here is a husband, here is a teacher. Nothing is more irritating to Pirandello's characters than to be enclosed in these false concepts that destroy in them what they really are. For Pirandello the poet is not only a poet but the aggregate of other aspects of his self. The father in *Sei Personaggi in cerca d'autore* (Six Characters in Search of an Author, 1921) refuses to be branded immoral, as his stepdaughter contemptuously calls him, thus reducing all his self to the image she formed of him when she met him in a house of questionable repute. Mrs. Morli, in *La signora Morli, una e due* (Mrs. Morli, One and Two, 1920), informs us that an individual cannot be categorically said to be serious or lighthearted. Speaking from her own experience, she confides to us that she is joyous and carefree with her former husband Ferrante and serious, silent, and subdued with her lover Lello Carpani. The mother in *Come prima, meglio di prima* (As Well As Before, Better Than Before, 1920) resents the fact that, when she left her home because she was disgusted with the sensuality of her husband, the latter told their daughter that her mother had died, picturing her as a saintly woman whom the Lord had called back to Him. When she returns home, this false image prevents her from revealing her identity to her own daughter, who looks upon her as an intruder. Whereupon she leaves home again, but this time takes with her her newborn child who will thus not grow up entertaining any false concept that the husband might nurture in his mind.

The conclusions that Pirandello draws from the contrast between the cosmic and the individual lead him to a destructive critique of man and society. When projected into his characters, this critique constitutes the backbone of his art. Man is pictured as a pitifully carnal being, walking desolately on the bleak road of life. He is unknown to himself, since his consciousness is in a constant state of flux. He is incapable of communicating with others, since words are too inadequate to express his innermost thoughts. In *Come mi vuoi* (As You Desire Me, 1930) Pirandello has dwelt on the tragedy of the soul in its inability to find shelter on this earth. Elma, a dancer, is placed by the whim of destiny in the situation of being Cia, the beautiful and lofty wife of Bruno Pieri, who mysteriously disappeared during World War I. Elma wants to make live again in herself the soul of Cia, but alas! those who surround her are more interested in her physical identity than in her soul. So she returns to her life of torment and passion with Carl Salter, a revolting German whose mistress she is.

Pirandello's vision of society is not very consoling. If man in his intimate nature is cosmic and therefore can live only in absolute freedom, what is the value of organized society with its well-regulated bureaus, its strict laws, unbending codes, and conventions? Why so many temples in our cities when the universe is the best place to worship God? Why so many gods, as many at least as there are religions, if the divine personality of God is one? Pirandello has reflected his political thought in *La nuova colonia* (The New Colony, 1928) that hinges precisely on the impossibility of creating a perfect society on this earthly planet. The religious aspect of his inquiry is projected in *Lazzaro* (Lazarus, 1929), in which the author, rejecting the idea of the personal survival of the soul, beautifully concludes that through death man re-enters the realm of the cosmic.

An interesting conclusion that Pirandello reached in his musing on life is the one relating to art. He saw a violent clash between art, which is life caught in a mold, and actual existence, which is fluid and rebellious against immobility. This motif is diffused in several plays, but is particularly well developed in *Tuda* (Tuda, a Model, 1927) and *Trovarsi* (She Wanted to Find Herself, 1932). The concept of the mobility of life and the immobility of art is viewed in Tuda in terms of her drama as a model and as a woman who loves Dossi, the artist for whom she poses. The tragic in the play is reached when Giuncano, who represents fluid life, in defense of Tuda strangles Dossi, who stands for static art. The same motif is developed in *Trovarsi* through Donata Genzi who, as an actress, has lost the spontaneity of her emotions, and Elj Nielsen, a youth who symbolizes life in the freest forms. The clash that ensues ends in a positive way in that Donata, being a perfect embodiment of womanhood, succeeds in finding her real self as an artist in Elj's love.

It is natural for the reader to ask himself what attitude toward reality in general Pirandello reached with such a pessimistic view of man and society. Pirandello distinguished between the angular reality of the everyday life that surrounds us and the formalistic reality of our concepts. Both are absurdly limited. But there is another reality which he calls that of the imagination. Through it he refers to the capacity of man to mold the most unbearable situation into one which becomes livable. In this manner he places his faith in the individual efforts directed toward the overcoming of the tragedy of life. This is the most fertile idea that he has exemplified and made living in his plays. *Così è, se vi pare* (Right You Are, If You Think You Are, 1917) is a very clear exemplification of this motif. In it the author does not reveal the actual truth concerning the Ponza family that has recently arrived in a small city and has disturbed the peace of its curious and gossiping citizens. The actual truth is of no consequence to him. Reality lies in the pitiful but compassionate deception that Ponza exercises toward Signora Frola, his mother-in-law, and she toward him, concerning the identity of Ponza's wife. The play reaches a climax of touching and exquisite beauty when the latter appears and announces that for Ponza she is the second wife, for Signora Frola she is her daughter, and for herself, no one. In her infinite compassion she has obliterated her very self. The same motif is found in *Il berretto a sonagli*, although the tone of the play in its humor does not reveal so effectively its intellectual motivation.

Pirandello most often describes individuals who try to escape from the tragedy of their existence. The means which he places at their disposal were perhaps those that he himself used in the unhappy life that he lived with his demented wife while earning a living as a teacher of Italian literature in a college in Rome. Some of his characters try by deceit to find a way out of the situations in which they are placed, as in *Ciascuno a suo modo* (Each in His Own Way, 1924). The father in *Sei personaggi in cerca d'autore* uses voluble words to justify his conduct. Ersilia Drei, in *Vestire gli ignudi* (Naked, 1922), tries through a pitiful lie to place a halo of romance around her attempt at suicide. Ciampa resorts to pretending ignorance in order to face the fact that his wife betrays him. Martino Lori, in *Tutto per bene* (All for the Best, 1920), carries on through passivity. Henry IV resigns himself to play the role of a madman when, after fourteen years of real madness, he finds that he cannot resume his true personality. These artificial but human devices were accorded by Pirandello to his characters, although he knew how painful and imperfect they were.

Deep in Pirandello's heart there was another means of overcoming the tragedy of living: to accept with humility one's human plight. In one of his most tormented plays, *Ciascuno a suo modo*, he writes:

Detach from yourself the little puppet that you create with the fictitious interpretation of your acts and sentiments, and you will immediately see that it has nothing to do with what you are or what you may truly be, with what is in you that you are not conscious of. He is a terrible god, understand, if you oppose him, but he becomes immediately compassionate of every form of guilt if you abandon yourself to him and do not wish to find excuses. . . . Here we teach that you have to build a road on which you walk alone for every step you wish to take, battering down what does not belong to you, because you have not built it yourself, and you have walked on it as a parasite.

In the development of his art Pirandello departed from the elementary naturalism that was prevalent in his youth, and veered more and more toward a psychological art that could adequately express the thought he entrusted to it. Following the precepts of his friends, Luigi Capuana and Giovanni Verga, he first wrote short stories and novels, the settings of many of which are typically naturalistic. He presented in them men and women whom he observed, or had observed, in his native Sicily. In these works there is a sharp contrast between the insignificance of his characters and the intellectual motivation of his stories. This is also true of Pirandello's first attempts at drama around 1915. He recast in dramatic form a great many of his short stories. The humble and elementary characters in whom he enclosed his tragic sentiment of life were not big enough nor possessed of an intellectual stature sufficient to convey his thought. The fullness of Pirandello's art was achieved when he created psychologically complex characters that were capable of carrying in a clear form the weight of his thought and pathos. Then such figures as Henry IV, Elma, the Father, Baldovino, and Donata Genzi appeared to give evidence of the full measure of his art. He had become identified with his characters and merged with them.

Pirandello has received greater recognition abroad than he has in Italy. It was owing to a Frenchman, Benjamin Crémieux, and an Irishman, James Joyce, that the international world of letters took cognizance of his art around 1915. Even when fame was accorded to him, the Italian public did not share the enthusiasm of the theater-going public of France, England, Germany, and the United States. He visited this country in 1925 and witnessed the successful staging of *Six Characters in Search of an Author*, *Henry IV*, and *The Pleasure of Honesty* in the Forty-fifth Street Theatre in New York. These plays, followed later by *As You Desire Me*, with Judith Anderson in the star role, created a real stir not only in New York but also in other major cities of the United States. The reception accorded these plays contributed greatly in establishing Pirandello's reputation as a great playwright.

It is strange that Pirandello should have been called an abstruse and cerebral author. Ultimately there is a strong anti-intellectualistic trend in his thought. His attitudes and conclusions merge with those of thoughtful men who, in the course of centuries, have had the courage to look at life with clear eyes and conclude that human existence is a tragic and short-lived experience.

The basic attitudes that form the nucleus of Pirandello's plays had been expressed by him in 1908, in his *Umorismo* (Humor). The book attracted little or no attention when it was first published. In subsequent years it has served as a point of reference for a great many contemporary playwrights. We do not claim that Pirandello invented the new psychological form that characterizes the contemporary Italian drama. Its antecedents are to be found not only in Ibsen and in French playwrights, but also in Giacosa and Bracco. But Pirandello developed it and used it more consistently and more successfully than did any other Italian playwright. He firmly established a trend that was felt by his contemporaries both because of his fame and because he founded a company of his own in 1925 that encouraged young playwrights by producing their works. In the plays we have already examined this trend is often visible. It is obvious that it was followed by each author according to his temperament and artistic capacities. At times it was even misused in that it received a mechanical application that hampered rather than helped the artistic effort of the writer. We have seen that the authors of the grotesque theater often reflected the theory of humor and pathos that Pirandello elucidated in his *Umorismo*. In spirit they are very far from the master.

It is of interest to single out plays and contemporary authors in whom the dramatic forms of Pirandello are very clearly visible. Even an author such as Lucio D'Ambra, who had started from an entirely different concept of art, in recent years has veered toward a psychological form that reminds one of Pirandello. In *Solitudine* (Solitude, 1936) a father, having discovered that one of his three children is the fruit of his wife's adultery, keeps his love for the bastard child upon reflecting that for so many years he had looked upon him as his own son. In Pirandello's terms the image of the child obliterates the actual datum of illegitimacy. Likewise, the theme of the reversal of the value of reality through the play of imagination is found in Rosso di San Secondo's *L'illusione dei giorni e delle notti* (The Illusion of Days and Nights, 1926), but here it is grotesquely distorted. Rosso imagines that an old man is visited at night by a young woman who gives herself to him because she sees in him an ardent youth, the projection of her dreams.

The author who shows most often, and not in an original form, the influence of Luigi Pirandello is Massimo Bontempelli (1878–   ). Bontempelli appeared as a sort of literary phenomenon in the twenties. He was the originator of the Novecento School through his journal *Novecento*, written first in French and then in Italian, in which he proclaimed with theatrical insistence the value of imagination. He baffled his contemporaries in that, being a man with a thorough classical training, he showed typically futuristic tendencies. In effect, Bontempelli's case can be easily explained through the active part he took in politics and because he carried to absurd extremes the premises of the new psychology. Since unquestionably he has talent, he has succeeded in making an impression on many, and hence his literary notoriety.

In *Siepe a nordovest* (High Hedge in the Northwest, 1923) he has complicated the contrast between the mask and the face by presenting the characters, no longer in the dualism of man and marionette, but in three groups: actors, marionettes, and puppets. He has also reversed the role of marionettes, which are supposed to perform for the amusement of men, by having marionettes and actors perform for the enjoyment of puppets. Two actions take place simultaneously on the stage, one carried on by the actors and the other by the marionettes. Both groups move, speak, and act but they are unaware of each other. The Pirandellian idea of the diverse interpretation that can be given to the same act is cynically expressed by making a screen, used by two lovers to cover their tryst, appear to the marionettes as a high hedge to protect a recently built city from the high winds that lash it. The play reduces itself to a banal plot: the love affair of Carletto and Laura.

In 1925 Bontempelli wrote and published *Nostra Dea* (Our Goddess) in which the automaton-like condition of man is exaggerated by making Dea change her personality completely, according to the clothes she wears. When she wears a turtle-gray dress she is gentle and sweet; when she changes to brown with red flowers and a red hat she is voluble, mocking, and masculine. As for herself, she is nothing, by the confession of the author. In substance *Nostra Dea* is an old comedy with the usual ladies, their lovers and jealous husbands, set against the background of an immoral and artificial society.

Likewise, in *Minnie, la candida* (Minnie, the Pure One, 1928), we find the current idea of man reduced to an automaton presented in a grotesque form through a woman who fails to distinguish between real men and marionettes.

The only play of Bontempelli that has achieved any degree of significance is *La guardia alla luna* (Watching for the Moon, written in 1916 and performed in 1920). The lyrical theme that forms its nucleus is that of a mother who, demented after losing her fifteen-month-old daughter, imagines that the moon has stolen her. After long wanderings among strange people, she goes to the top of a high mountain to kill the moon, but she herself dies of exhaustion and exposure.

Marionettes, which have played such a large part in the Italian theater, also appear in Ugo Falena's (1875–1931) play, *Il raggio di luna* (Moonbeam, 1927), where they are allowed to become animated into real human beings, only to want to become marionettes again. It is evident how far we are from the spirit of Pirandello's sense of the tragedy of man.

The theme of the split personality that so often appears in Pirandello is visible also in the work of Cesare Giulio Viola (1887–   ). In his *Il cuore in due* (A Heart in Two, 1926) a girl, who becomes infatuated with the author of a book, is made to discover that the book is the work of two brothers. She succeeds in meeting them and finds them quite different one from the other. Giovanni is a sensitive and almost sickly person whereas Andrea is manly and strong. As might be expected, she chooses Andrea. The conclusion is complicated by Pirandellian considerations of personality that makes heavy reading in this otherwise interesting work. The situation in which Giovanni's peaceful existence with his brother is disturbed by the love of the girl is well presented, yet the mechanical character of the theme is very evident if compared with the deeply human treatment that Pirandello gave to it in *La Signora Morli, una e due*.

A better treatment of the Pirandellian idea of the image that destroys the reality of man is found in the well-received play *La vena d'oro* (The Vein of Gold, 1919) by Guglielmo Zorzi (1879–   ). Zorzi presents the reaction of Corrado Usbeti upon realizing that his mother has fallen in love with Guido Manfredi, a poet. His reaction is created by the contrast between the image of a mother, through which he had always looked at her, and the sudden apparition of the woman in her. After a long struggle the son is made to accept the situation by the family physician, an old and trusted friend. Even more evident is the influence of Pirandello on Zorzi in his play *L'immagine* (The Image, 1929), in which the love that a woman feels for her adopted son is kindled and kept alive by the image of her real son from whom she was separated when she left her husband. When her real son dies, she feels her love for her adopted son die, too.

Orio Vergani (Milan, 1899–   ) has developed in his plays the idea of reality projected on various planes, a concept on which Pirandello strongly insisted and which he beautifully exemplified in his *Sei Personaggi*. Vergani centers his plays on the clash of the actual and the fantastic realities. In *Un vigliacco* (A Coward, 1923) he studies the reactions of a sensitive mind as determined by the reading of a novel. The author analyzes subtle states of mind but no action is determined by them. A better play is *Il cammino sulle acque* (Walking on the Waters, 1926), in which a husband tries to reconstruct the causes which five years before had brought about his wife's madness. It is really a play within a play, since we witness the past through the reconstruction of it made by the husband as he succeeds in ascertaining that what brought about his wife's tragedy was the discovery that her stepmother had a lover. Unlike Pirandello, who knew how to create drama from the clash of the various planes of reality, Vergani remains static in his plays, since in him the past has no telling influence on the present. These examples, even when not significant, show how persistently contemporary playwrights have sought to treat the themes and forms that Pirandello typified in his art.

Whether in comedy or in lyrical and historical dramas, the outstanding trend in the modern theater has been characterized by a passionate search into the baffling workings of the human mind. Through it the theater of our age has assumed forms that distinguish it from those of the nineteenth century.

Grazia Deledda
and Her Early Literary Contacts

THIS essay is based on the personal correspondence that we have been privileged to have with Professor Guido Costa, son of Enrico Costa, the Sardinian novelist whom Grazia Deledda has acknowledged to have exercised a definite literary influence on her in the years of her youth.

Professor Costa reveals in his letters the unbounded admiration that he, as a citizen of Sardinia, felt for the writer who had brought so much honor to his island. In reference to this he writes: "Grazia Deledda honored me with her esteem and affection, and I was deeply grieved by the great sorrows that she suffered as an artist and as a mother. Her death was a personal loss to me."

Professor Costa's letters throw a revealing light on the intimate life of the Sardinian novelist. Dictated by deep and sincere feelings, they illumine it without going beyond the boundaries of discretion. One of these letters, dated April 13, 1938, makes it clear why the announcement of her death, that took place on August 15, 1936, deeply affected those who admired her art. Professor Costa writes thus: "The great Sardinian author died of cancer of the breast, a disease that she kept secret from all, even from her children." This tragic fact explains her last novel, *La chiesa della solitudine* (The Church of Solitude, 1936), in which Deledda presented the drama of Maria Concezione, a beautiful and lonely young woman who renounces the love of Aroldo because she suffers from cancer of the breast. This is no longer fiction. It is life painfully and tragically lived and transcribed.

But the greatest grief that tormented the heart of Deledda was, perhaps, the sickness of her son, Sardus. We quote from the same letter: "Her first-born child, whom she worshiped because he had inherited her love for literature, was doomed because of a disease that does not spare even the young: tuberculosis. The unhappy youth, one year after his mother's death, followed her on the way to the tomb. How many hopes were thus deluded!"

Deledda had two sons: Sardus and Franz. Franz is a doctor in chemistry. He and Signor Madesani, whom Deledda married in 1900, are the only survivors of a once very happy family.

Still gleaning from his letters, we learn of the death of Deledda's sister, and that she left "three children, among whom charming Mirella, who was most beloved by Deledda, to the point that it could be said that she literally lived in the novelist's household." The presence of the exquisite child in Deledda's home is a living document of the acute sensitivity of a writer who has created in her books so many passionate souls. Few authors follow the vicissitudes of their characters with the sympathy and compassion that Deledda evidences in her novels.

Professor Costa's letters throw a vivid light on the early youth of Deledda and on the literary contacts that determined, in part, the character of her art. In a letter dated January 21, 1939, we learn that two old friends of Professor Costa were among those who encouraged young Deledda to write novels: Antonio Scano and Luigi Falchi. Here is what Professor Costa writes about them: "Falchi and Scano are two friends of mine, both well known to Deledda. The former is a man of my age [in his sixties], but the latter is nearing his eightieth year. When Deledda was a mere girl and lived at Cagliari, Scano never failed to encourage and spur her on. He has kept a great admiration and affection for her." Both admirers of Deledda have each recently published a book on her fiction. Scano's work bears the title of *Versi e prose giovanili* (Verse and Prose Writings of Deledda's Youth).[1] That of Falchi is entitled *L'opera di Grazia Deledda con due appendici di lettere inedite* (The Work of Grazia Deledda with Two Appendices of Unpublished Letters).[2]

Of greater significance is what Professor Costa writes about the literary contacts between Deledda and his own father, Enrico Costa. The latter wrote a novel, *Il Muto di Gallura* (The Deaf Mute of Gallura), whose value Deledda directly and explicitly recognized, stating that it had had a definite effect on her in the formative period of her art. Professor Costa has most kindly sent us a copy of his father's novel with an inscription that reveals his lofty sentiments, his thoughtfulness, and the warm friendship with which he honors us. One of his letters refers to this novel, and in transcribing his words we listen to what the son has to say about his own father's work: "The novel was published in 1884, and a second edition appeared in 1912, three years after my father's death. The edition that I am sending you could be called the third one. It was published without my knowing anything about it, and I did not resent it at all, all the more that the preceding editions were all sold out. It is the one, among my father's novels, that Grazia Deledda prefers. Together with Verga's novels, with which Deledda became acquainted later, it strongly contributed to guiding her on the road that has made her celebrated."

This opinion is shared by Deledda herself in an article written a few months before her death, in which she testified to what a degree she was indebted to Enrico Costa. This article has escaped the attention of the latest critics of Deledda: Antonio Scano, Luigi Falchi, and Eurialo De Michelis. The latter author published a study on Deledda in 1938: *Grazia Deledda e il Decadentismo*.[3] None of these students includes this important article in the detailed bibliography dedicated to the Sardinian author. This omission is probably due to the fact that the article in question appeared in the *Illustrazione del Medico*, a medical journal that contains discussions of both scientific and literary topics, such as this important statement by Grazia Deledda concerning her youth. In the essay she nostalgically looks in retrospect at the years of her past at the time when she received the early impressions that molded her into the future novelist of Sardinian themes.

Let us recall at this point that Grazia Deledda dedicated her long career to the passionate evocation of the landscape of her beloved island, its customs, and picturesque inhabitants, often observed and studied in actual life in the fields and towns near Nuoro. It is this countryside and these very people, who had been a part of her existence, that her memory cherished and her fancy embellished in her novels, while her heart lent deep sentiment and passions to them as characters in the plots so beautifully developed.

In the above-mentioned article Deledda acknowledges that, to her, Sardinia was "still a country of myths and legends," and she adds, "At that time, the novels of Enrico Costa were very much in vogue in the island." [4] There follows in the article a short but vivid sketch of Enrico Costa and his literary career. It behooves us to study it because it possesses a documentary value since it is written about one who contributed in forming the literary atmosphere that predominated in Italy in the days of Deledda's youth.

Those were the days of *verismo*, a movement characterized by an ardent thirst for truth in art. Young Deledda was attracted to it, and she infused in it the treasures of her fancy and of her deep soul. Here is what she wrote on Enrico Costa and his works: "He was a historian, a poet, and an honest and colorful writer. He had written a *Storia di Sassari* (History of Sassari), a carefully documented and very exact work, as well as other scientific books. But he was also known for his fiction dealing with historical figures, very romantically presented. He had written a novel on Rosa Gambella, a lady from the city of Sassari, who had had a very adventurous existence, and on Adelaide Torres, the beautiful but unhappy Sardinian princess who, in the thirteenth century, married King Enzo of the Swabian kings. She was a very romantic figure whose legendary deeds still illumine the countryside near the castle of Burgos, where she was imprisoned and ended her unhappy life. The novel by Enrico Costa that influenced most my young mind was *Il muto di Gallura*, a novel made up of a very passionate adventure, the idyllic and tragic story of two hostile families, led by their hostility to destroy each other throughout several generations."

Enrico Costa always remained faithful to the principles of *verismo*, a young shoot that had germinated at the foot of the leafy plant of the historical novel, such as cultivated by Grossi, d'Azeglio, Cantù, and Guerrazzi. In dedicating his novel to his friend, Medardo Riccio, Enrico Costa insisted, with passionate earnestness, on the principle that he, as a child of *verismo*, had scrupulously followed, the principle of absolute respect for truth and truthfulness, to the point of reproducing even the dialect of the characters modeled on the inhabitants of Gallura. The comments of Deledda on this passage are extremely interesting: "That novel touched me because it was so tragically true. At Orune, Orgosolo, and other places of my primitive island these hostilities between families, accompanied by vivid flashes of hatred, love, vengeance, pitiful and cruel vicissitudes, were very frequent and they involved entire sections of Sardinia. Magistrates and bishops intervened in order to put an end to them. Thus I recall that, at Orune, peace was realized between two powerful, hostile families with unforgettable solemnity. A poet wrote about it in a style possessed of biblical grandeur. The poem together with the novels of Enrico Costa delighted me in the dawn of my literary career."

The faith in what was "true" (*il vero*) was the flame that at that time kindled the souls of those who hoped in a new art. They wanted literature to take its themes and its sense of reality from actual life; just as they had resolved that the new Italy should enter modern life resolutely and boldly. For them, modern life was the creation of great masses of people, the result of work and new struggles, unknown to the generations of the past. It meant especially to break away from the idylls and dreams of former days.

It is natural that we should look upon the interest in truth on the part of Enrico Costa and his contemporaries as a document of the aesthetic principles that the young writers of the last decades of the nineteenth century formulated and followed in opposition to those who tenaciously clung to the dictates of tradition. Truth, a truth, must always kindle the heart of men, no matter of which generation, and every generation fashions for itself a concept of reality that has validity in art only in that it is capable of kindling a new faith in original minds. Doubtlessly, the heart of Enrico Costa felt a great interest in the historical reality, that he enlivened with sentiment and passion accompanied with a keen study of the environment in which the plot of his novel developed. The emotions and sentiments that stir the hearts of his characters in *Il muto di Gallura* are painstakingly evoked and made to center in the events that saddened the town of Aggio from 1848 to 1856. The name of the main character, Bastiano Tanzu, is historical, and historical is his love for beautiful and young Gavina, as is the death of her father when he refuses to allow her to marry Bastiano. It is hardly necessary to add that the action that unfolds in the novel, the sentiments of the unfortunate youth, the situations in which he finds himself are due to the fertile imagination of the author, and they reflect his sensitivity, just as the characters of every work of fiction reflect the temperament and experience of their creator.

The opinion that Grazia Deledda entertained of Enrico Costa assigns to him a distinct place in the history of Italian fiction. He can justly aspire to this place because his novels are well constructed and he is capable of expressing in a very strong and dramatic manner the events that he relates. The interest of his readers is constantly kept alive by him. The novel that impressed young Deledda so deeply and encouraged her to write fiction is still read in Sardinia today. Professor Costa informs us that especially in Gallura "there is no *stazzo* (an aggregate of farmhouses) where one does not find a copy of this book."

The desire to pattern his characters on persons known, observed, and carefully studied helped Enrico Costa in the process of transforming his experience into his fiction. He constantly strove to render the landscape and the people of Sardinia with the utmost directness and simplicity, a reflection of the integrity that characterized every act of his existence. Deledda, too, patterned her fiction on the actual forms of man and nature, tempering the flights of her imagination with the memory of the existence that she had lived and that she reflected in her characters.

The two novelists, naturally enough, are very different. Artists strive to be different, and they are different, not only in terms of their culture, but also and especially in those of their personal temperament. Enrico Costa, who wrote around 1880, adhered more faithfully than Deledda to the creed of *verismo*, and focused his attention on life in the various parts of Sardinia, creating characters that are historical, at least in name and in the central action which is developed through them. Deledda definitely abandoned historical themes in order to study and render the actual reality that she had observed and lived directly and passionately. Her novels possess a richer gamut of colors and passions than those of Enrico Costa. The life that unfolds in her novels is more passionate, and the landscape infinitely richer. Deledda was more definitely a product of modern life, with its web of doubts and uncertainties about ideas that gave to the existence of our ancestors a quieter rhythm and tempo. Grazia Deledda experienced the fury of the storms that ravage our modern souls, storms that the serene countenance of Enrico Costa seemed capable of keeping at a distance or, at least, of controlling.

In spite of these marked differences, Enrico Costa can be called the first teacher of Grazia Deledda in that he guided her in her youth and directed her toward the fiction that has enriched narrative art in modern Italy.

Pirandello As I Saw Him

THESE are recollections of my meetings with Luigi Pirandello in New York during the months of July and August 1935, and they are offered here as a historical document of what he said in many hours of intimate conversation. The term "historical" is advisably used. I am fully conscious of the stateliness and importance of history as well as of the humble media that are often used in its making. That Pirandello belongs to the literary history of the last fifty years there is no doubt. He created such a stir in the dramatic circles of our time as to cause his name to be known outside of Italy; and many a playwright took his intuition of human personality to the point that "Pirandellian personality" became a byword in our generation.

I first met Luigi Pirandello at the reception that was tendered him aboard the steamship *Conte di Savoia* on July 20 when he arrived in New York for a three-month stay in the hope of having his well-known play *Six Characters in Search of an Author* made into a film. As I stood on the pier, bewitched by the beauty of the New York skyline, the majestic ship slowly advanced like a fantastic and huge bird, dazzlingly white, and moored at the Eighteenth Street dock. Once on the ship, the thought that I was shortly to see the man whose work I had always admired keyed me to a high nervous tension. When I confided my nervousness to a young colleague of mine, he, with characteristic modern indifference toward greatness, almost shouted, "For heavens' sake, man, do you think that Pirandello is a god?" Mindful of the Pirandellian precept that reality is something very subjective, I did not answer, but hastened toward the other end of the salon where the smiling and wistful countenance of the maestro had appeared. He was accompanied by the ship's officers and the New York City dignitaries who had gone to meet him at quarantine.

Pirandello was of medium height, rather heavy-set, with an oval face and a short, pointed gray beard. Although sixty-seven years of age, he moved very swiftly, and his person bore the marks of a robust manhood. What attracted me more than anything else were his mobile eyes. They had a way all of their own of converging on you as if to penetrate your innermost thoughts, and then they suddenly became hidden by an impenetrable veil as he relaxed his attention and withdrew within himself. Introspection was not a pose with him. It was an instinct and a habit that are reflected in many of his characters. There was something shy and timid in him as he stood in the midst of the reception committee. While grateful for the reception accorded him, he seemed to have to force himself to listen to the oratory profused in his praise.

As I stood a little to one side, interested in observing his reactions in meeting people, I saw him turn and beckon to me with his crooked finger, evidently having been told that I was eager to have an interview with him. He was very cordial in thanking me for my interest in his writings and expressed gratification at the manner in which I had presented him in a long article that had been published in the journal *Ateneo Veneto* a year before. He gave me an appointment for the following day at the Waldorf-Astoria at ten o'clock.

The next morning, as I waited in the magnificent lobby of the Waldorf-Astoria, it was hard for me to picture Pirandello, who had always indicted the splendor and the hustle of modern civilization, on the forty-first floor of a hotel that has no rival anywhere in the world for size, beauty, luxury, and comfort. He received me in the large living room of his apartment. The maestro seated himself in a rather high armchair against the open window, and I was happy to look up to him. As we discussed his art and plays, he seemed gradually to recede miles and miles from the luxury that surrounded him. I had with me the page proofs of my book that appeared in the fall of that year, *The Drama of*

Luigi Pirandello. I submitted to him my plan of work, my interpretations of his plays, and my main conclusions. He was very interested and eager to hear what I had written. I translated into Italian the passages in question, because he confessed that, although he could read English, he found it difficult to understand spoken English.

My first interview almost went awry at the very outset when I showed him the index of the various chapters of my book and told him that in the first chapter I dealt with his contacts with naturalism. The maestro was very indignant. "My art has no connection whatever with naturalism," he almost shouted. "Giovanni Verga, the great representative of that movement, wrote me that there was a new force and a new light in my art. I have a letter written to me by him after the publication of my novel, *The Outcast.* Indeed I feel that I am at the opposite pole from naturalism. I have battered down blind faith in clumsy, tangible reality. My characters, through imagination, conquer and break the fetters of everyday reality. I have shown the stupidity of placing our sense of reality in this material world of ours, which was the pivotal point of the art mode created by the naturalists." I confess that I saw myself lost. I pleaded that I considered naturalism only as a point of departure for his art, and that my book aimed at showing how later he had developed into the artist so uniquely psychological that we all admired. I cannot say that the maestro looked convinced, but he became more approachable.

"Certainly it is due to naturalism," I continued, "if your early characters are small figures caught in the ebb and flow of everyday life. Indeed I feel that they are not so capable of carrying the intellectual motivation of your art as the more complex personalities that one finds in your later works." I referred to the dramatization of early short stories that are typically naturalistic, and I singled out "Liolà" and "Man, Beast, and Virtue."

"Yes," agreed the maestro. "These are developed along the lines of the traditional comedy of the sixteenth century." Of

"Man, Beast, and Virtue," he said, "It is tragedy stifled by comedy."

The reason why Pirandello was so resentful about my mention of his contacts with naturalism was the fact that Benedetto Croce, in an article published in *La Critica*, had reduced Pirandello's art to the form and substance of the naturalism of the eighties. The maestro in his outburst had not referred to Croce, with the prudence of one who is not interested in having a hostile opinion known.

"Croce has failed to see that naturalism was only a starting point in your art," I pressed, "and my conclusion is the very opposite to Croce's." The maestro was now somewhat mollified, but the name of Croce had been like a red flag before a bull. Pirandello used the foreword that he wrote for my book to take his revenge on Croce, an unhappy choice for me since I happen to admire both men.

"Croce, in his obtuseness," went on Pirandello with ill-repressed anger, "has failed to see the human strain that runs through my art. I have been and am the enemy of formalism and hypocrisy. My idea of *costruirsi*, to build up oneself, is the fundamental tenet of my art. Marriage, fatherhood, motherhood, and personality have no meaning except that which we give to them. In my plays I have shown how unreal marriage is if held together only by the civil and religious ceremonies. I have shown couples who quarrel at home but stroll through the city streets arm in arm as the embodiment of marital perfection. Such people are not alive or real. They are self-constructed, empty concepts. I have compared one such man to a cigar that has smoked itself out, keeping its shape but being only ashes."

I told the maestro that I had taken the liberty of pointing out in my book the anti-social undercurrent of his thought. An expression of resentment passed over his face as he replied, "Society is necessarily formal and in this sense I am anti-social; that is, I am opposed to social hypocrisies and conventions. But my art teaches each individual to accept his human lot with candor and humility, and with full consciousness of the imperfections that are inherent in it."

Pirandello was very happy when I revealed to him that I had definitely stressed the positive side of his thought, quoting especially from the interludes of *Each in His Own Way*. "All true art contains a philosophy of life that tends toward sound living," he concluded.

"What about the 'drama of mirrors,' as your drama has often been characterized?" I asked on another occasion.

"It is an exaggerated view of a situation that exists in many of my plays," he answered. "If we present ourselves to others as artificial constructions in terms of what we really are, it is logical that, upon looking at ourselves in a mirror, we see our falseness reflected there, made galling and unbearable in its fixity. That's all that I mean by placing my characters before a mirror and making them say that they would like to spit at themselves."

Pirandello complained of having been misunderstood, or not understood at all, especially in Italy. "How many do really understand what I have tried to do and say?" he asked, raising his shoulders and closing his eyes in the typical Italian fashion that expresses resentment and mortification as well as a bit of contempt. I called to his attention how much the criticism of Adriano Tilgher in *Voci del Tempo* and in *Studi sul Teatro Contemporaneo* had contributed in blurring the clear profile of his drama. Pirandello seemed unwilling to dwell on Tilgher, undoubtedly because he had accepted Tilgher's presentation of his art in the early twenties. However, he agreed with me that Tilgher had unintentionally misrepresented the philosophical content of his drama by stating that his art pivoted on the obliteration of reality and of human personality. He also agreed that dramatic art is not conceivable without a clear-cut personality, and that the conscious madman that appears so often in his plays is a well-defined dramatic character. He added with a gesture of resignation, "Tilgher is not the only one!" Yet I have a slight suspicion that his managers, at least, if not he himself, did not regret the quibbling and shouting that accompanied the performance of his early plays after World War I. It certainly helped theater receipts. There is an echo of those disputes in two of Pirandello's plays: *Six Characters in Search of an Author* and *Each in His Own Way*.

Pirandello departed from the discussion of Tilgher to inform me that what he thought of life and art had been expressed by him in a book that bears the title of *Umorismo*, published in 1908. Neither his life concept nor his art had substantially changed, he insisted. And he plunged into a wonderful discussion of what life was to him. He said with a force that bespoke his inner conviction: "Man moves in an impalpable atmosphere of dreams, whether he is conscious of it or not. Because of this, he walks over the bleak planet of the earth as a bewildered stranger and a grieving vagabond. Beyond the boundaries of time and space, above the arched, blue curve of the sky, there is life, unformed and unfettered, life out of which a strange god has carved man, the earth, and the universe. No laws, no limitations, no boundaries exist there. Life is a ruinous stream that roars into dazzlingly white stretches of infinite space. Woe to us if we have a glimpse of that primeval life! We become both terrified and deified by it. We cease to be human, and our contact with the average man becomes impossible. My art is the expression of what happens to universal life when it becomes individual existence."

I showed him various passages in my page proofs that brought out the tragedy of being human as he had expressed it. He added, "There are four great forces in life whose urge man constantly feels: love, hatred, mystery, and the acquisitive instinct." He turned toward the little table near which we were seated and grasped a small and exquisite ash tray that was there. "We say as fiercely as in the days of the cave man, 'This is mine. This woman is mine.' As to mystery, this is to me the greatest force of all. Man speaks, and he does not know whence his words come. We are the prey of forces that emanate from a world that we feel moving beyond time and space, a world whence all life springs, whence all the forces of instinct issue."

This was a golden opportunity to have Pirandello explain his concept of personality. Here are his words that I wrote almost verbatim as he spoke: "The last generation looked upon nature and man as something existing in unchanging, clear-cut, and solid forms outside of us. To me, reality is something that we mold through the power of our imagination. I have given a quixotic treatment of this concept, especially in *So It is (If So It Seems to You)*; but this idea is fundamental in my art and it enlivens most of my works."

Fully in agreement with him, I showed him what I had quoted from his *Umorismo:* "Man does not have an idea, an absolute concept of life, but rather a changing and varied sentiment according to time, cases, and circumstances."

With a slightly ironical smile the maestro countered, "You see that this was said by me long ago, and that applies also to my idea of personality. We say, I am one, and we look upon our fellow men as solid and clear-cut personalities, while in reality we are the juxtaposition of infinite, blurred selves. We are multiple personalities. Take the case of Mrs. Morli in *Mrs. Morli, One and Two*. Yes, she was one while in the company of her husband Ferrante, and another when she was with her lover Lello Carpani. That's an experience that we all have."

The maestro was so serious as to seem almost aggressive. "Those who deny the reality of Mrs. Morli are deprived of understanding and feeling."

"The strange thing in that play," I added, "is that she is carefree with her husband, and serious, almost sullen, with her lover."

With a gleam of mischief in his eye Pirandello said, "That's a trick of the trade!" He went on, "My idea of personality is clearly expressed in my latest play, *One Does Not Know How*."

I had not read the play, and felt lost. I though that I had read all his works. He informed me that the play had been given in Germany before being performed in Italy. Stefan Zweig had translated it beautifully. Pirandello gave me the German translation that I might add the analysis of that play to my book.

"Yes," continued Pirandello, "we pass most of our time outside of ourselves rather than in a state of full consciousness. We constantly lapse into subconscious reveries that detach us from our surroundings. It is the call of primeval life. How can our personality be one when so suddenly we are capable of re-entering primeval life and of being reabsorbed by it?"

When I told the maestro that this seemed a sort of flimsy mysticism that clashed with the central theme of the play in question, which presents a strange case of adultery, he exclaimed, "Sexual instinct in its origin is a cosmic force; yet when it enters individual life it leads to the most terrifying complications. It makes us betray our friends, break moral laws and conventions."

"But thus you destroy the moral code," I interrupted.

Pirandello was on the defensive. "I cannot help it," he said. "There are emotions and acts that are uncontrollable because of the blurred character of our personality. It is so, and I should not be honest with myself and with my art if I did not say so."

"You actually reach the same conclusion as D'Annunzio," I added.

Pirandello was furious. "No, no!" he shouted. "D'Annunzio is immoral in order to proclaim the glory of instinct. I present this individual case to add another proof of the tragedy of being human. D'Annunzio is exultant over it; I grieve over it."

I remained silent and convinced in the face of this rebuke.

This discussion brought us to the maestro's religious point of view. He stated that Pietro Mignosi of the University of Palermo was trying to make a Catholic mystic out of him, but he added that he could not recognize himself in that role. "In my system of thought," he said, "there is no place for any organized religion." Then turning sharply toward me he added very seriously, "Don't you see that even God has built up Himself?"

I must have looked puzzled, for the maestro continued, "I am not sacrilegious. I mean that God is a universal concept existing outside the partial constructions of Him that each religious sect makes. When this universal concept is enclosed in the Christian God, the Hindu God, and in as many other gods as there are tribes in Africa and peoples on the earth, the universality of that concept is necessarily offended and dwarfed."

I understood and, by way of comment, added that there was the same relation between the concept of God and the many gods that man has fashioned as between universal life and individual existence. The maestro agreed.

"This relationship exists also between the ideal state and the actual realization of a form of government, whether you call it democracy, fascism, or communism," said Pirandello another day in telling me of a request he had received to grant an interview to a group of American newspapermen who wanted to know what he thought of the Ethiopian campaign. In spite of his political relativism, he took the defense of Italy with the result that the American press assumed a very hostile tone toward him. He explained to me that, since he was a member of the Fascist party and traveled with the permission of the Fascist government, he had no other alternative.

He was actuated by the same practical considerations in refusing to see Samuel Putnam, the translator of *As You Desire Me*, who had recently joined the Communist party. Pirandello had the deepest affection for Samuel Putnam, whom he had known in Paris in 1923, but he confided to me that he could not see him because of political considerations.

Concerning *As You Desire Me*, he was indeed provoked upon hearing that in the English version the translator had blurred the identity of Cia and Elma. In the Italian original there is not the slightest doubt about the identity of the actual Cia and of Elma, who consciously set before herself the task of reincarnating the soul of Cia. I told Pirandello that I had set the question aright in my book, and he was very grateful.

Another play on which his comments should be recorded is *As Well as Before, Better Than Before*. In my analysis of it I had failed to see the point in the denouement of the play. Fulvia, the heroine, frustrated in her motherhood, leaves for the second time the home of her husband, a famous surgeon, but a man of very low moral character. Her only alternative is to return to her lover Mauri, a quixotic dreamer who can offer her only an existence of passion and torment. But this second time she takes with her the child born to her after her return home, something she had not done the first time. What I had not perceived was the significance of her taking her new child with her. Pirandello explained: "Don't you see? The first time she deserted her husband, she left her daughter Livia with him who, not desiring to tell the truth of the situation, allowed Livia to grow in the belief that her mother was a saintly person who had died when she was born. Fulvia rebelled at the idea of having lived in the conventional and false concept of a saintly woman in the memory of her daughter. That was an imposture and had made a puppet out of the living Fulvia. The second time Fulvia left her husband, the latter will not have the chance to contaminate her child's mind and falsify her personality." As to Mauri, Pirandello said, "I actually met that man in a small town in Umbria. I transported him into my play as I studied him in real life."

He spoke at length of *Six Characters in Search of an Author*. He did so especially one afternoon after having had a long conversation the previous evening with Mr. David Selznick concerning the possibility of filming this play. Pirandello was highly excited. "I could not convey to him, no matter how hard I tried, my idea of the three planes," he kept saying. I read to him what I had written in my book, after having asked him whether I was correct in believing that the nucleus of the play was the clash between actual reality and reality in art. I translated for him: "The six characters oscillate with perfect balance between the artificial life of glorified marionettes and the moving, stirring existence of tragic human beings."

"Yes," interrupted Pirandello, "but it is more than that. I have portrayed their life on three planes that could be expressed in the cinema even better than on the legitimate stage."

I agreed, and I added that to me the three planes were that of the solid and angular reality of actual life, the one portrayed by the actors who take the roles of the six characters in re-enacting their tragedy, and finally that of imagination that bridges the former two, thus creating a new reality which is "life lived with passion, illumined by fancy, made immortal by true art."

Pirandello commented that this sort of three-dimensional art was the salient feature of that play, and expressed his disappointment that I had not read this to him before his meeting with Mr. Selznick. From his rather bitter reference to his conversation with Mr. Selznick it was evident that he had no desire to reopen his negotiations with the movie magnate.

Pirandello also commented on *The Life That I Gave You*, that had failed even in England, where his plays had usually been very well received. "They do not understand the fact that for that poor mother who lost her son the only reality was the image of him as a child that she held in her memory. After all, that was all that was left of him."

In reply to my question as to which he considered his best play, he showed his preference for *Henry IV*.

It may be of interest to record what he had to say about Italian literature in general and about criticism. When I asked him to give me accurately the dates of his plays, he was definitely impatient. "What does it matter?" he asked. I told him that one could thus trace better the development of his art. He retorted, "Dates do not count. An author should stand before the critic as a complete whole." He added that he would soon write an autobiography, the title of which would be *Of My Unasked-for Visit to This Planet*. He continued to speak animatedly and even volubly of his future plans, but I never got the dates of his plays.

He was very happy when I told him that I had presented him, in the introduction of my book, as the antithesis of D'Annunzio, and he added, "In the whole course of Italian literature, one constantly finds such contrasts: Dante and Petrarch, Ariosto and Tasso, Goldoni and Metastasio, Leopardi and Monti, and today myself and D'Annunzio." He had words of deep contempt for D'Annunzio.

Of contemporary writers in Italy who had significance for him he mentioned Alberto Moravia, author of *The Indifferent Ones*, and his own son, Stefano, who writes under the pen name of Stefano Landi in order not to exploit the fame of his father. He spoke with great admiration of the American authors Edgar Allan Poe and Mark Twain.

Of his personal life he said little. He appreciated greatly my defense of his relationship with the actress Marta Abba in a conversation with former ambassador to Italy Richard Washburn Child. It happened in 1927 at a luncheon at Buck Hill Falls, where I had lectured on modern Italy and had presented Pirandello as the embodiment of the new consciousness that had emerged from the tragedy of World War I. Mr. Child in his cynical humor warned me not to be so sure about the "new consciousness" as embodied in Pirandello, and added, "He is having a good time just now with a young and beautiful actress, Marta Abba."

Pirandello interrupted me, "Why didn't you tell him that Pirandello has never had a good time in his life?"

Those words still echo for me as an exemplification of the art and life of Luigi Pirandello. He then confided, "She is like a daughter to me. She is younger than my own children. She is twenty-seven years of age and I am an old man, nearly seventy." I told him that I had singled out the plays in which I had felt the presence of Marta Abba: *Their Wives' Friend, To Find One's Self, When One Is Somebody*. He confessed that he had written them thinking of her, and a smile shone in his brown eyes that were now soft and affectionate.

Before leaving New York he was gracious enough to send me the following foreword for my book, which I give in the English translation:

Dear Vittorini:
The world of international literary criticism has been crowded for a long time with numerous Pirandellos—lame, deformed, all

head and no heart, erratic, gruff, insane, and obscure—in whom, no matter how hard I try, I cannot recognize myself, not even in the slightest degree. (The most senseless of these phantoms I believe to be the one fashioned by Benedetto Croce.) You, too, have now decided to present your own Pirandello, not for the pleasure of maiming me and then exposing me as I limp along; not for the pleasure of showing me masked with the head of an elephant and my heart atrophied by that infernal pump which is the machine of logic, lost in the clouds or wandering in the murky bowels of the earth. Indeed you have done just the opposite of this, and, as is natural and as you can well imagine, I am very grateful to you, dear Vittorini. I am very grateful because, among so many who think they know so well what I am, I, who have no conception of what I am and have always refrained from trying to find out, for fear of offending all the life which continually seethes within me, find in you one who makes me walk upright on my own legs and grants me as much heart as I need to love and pity this poor humanity of ours, both when it is rational and when it is irrational; one who tries to explain that if so many believe me erratic, it is because I move in my own way and not as others would like me to; gruff because I grow indignant with their affectations; incomprehensible because they do not yet know how to see, to think, to feel as I do.

At any rate, dear Vittorini, lame, deformed, all head and no heart, erratic, gruff, insane, and obscure, I exist, and I shall continue to exist, while they will not. It is true that this is not a matter of great importance for me. A man, I have tried to tell something to other men, without any ambition, except perhaps that of avenging myself for having been born. And yet life, in spite of all that it has made me suffer, is so beautiful! (And here is another positive statement without even a shadow of logic, and yet so true and deeply felt). Well, I thank you cordially, dear Vittorini, for the mirror, that with this book you place before me, in which I can behold myself with so much gratification.

LUIGI PIRANDELLO

I never realized more clearly than in those conversations the close relation that exists between Pirandello the man and

Pirandello the artist. I felt it again when I read with grief in our newspapers that on December 10, 1936, Pirandello was taken to his resting place in a coffin of plain wood, in accordance with his request that he be buried without any pomp and ceremony whatsoever.

Pirandello and the Concept of Reality

THIS short chapter is primarily concerned with the meaning that such terms as *real*, *reality*, and *realism* assumed in the mind and art of Luigi Pirandello.

The meaning of these terms has varied throughout the ages. One of the first to focus his attention on the relationship between life and art was Aristotle, one of the great men of antiquity. In his famous booklet, *Poetics*, he defined poetry as "mimesis or imitation of nature." By nature, however, he meant the immutable and eternal pattern that underlies the phenomenical world. He followed the Platonically conceptual point of view that had blossomed in the perfect creations of the classical era, represented by Homer, Phidias, and Sophocles. Not much was added to this investigation during the centuries of the Renaissance, when the term *verisimilitude*, as applied to art, reflected the same attitude as that of the author of the *Poetics*.

Pirandello, as a teacher of Italian literature in the Istituto Femminile di Magistero, a sort of teachers' college in Rome, was very much interested in aesthetics and reacted against the Renaissance sense of realism as well as that of the naturalism of the late nineteenth century. He pronounced himself, with unmistakable clarity, against both the Humanistic trend in the Italian literature of the Renaissance and against the narrow sense that the naturalists of the late nineteenth century gave to the term *realism*.

Luigi Pirandello was born in Sicily in 1867 and died in Rome in 1936. He was awarded the Nobel prize in literature in 1934, a clear recognition of the universal appeal and significance of his art. Pirandello lived his not-too-happy life astride the last century and our own, bridging two very distinct ages, that of the objective naturalism of the late nineteenth century and that of the imaginative or subjective naturalism of our own. His early literary work, short stories and novels, bore marked traits of the objective naturalism of the last century. His later works, mostly in the field of drama, were and still are an outstanding exemplification of the literature of our epoch.

Pirandello's major and significant plays can be best understood if viewed as the projection of a theory of art that has distinguished modern aesthetics from those of the ancients and from those of the late nineteenth century. He has contributed to both the modern concept of art and its reflection in works in which we men of today can recognize ourselves in ideas, feelings, and passions.

Pirandello was so deeply concerned with the creative character of art as to believe that the influence of classical antiquity on the Romance literatures had been very obnoxious. In 1906 he wrote a critical study that serves as a preface or introduction to a novel by an Italian humorist, Alfredo Cantoni (1841–1904), whom Pirandello admired very much. Regretting the vast role that rhetoric had played in Italian literature, he stated: "The harm that it [rhetoric] has caused in every age, not only to our literature but also to Latin literature and, hence, in varying degrees, to all Romance literatures, is incalculable." The pages that follow this statement insist on the necessity of originality in art. Condemning imitation, he stated: "In imitating a preceding model, one denies his own identity and remains of necessity behind his pattern. The best is to affirm one's own sentiment, one's own life." He believed that each work of art has in itself its own laws and rules. There are no "eternal principles" in literature. The task of criticism consists in "discovering the principle that determined and gave a personal character to the specific work of art." And again: "The work of fancy is a work of nature, an organic and living whole.... A work of art is nature itself that makes use of the instrument of human fancy in order to create a work of a higher order, more perfect because elements that are too common, obvious, and fleeting have been pruned away. A work of art lives by its own essential ideality."

As to the attitude of Pirandello toward the aesthetics of the naturalists, to hear himself classified as a naturalist was enough to cause him to explode with typical Italian vehemence. His art, he believed, was a complete departure from the aesthetics of the naturalistic school as exemplified by his personal friends and predecessors, Giovanni Verga and Luigi Capuana. He was wont to quote from Verga who, upon reading his novel *L'Esclusa* (The Outcast), had written to him that with his novels a new light was shining in contemporary fiction.

Pirandello, in his aesthetic views, resumed contact with Gian Battista Vico (1688–1744), who ushered in the romantic age with a fundamental distinction between the role of logic and fancy in art, a distinction that is still the cornerstone of modern aesthetics. Vico proclaimed in his *New Science* (1725) that art is the product of fancy and, if so, by inference, art is not conditioned by actual life. A character is not *real* simply because it is modeled on a man actually existing, actually known and studied in the world close at hand. If art is the product of fancy, Pirandello felt, a complete definition of aesthetics should embrace not only the use of Greek myths (classicism), not only historical material (romanticism), not only material observed in the society and environment in which the artist lives (naturalism), but also whatever dreams and enchanted or awesome places the artist evokes from his imagination (contemporary art). *Reality* resides not in the material used, but in the life that the magic power of imagination can awaken in it.

In many of Pirandello's plays, *Six Characters in Search of an Author, Henry IV, Tonight We Improvise, When One Is Somebody, To Find Oneself,* and others, one reads beautiful pages dedicated to his art concept. I quote at random a passage from *Six Characters* that echoes the very words of the essay on Cantoni: "Nature uses the instrument of human fancy to continue, even in a higher form, its creative work." Art rests on a higher plane than actual life. It is capable of giving to the creative artist a completeness of existence that actual life does not give him. The vision and realization of this more complete and different form of life constitute *realism*.

Realism is an aesthetic category and not the material that some artists have used. An artist can reach realism either by using ideal patterns or actual ones. He is completely free in his choice that is dictated only by his own temperament, mood, and experience.

The clash between Benedetto Croce and Luigi Pirandello that started with the publication in 1902 of the *Aesthetics* of the Neapolitan philosopher ultimately rested on the fact that Croce, through his definition of art as expression of a subjective intuition of reality, still clung to *objective reality* as the model or pattern of art. Pirandello felt that *imaginative reality* is as real as the tangible, solid, and angular reality of the world close at hand. Hence, the insults and recriminations that each heaped upon the other until the very end of their lives.

The new meaning of reality in art is more than a theory in the late Pirandello. It served as the fertile seed from which developed the new drama that our age has admired with almost universal consent.

Pirandello was a very patient and stubborn worker. He worked very slowly, and his plays clearly show the moment when he departed from the naturalism of his youth, as exemplified in his short stories, "The Old and the Young," and even in "Mattia Pascal," in order to rise toward a type of realistic drama, the glory of which is a more searching and subjective study of man and life. His essay on humor, written in 1908, can only serve as a basis for his fiction and for the section of his drama formed by plays that were the dramatization of previously written short stories. An attentive study of the two sections would show how close Pirandello was, in inspiration and technique, to the tenets of naturalism, and how different and new are such plays as *Henry IV* and *Six Characters*. Naturalism, with its precepts of closeness to actual life, hindered and fettered Pirandello in realizing an ideal of art that had loomed even in the days when he wrote his *Umorismo*. How is it possible to correlate the events in Pirandello's early fiction and old plays with statements such as the following that is found in his just-mentioned critical work? Here we read: "Life is a conscious and fluid entity that we try to stop, to fix in unchanging and definite forms, inside and outside of us, because we all are fixed forms, forms which move along others equally fixed." We are, he continues, the result of concepts reached through an infernal machine called logic, which pumps our sentiments from our hearts up to our brains and reduces them to lifeless abstractions. Only now and then, in rare moments of inner illumination, do we resume contact with real life, life as a cosmic flux that suffers in being enclosed in its human molds: rocks, plants, animals, men. Then we experience a terrifying shock, as we see ourselves live suspended in the inner void created by the contrast between cosmic life and its earthly and human forms. Pirandello's fiction reflected in his puny and strange-looking characters the ludicrous embodiments of this ideal life concept. We must not wonder that this fiction was never popular. It was this intuition of life that was developed in the works written after World War I. He uncovered a new and deeper stream of creativeness only when he forsook the tenets of naturalism and entered the precincts of stately tragedy. Then he penned such works as *Henry IV*, *Six Characters*, *As You Desire Me*, *When One Is Somebody*.

A perusal of the preface to *Six Characters*, written in 1927, seven years after the play which had sent the name of the author all over Europe and South America, can serve as a document to illustrate the art concept that led to the new art. Here Pirandello differentiated between "historical" or descriptive authors and "philosophical" ones. He ranked himself as one of the latter type. Art had become for him the medium of expression of the unspeakable loneliness of his soul, as befitting a man who had lived for years in the company of a wife who was demented and in a period of history made up of wars, hatred, and destruction.

Such an intuition of art as Pirandello revealed in his new plays helps us to understand our contemporary art or, at least, that section of it that refuses to accept the principle that art must be molded on models found in actual life.

Pirandello's theoretical attitude, as exemplified in works that men will never forget, shows how limited is the current use of the term *realism*. If realism is associated with the idea of art as the closest approximation to actual models, then the significance of art rests on accuracy and not on creativeness. In a way such a restricted view of realism proclaims the uselessness of art in that it is unquestionably true that no reflected object is more similar to itself than the very object that the artist wishes to represent. Why waste time in reproducing imperfectly in art what exists perfectly in life?

Pirandello visited the United States in 1935 and spent three months in New York, at which time I had the opportunity to discuss his plays during several hours of intimate conversation with the kind maestro, for I had with me the page proofs of my book on his drama.

In our discussion it became clear that the term *reality*, as used in his works, was often confusing. Drawing on what I had learned from him more than from any other author, I suggested to him that in order to distinguish between *reality* in life and *reality* in art, one could use the term *actuality* for the former and *reality* for the latter. Art transforms the actual into the real. The actuality of life is outside the realm of art until the fancy of a poet gives to it the new life to which Pirandello constantly referred. The logic of life is different from that of art in the same way as that of primitive peoples and children is different from that of highly civilized beings. "Vico discovered this long ago," interjected Pirandello, looking very wistful.

One of the most unforgettable conversations that I was privileged to have with the maestro took place the day after he had had a very stormy session with Mr. Selznick, the Hollywood producer, about the possibility of filming *Six Characters in Search of an Author*. I found the maestro in a highly excited state. "I could not convey to him, no matter how hard I tried, my idea of the three planes," he kept saying. I read to him the chapter in my book that dealt with *Six Characters*, asking him whether or not I was correct in believing that the nucleus of the play lay in the clash between *actuality* and *reality* in art. I translated for him from my chapter on that play. "The six characters oscillate with perfect balance between the artificial life of glorified marionettes and the moving, stirring existence of tragic human beings."

"Yes," interrupted Pirandello, "but it is more than that. I have portrayed their life on three planes that could be expressed better in the cinema than on the legitimate stage." It was this intuition that he was unable to convey to Mr. Selznick, owing largely to the fact that Pirandello did not speak English and Mr. Selznick did not know any Italian. The conversation was heatedly carried on in French, with Pirandello's secretary as interpreter.

Our conversation resumed its usual pleasant character when we returned to the discussion of *Six Characters*, and I told him, much to his satisfaction and even joy, that, to me, the three planes were conveyed by his consideration of the characters as actual human beings in the snares of nature, by their resentment upon seeing themselves represented by professional actors when the stage director decides to use their tragic case as art material of an improvised play, and, finally, as they live now in Pirandello's play.

To understand fully Pirandello's art one must be aware of the efforts through which his characters are made to replace their actual existence by one created through illusion and fancy. The two planes are constantly and clearly visible in his best plays. To restrict ourselves to *Naked Masks*, a collection of his plays translated into English and now available in the Everyman's Library edition, one finds a great variety of situations, all characterized by this pitiful attempt to put on a mask that covers a scarred human countenance, seared by shame and contorted by suffering.

The nucleus of *Henry IV* is precisely this: an imaginative and hypersensitive gentleman who, while impersonating the famous emperor, Henry IV of Germany, falls from his horse and strikes his head. When he opens his eyes, he has lost the consciousness of his actual personality, as a man of today, and feels that he is the historical character of the eleventh century, who lives again in his mind the struggles against Pope Gregory VII, the other rulers of the time, and the intrigues of Peter Damian. A wealthy sister places him in a palace and surrounds him with counselors, guards, and pages who keep that illusion alive. One day he recovers consciousness of his actual identity. Never has human fancy so exploited the artistic possibilities of the clash of the two planes, the actual and the fantastic, and seldom have the two planes merged into a more tragic and heart-rending unity of artistic reality than in this play.

In *Naked* the contrast between the actual and the self-imposed illusion is projected into the attempt of Ersilia Drei to fabricate the tale of a little romance in a life that has never known the joy of love. When the iridescent bubble of the fiction that has become her whole life is destroyed, she commits suicide.

In *The Pleasure of Honesty* Baldovino, at the end of his resources, financially and intellectually, decides to become the husband of a young woman with social position and wealth who has had to hide the fact that she, unwed, is going to give birth to a child. Baldovino is fully conscious that he wears only the mask of a husband, and that he lives in the home of Agata as a phantom. Pirandello makes him take his role as a husband so seriously and with such telling effect that eventually the form of the husband in Baldovino becomes the reality of the husband of Agata Renni.

The nucleus of Pirandello's dramatic art lies precisely in the transformation of the *actual* into the *real*. It represents one of the most beautiful and perfect embodiments of realistic art, as the playwright understood realism. He was so successful in presenting this to his readers because existence and art in him became fused into one. Confronted by the angular and hard existence that was his because of his temperament, sensitivity, and the circumstances that surrounded his life, he took refuge in the reality of art, just as his characters took refuge in the reality of illusion. He lived the last years of his life believing that true art portrays life lived with passion, illumined by fancy, and solidified in the joy of creative art.

It was an unforgettable experience to have been privileged to know one of the greatest men of our time. In my personal life it has been an even greater gift to have been able to study his works in which he still lives, the only kind of survival in which he believed.

Benedetto Croce and Criticism

Apropos of his book, *Poesia popolare e poesia d'arte*

THERE are attitudes in the mind of an author which, because they are determined by a violent reaction against some aspects and trends of the historical moment in which he lives, are most visible in his physiognomy as a thinker or an artist, without, however, representing, of necessity, the central part and very marrow of his thought. A monstrous nose attracts our attention much more than a normal nose, but it remains, nevertheless, a calamity for anyone who has to spend his life with it. People will notice it, even if the other features of a man's face are normal or even beautiful.

Francesco De Sanctis and his follower Benedetto Croce reacted most violently against the philosophy and aesthetics of the last decade of the nineteenth century. They resented, above all, the way of gaging art in the light of patriotism, just as men of other generations had assigned to art a moral aim. Croce attacked very vigorously the followers of the historical school that to him reduced the historical process and criticism to a mechanical process, inconsistent with the mobility and creativity of the human mind. In the same manner that Francesco De Sanctis fought both the abstract conceptualism and utilitarianism of his contemporaries in the name of his exalted yet human sense of reality, Croce took issue with the historical school through his concept of pure art. Art was to him the expression of a subjective intuition of the actual world and man's experience in it, without any preoccupation of ethics, practicality, or religion. He believed to such an extent in pure art that he never admitted that religion, as an instance, could have stirred very deeply the heart of a specific author.

A shortsighted critic could find numerous passages in the two men with which to confirm such conclusions; yet the greatness of the two masters does not rest on such extreme attitudes. Those who wish to find with clarity and thoroughness the significance and originality of De Sanctis's and Croce's doctrines must seek other aspects of their aesthetic conclusions. Who could accept today the value of "irrationality" given by De Sanctis to the term "ideal," when one realizes how deep, lofty, and virile was the ethical sense of this man? Who can today accept Croce's view of "pure art," as separate and distinct from any other human activity, when it is so evident in his philosophical system, whether called "philosophy of the spirit" (*Filosofia dello spirito*) or "absolute historicism" (*Storicismo assoluto*), that the great thinker constantly sought to integrate pragmatic and ethical life? His great merit lies in having conceived life as a magic circle within which each thinking man constantly strives to realize a sense of unity in all his actions and tendencies. What he calls "expression" (*espressione*) is a felicitous term to refer to a totality of human existence constantly tending to harmonize nature and mind, instinct and thought, or "spirit," the term he prefers to use.

To have called Croce's philosophy "idealistic" has been a grave error, and, for this reason, in the maturity of his intellectual life, he changed the term into "absolute historicism." That which is "real" in life is that which has become "real" in history. There are in life boundless streams that flow on and on without being recognized and studied by thinking men, and these do not belong to history. They possess only the physical existence of "facts," without having acquired historical significance. They are neither history nor real life. Such terms as "activism" and "real action" express much better the intimate and basic force and the virile profile of Croce's philosophy. They illumine the role that Croce assigns to the spiritual forces that originate progress, and represent the sum total of what man has added to the primitive and initial energies of nature throughout the centuries of his history.

Benedetto Croce's book, *Poesia popolare e poesia d'arte*, published in 1933, is the clearest proof of the deeply ethical and universal character of Croce's aesthetics. This work redeems its author, not so much from the accusations of his enemies, as from those of his admirers who look upon him as a "pure man of letters" and a "pure aesthete." These admirers have made of Croce the defender of pure expression, the enemy of culture, in that he constantly attacks "rhetoric" in the Italian literary tradition. No greater offense could be addressed to Benedetto Croce, a man saturated with culture, who has constantly searched in Italian archives and has so largely contributed to the vast reservoir of Italian cultural life. What Croce constantly resisted was the confusion between culture and art, cultural elements used to becloud the clear profile of a work of art.

His book on popular and courtly poetry contains a clear and strong declaration of his tenets. Here are the author's words: "La linea del mio pensiero è stata costantemente quelle di accogliere i motivi romantici dell' antintellettualismo e della passionalità; ma soltanto per serbare e per restituire al classico la sua linfa e la sua forza vitale, impedendogli di pervertirsi nel classicistico ed accademico, e non certo per mortificare la poesia condannandola a una sorta di povertà mentale o addirittura d'infantilismo" (p. XI) (My attitude has constantly been that of accepting the romantic aspects of spontaneity and passion, but only in order to preserve or to restore to classicism its living force, preventing it, thus, from deteriorating into pseudo-classicism and academism. Nothing could have been more remote from my mind than to mortify poetry by condemning it to a kind of intellectual poverty or to downright infantilism). He could not have been more explicit in drawing a line between classicism and pseudo-classicism. He accepted the subjective aspects of spontaneity in art, in the same way as the immortal classical authors had done, in order to prevent the clear-cut contour of true classicism from being contaminated by pseudo-classicism, whether baroque, Arcadian, or rococo. Croce has kept his faith in true classicism in every respect in his mental processes and activities. He has constantly rejected the empty praise of having destroyed literary genres in literature, by way of an example, and of the categories in which older students of aesthetics delighted. In reality, he never denied the validity of literary genres. How could a man so conversant with history do so? What he did was to make a clear distinction between the historical and the aesthetic fields. Literary genres are significant as historical facts, but on the aesthetic plane they have no validity. In this manner he went beyond the conclusions of the critics of his youth who belonged to the erudite school, and he focused his attention on the human reactions of the artist which stir and live in his work.

This book proves more clearly than his other works that Croce never sought popularity through brilliant paradoxes. He does not hesitate to use the traditional tenet that poetry aims at reaching the universal (p. 3), but, while using this criterion, he has revealed to us better than any other critic the basic traits of such enigmatic ages as the fourteenth, fifteenth, and sixteenth centuries. It suffices to read the essays on the *Fioretti*, Petrarch, Sacchetti, on Passavanti's legends, the comedies of Aretino and Lasca, to realize what a practical use he has succeeded in making of generic and traditional definitions, revealing through them the human qualities and beauty that enrich these works.

Likewise, Croce has not hesitated to accept the division between popular and courtly literature, even with the danger of seeming to deny the value of popular poetry. What he has achieved, however, is to reach the basic characteristics that clearly divide these two modes of poetic expression. He has stressed the difference of "tone" that distinguishes the two facets of poetry, the spontaneous and elementary quality of popular poetry and the complex and more conscious quality of courtly poetry. In this discussion Croce has inserted an essay on the development of Italian literature (pp. 46–49), which deserves to be placed side by side with the famous one that students owe Giosue Carducci.

This volume on poetry of the fourteenth, fifteenth, and sixteenth centuries illumines a large zone of that vast canvas of Italian literature on which Croce has laboriously worked in his long and fruitful career as a critic, and which embraces the development of Italian letters from Dante to the early decades of our century.

This great master of criticism has given particular attention to the cultural currents that form the background of Italian literature. He has tried to seek the living elements of such movements as Petrarchism, Humanism, Platonism, and even in the theory of imitation (pp. 339–54). In view of the defenses of such imitative tendencies it is hard to understand why he denies the poetic quality of religious experience in the poetry of Dante and of Petrarch. He is unable to follow Petrarch when he tells us that Laura led him to God. Croce goes so far as to doubt the sincerity of Petrarch (p. 68), while he can see the reality of the relation between Girolamo Muzio and the public woman Tullia d'Aragona (p. 348). On this point the reader is forced to admit that Croce, while accepting the validity of rhetoric, rejects that of religious experience, and shows greater sympathy toward the sixteenth-century Platonism of the followers of Petrarch than toward that of Petrarch himself. Croce answered this criticism in a personal letter to me by stating that religious ideas tend toward didacticism. This statement, however, does not destroy the necessity of investigating and concluding whether religious sentiment actually became a pedagogical treatise in Petrarch or flowered into beautiful poetry. If, as Croce constantly reminds us, poetry germinates in the heart of man, if it is the very flower of his humanity, why coldly separate this humanity into its composing elements and consider it above or below its aesthetic possibilities? If man is a mysterious result of instinct and intellect, of sensations and emotions, most assuredly religious feelings can claim the right of artistic representation as well as the domain of the senses. It all depends on the man who experiences the religious experience, on the depth of his soul, on his sensitivity, and the resonance that his experience acquired in him when he brought it within the circle of his art. True realism embraces the whole of man, man in his various and even contradictory attributes. As such, realism accepts the realm of the senses as well as that of the spirit. The pivotal center rests on the definition of the spirit.

Every thinker has given to it a different value, but every poet has done the same, too. The best critical method suggests that we look at the human reactions of the poet from his own standpoint. If we refuse to believe what Petrarch tells us of himself, how can we claim that our readers will believe what we, as critics, tell of him and his experiences, religious or sensuous, whatever they may be?

It is not with disrespect that it is here stated that Croce was extreme and unjust in his hostility toward religion. In this he shared an attitude no longer found today, but very common in the second half of the nineteenth century. It was engendered by the resistance that the Church offered to the dream of the liberal patriots who wanted Rome to be the capital of a unified Italy. Croce's politically inspired attitude of hostility led him astray every time he tread on the religious terrain. However, this should not obscure the debt of gratitude that our generation owes to the man who has so largely contributed to the theory and practice of sane criticism.

Benedetto Croce and Luigi Pirandello

BENEDETTO CROCE and Luigi Pirandello were the most significant men who reflected luster on Italian intellectual life from 1900 to the day when death claimed them. Pirandello died in 1936; Croce in 1952.

We propose to discuss the enmity that existed between them, an enmity in which we were, in a small and indirect way, involved. Ours is not an easy task, nor is it a pleasant one. Disagreements and clashes, even literary ones, are always unsavory and distasteful. It is very sad, indeed, to think of the long feud that embittered the two men and to realize its futility now that both have disappeared behind the heavy curtain that fringes human existence. We dwell upon it only because our personal contacts with both Benedetto Croce and Luigi Pirandello enable us to gage their temperaments and their attitudes in an intimate way not granted to many. Having had the privilege of corresponding with Benedetto Croce for many years, we are able to publish direct statements taken from letters written by Croce about Pirandello. We also clearly recollect conversations held with Luigi Pirandello when he visited the United States in 1935, in the hope of having his play *Six Characters in Search of an Author* filmed in Hollywood.

The first letter addressed by Benedetto Croce to us bears the date of 1937 and came from Naples. In it the philosopher thanked us for what we had written and published on his book *Poesia popolare e poesia d'arte* (Popular and Courtly Poetry). He tarried especially and gratefully over our attempt to defend him against those who overstressed the subjective element in his aesthetics and attributed to him anti-traditional and anti-historical attitudes. Croce, agreeing wholeheartedly with what we had written, added: "What you write in your letter is correct. How could I be anti-historical, I who am spending a large part of my life in the study of history and in historical research? The historical school was not historical, but positivistic and anti-realistic, and showed its incapacity in writing the history of civilization from an ethical and political point of view. Nor were its followers capable of understanding philosophy and art. I have reacted and am still reacting against that pseudo-historical school, entirely deprived of constructive criteria. After all, in my book bearing the title of *Poesia* (Poetry) I have explained this point with a clarity that, as far as I am concerned, could not be greater. If I am not understood, I accept the situation, repeating the saying: 'Qui vult capere capeat.' " It is useless to add any comment to this precious document that allows us to see very clearly and deeply into the illumined traditionalism of Croce, the last great and true Italian humanist.

Croce was very kind to us from the date of this letter until his recent death. In two letters which we hope to publish on another occasion the maestro revealed with frankness and indignation his feelings about the character and political conduct of Arturo Farinelli, a fascist, and Giuseppe Antonio Borgese, who had recently published his anti-fascist *Goliath*. Croce did so with that irony engendered by moral indignation that, in him, more than goading or cutting, actually annihilated those against whom it was directed.

The hostility that existed between him and Pirandello is too well known to require tracing its history. We followed its vicissitudes with deep regret, a feeling that is even heightened in this moment as, in order to study their clash, we review this sad episode in the life of the two men.

The hostility began with bitter remarks on the part of Pirandello immediately upon the publication by Croce of his *Estetica* (Aesthetics) in 1902. Acrimonious comments were continued in *Umorismo* (Humor), that appeared in 1908. Croce censured the book in *Critica* in 1909, and later censured Pirandello's dramatic activity while the latter's fame was gaining ground in both Italy and abroad.

284 HIGH POINTS IN THE HISTORY OF ITALIAN LITERATURE

One of the central points of dissension was their concept of humor. In reality, it was a trifle, one of those trifles that are hardly mentioned when the two disputants are on friendly terms. At the most, in such cases of divergent points of view, one might say: "I clearly see what you mean, although I don't quite follow you," and all ends there. But when friendly feelings or a benevolent attitude are absent, the most insignificant detail can become a serious cause for attack.

As to Pirandello's theory of humor, as expressed in his book *Umorismo,* Croce denied that humor can be considered a special category of literature. He looked upon it as upon any other art content in order to focus his attention, as a philosopher does, on the intimate nature of art. Pirandello, on the contrary, saw in humor a special form of art. He stated with feverish enthusiasm and faith that humor, in that it is engendered by the contrast between life as an ideal form and life as an actual realization, is based on the clash of two opposite sentiments. While thought in general composes and harmonizes contrasting elements, humor breaks the situations considered into their composing parts. Humor lives on contrasts and contradictions. To be sincere, what artist has ever admitted that his own art can be reduced to art in general? And how could Luigi Pirandello agree with such a conclusion when, in the solitude of his existence, he was gradually and passionately elaborating the ideal of an art based on the belief that every human life and every individual are "constructions," destined to suffer precisely because each person builds himself up in the presence of a deeper self from which he is excluded? Life as a primeval entity, Pirandello believed, is fluid and uniform. Yet, as such, it cannot exist in the actual world, and when it takes form in man, plant, or animal, it cannot forget its divine origin, but must exist in a state of torment and strife with itself as well as with its environment in terms of society or its fellow men. Man is in a constant state of rebellion even against the fact that he is whatever he is, his actual form as an individual, without mentioning the contrasts that he experiences in his contacts with other men and groups among which he lives. To an objective philosopher such a conclusion borders on insanity. But this philosophy of contrasts and clashes was true and real to Pirandello, even to the point where he claimed that man adds to the basic "construction" other "constructions" through his prejudices and false concepts of himself and others. This was the creed that he, desperately lonely, all closed within himself, tenacious and stubborn like many of his characters, molded for himself, and through which he wished to transform the naturalism of Verga and Capuana into a new art mode, infinitely more tormented and complex.

Basically, Croce looked at humor from a philosophical point of view, while Pirandello considered it purely as an artist. He had already reached this conclusion as he penned the *Esclusa* (The Outcast, 1901) and *Il fu Mattia Pascal* (The Late Mattia Pascal, 1904). It is not to be marveled at that they could not understand each other.

In fact, Benedetto Croce, looking at art from the height of his philosophical investigation, concluded that Pirandello's art constituted nothing more than a continuation and conclusion of the Sicilian *verismo*, such as is exemplified in Giovanni Verga and Luigi Capuana. This was a bitter morsel for Pirandello to swallow. One can easily imagine his wrath! He even vented his fury on us when, in one of our many interviews with him at the Waldorf-Astoria in New York in 1935, we read to the maestro the first chapter of our book *The Drama of Luigi Pirandello*, which was then in the process of being printed. The chapter unhappily happened to bear the title "In the Wake of *Verismo*." We have yet to see anyone angrier than Pirandello when we translated the English title into Italian for his benefit. His eyes flashed with indignation, and a veritable torrent of words poured from his mouth. He protested most vigorously that he had in his possession a letter from Verga, received when *The Outcast* had appeared, in which his beloved friend stated that with that novel a new light had shone in the annals of Italian literature. It took all the powers of persuasion at our disposal to put the maestro in a state of mind that would allow him to hear what we had written concerning his connections with *verismo*. Overcoming our confusion, we read to him that *verismo* had been only the starting point of his narrative art from which he had risen toward a psychological complexity that distinguished it from any other form of modern narrative and dramatic literature.

To be perfectly truthful and sincere, the art of Luigi Pirandello cannot be reduced to Sicilian *verismo*, as Croce wanted. Indeed, every time Pirandello returned to the canons and forms of *verismo* his art greatly suffered, for then the rudimentary quality of his characters was ill suited to the intellectual character of his short stories, novels, and plays. We told this to the maestro in the hope that he would give us the opportunity to read to him what we had written in our book. It was a hard struggle indeed to quiet down the fiery Sicilian. We finally succeeded in persuading him of the fairness of our presentation when we begged him to observe some of his plays that he had recast in dramatic form from short stories written in his youth. The typical example was *Il berretto a sonagli* (Cap and Bells) in which Ciampa, a modest bookkeeper, is assigned the task of enunciating philosophical propositions worthy of Hegel. Typical is his utterance that "the spirit enters into us and it becomes dwarfed." The maestro agreed somewhat reluctantly and resumed his cordial attitude when we added that this was no longer true in his immortal plays, *Sei personaggi in cerca d' autore* (Six Characters in Search of an Author), *Enrico Quarto* (Henry IV), and *Quando si è qualcuno* (When One Is Somebody), the plays in which the maestro revealed his tragic sentiment of life in complex and deep personalities, worthy of ranking with the great creations of all time. Even illustrious authors are very human when their vanity is at stake.

It is interesting at this point to read what Croce has to say in revealing his feelings about Pirandello. In 1938 he wrote us from Pollone (Biella), his summer place in the Italian Alps, and he referred to the injurious words that, much to our regret, appeared in the preface of our book, *The Drama of Luigi Pirandello*, penned by the playwright himself. Pirandello expressed in them his resentment against the negative opinion of his art repeatedly expressed by Croce. Here are the textual words of Croce: "That word of Pirandello was one of the many that he had usually uttered about me and which showed me the man he was, a man incapable of thinking problems through and reasoning in terms of logic. He always pretended to criticize my concepts that he was not in a position to understand. I did nothing more than to quote his words in *Critica*, and, since they were confusedly conceived, I interpreted them as not applying to me but to him. I thought that this was the best way to treat the silly incident, and I did not give it another thought."

To be just, we must confess that Pirandello had unequivocally expressed his thought in his preface to our book. We quote: "Among the many Pirandellos that for a long time have been wandering in the world of international criticism, lame, deformed, all head and without heart, strange, unkind, lunatic, and obscure, in whom, I, no matter how hard I try, don't succeed in recognizing myself, not even to the smallest degree (the most idiotic of all I believe to be that of Benedetto Croce), you, too, have wanted to add your own, not for the pleasure of ruining me, and then showing me as I limp along, not for the pleasure of showing me with a mask representing the head of an elephant and with my heart atrophied through the pump that is the infernal machine of logic, showing me groping among clouds or lost in dark grottoes. Your intentions have been quite different from these and for this, as is natural and as you can readily understand, I am very grateful to you, dear Vittorini." The blow, whether rightly or wrongly, was directed toward Croce, but the latter, in a human way, tried to divert it from himself without directing it toward his adversary, and this does honor to him. He merely stated that he had not qualified his contemporary Pirandello as an imbecile.

In another letter of October 10 of the same year Croce discussed with us the criticism that we had respectfully addressed to him concerning his attitude toward the religious content of Petrarch's poetry. We believed, and still believe, that religious sentiment, like any other art content, has artistic possibilities, and that it is up to a writer whether such a sentiment rises toward a lyrical height or becomes coldly and deadly pedagogical. It seemed to us that in this Croce was still close to the aesthetic position of Aristotle, in the sense that he, like Aristotle, still placed poetic quality in the content of literature. The Greek thinker certainly followed this principle when he declared epic higher than tragedy and comedy inferior to tragedy. Aristotle, in the dawn of aesthetics, had not reached the conclusion that the true source of epic grandeur lay in Homer and not in the subject matter that he developed in his *Iliad*. Croce, too, seemed to follow Aristotle when he extolled wholesome sensuality in Boccaccio and rejected the poetic quality of Petrarch's religious experience. We wrote this to the great philosopher in a letter in which we thanked him for having sent us an extract of the *Critica* in which he discussed the poetry of Boccaccio and Petrarch. To this effect he answered our objection thus: "As to the relationship of poetry and religion, my thesis is that religion, in becoming poetry, becomes an aspect and state of mind of our humanity, but in its quality and actuality of religion, shares the nature of our will and intellect, and is, therefore, deeply differentiated from poetic form. On this very point I have insisted with many proofs and examples, and quite recently in an essay, still unpublished, on the famous hymn, the *Dies Irae*." This is unquestionably true. But, we retorted, this is also true of sensuality and of every other human act and state of mind. As a part of Boccaccio's existence, sensuality was not art. It was an "actuality" that awaited the magic touch of fancy in order to be raised to the level of an artistic "reality." It is the artist who transforms the actual into the real. We learned this from Croce himself, who refers to this transformation by the term of "pure poetry."

After the reference to his essay on the *Dies Irae*, Croce, in his letter, referred again to Pirandello. Becoming even more abusive, he added: "Even in the case of Pirandello, I don't deny at all that we should look on him only as a poet, as pure fancy, and not at all from the logic of a philosopher. But I say that he has exhibited his despair and agitation without going beyond them in his fancy, without transforming them into poetry. For this reason I believe that Pirandello's work will not remain, except in a few fragments. Unhappily, he prided himself on being strong in logic, a philosopher, and I must confess that rarely have I found a man as unfit as he on this score: his books on aesthetics are a clear proof of this. When I compared him to my child (she is my youngest daughter), who could not understand why Latin, a dead language, should advance a claim to existence, the comparison was perfect. Only my daughter, by being disturbed and in despair, did not pretend to write a play." Pirandello was both childish and illogical for Croce, the philosopher.

There is a great deal of tenderness in Croce's reference to his daughter, as if he had felt the need of getting rid of the unpleasant feeling superinduced by the thought of his literary enemy. In the same letter, after his signature, in the manner of a postscriptum, Croce added these words: "I rejected the groundless insult directed against me by Pirandello in your book by interpreting his words as the accusation of having called him an imbecile. I naturally protested against it. And I was glad to have turned the matter into a joke, for not long afterward Pirandello died, and I did not have the unpleasant remembrance of a dispute with him on the eve of his death."

At this point it is dutiful and logical to ask ourselves whether there was a true and logical reason for the bitter animosity that existed between the two great men who have represented our age at its best in the field of aesthetics and dramatic art. Was there an essential difference in their concept of art or was their hostility due to diversity in temperament? Caught as we were in the hostility of the two men, allow us modestly to suggest that all the bitter feelings that existed between Croce and Pirandello were due to the fact that they did not realize that the world of the philosopher is not, and cannot possibly be, that of the poet. They had (or did not have) the right to accuse each other of showing (or not showing) the same attitude, in terms of the point of view from which each looked at the other. How could Croce, a philosopher, accept what he calls "the despair and agitation" of

Pirandello, that is, the agony that the latter revealed in his plays when he described the plight of his characters and which were, directly or indirectly, his own misfortune? How could his art have existed without that torment and despair and agitation? A poet struggles and feels tormented, precisely because he cannot understand his torment. A philosopher tries to understand it, and, having understood it, finds rest in his philosophical explanations. If the two contenders had come out of their passionate egocentricity, they would have realized that Croce needed his Olympian calm because he was a philosopher, and Pirandello could not have created his characters without the impossibility of comprehending the situations in which their creator placed them.

Croce accused Pirandello of not being logical. But the author of *Henry IV* and of *Six Characters in Search of an Author* confessed that he hated logic. In his *Humor* there is a most beautiful page dedicated to logic in which Pirandello compares logic to an infernal machine that sucks sentiments from life and reduces them to sterile concepts. Logic and concepts were indispensable instruments for Croce. For Pirandello they were the sworn enemy of his art. Even in the preface of our book he refers to logic as "the suction pump, which is the infernal machine of logic." Artists have followed, and follow, a logic of their own, in terms of the specific mood that dictates the work that they are engaged in writing. It is the *logica utens* and not the *logica docens,* to use the expression created by Peter of Aban around 1300, when he defended his logic as a philosopher against the theologians of his time. The logic of Pirandello was the logic that he, as an artist, needed, a logic inherent to his works in which he presented the weird situations in which he saw himself caught. Had Croce accepted this fact, he would not have called Pirandello deprived of logic. The logic of Pirandello does not aim at reducing life to a system, the great goal of the philosophers of all time. He sought contradictions, just as Croce spurned them. It is useless to add that Pirandello, too, was unjust toward Croce by forgetting that Croce was on theoretical ground.

Before dying, Croce expressed with simple words his attitude, strong and serene, before the inescapable tragedy of every life. He entrusted to these words his creed of faith and action as a philosopher and a teacher. How could Pirandello, an artist, have assumed such a serene attitude before this tragic human fate that has always engendered in man a feeling of dismay, not only physical, but intellectual? There are not many who, like Francis of Assisi, have reached the height of being able to praise the Lord even for having created death. In art, it would be even monotonous to repeat his heroism, since he expressed it in his *Hymn* in which he voiced his admiration for the wonders of creation. For this reason, too, death could not have for Pirandello the same meaning as for Croce, at least in his writings.

In another letter of 1938, Croce, referring through a classical image to the political maneuvers of G. A. Borgese, whom he did not admire, concluded with these words: "This [the political action of G. A. Borgese] is not a position conducive to meditate over life, to penetrate into it, and engage in useful deeds." There is the whole of Croce in these words, but the "action" that he sought and accomplished was not of the same nature as that sought and realized by Luigi Pirandello, a very great dramatist of our epoch.

The two men were most different, not only as thinkers but as individuals. Croce was a serene and strong figure. Pirandello felt constantly alone and not understood, a very introspective and tormented man. Although Croce and Pirandello were children of the same generation, and happened to entertain a philosophy of art not very different, they reacted very differently to the historical circumstances that touched them. They remain the same only in this, in the fact that they are the two Italian men of letters through whom our generation will be remembered in the days to come.

Notes

DANTE'S CONTRIBUTION TO AESTHETICS

1. "Il procedimento d'interpretazione [during the Middle Ages] si fissò nei quattro significati: letterale, allegorico, morale e anagogico, che Dante doveva poi trasportare alla poesia volgare." [The method of interpretation during the Middle Ages was focused on the four meanings: literal, allegorical, moral, and anagogical, that Dante later transported to poetry in the vernacular.] *Estetica*, fifth edition, Bari, Laterza, 1922, p. 193.

2. *History of Criticism*, Edinburgh, Blackwood, 1900.

3. *Ibid.*, p. 431.

4. *Ibid.*, p. 436.

5. *Ibid.*, p. 5.

6. *Ibid.*, p. 437.

7. *Ibid.*, p. 445.

8. A. Schiaffini, *Tradizione e poesia*, Genova, Orfini, 1934.

9. In *Essays and Studies by Members of the English Association*, Vol. III, collected by W. P. Keer, Oxford, 1912.

10. *Dante and the Grand Style*, p. 133.

11. *Ibid.*, p. 115.

12. "Gli esempi di superbia punita e il 'bello stile' di Dante" in *Poesia e storia nella Divina Commedia*, Napoli, Perrella, 1920, p. 251.

13. *Literary Criticism: Plato to Dryden*, New York, American Book Co., 1940, p. 200.

14. *Il Convivio* ridotto a miglior lezione e commentato da G. Busnelli, e G. Vandelli, con introduzione di Michele Barbi, Firenze, Le Monnier, 1934, II, I, 2.

15. Dante substantially repeats the exposition of the four senses by Garnier de Rochefort in the introduction to his *Distinctiones*. Quoted in *Convivio* (Busnelli-Vandelli), p. 96, note 4.

16. We do not agree with Michele Barbi, who does not believe that Dante attempted to clear himself in the *Convivio* of the accusation of immorality circulated by his political enemies. Dante states the reason for writing his *Convivio* thus: "Movemi timore d'infamia ...Temo la infamia di tanta passione avere seguita, quanta concepe chi legge le sopra nominate canzoni in me avere signoreggiata." I, II, 16. It seems logical to infer that among other charges his enemies had accused him of levity and immorality, especially for the episode of the *Donna Gentile* at the end of the *Vita Nuova*. In the *Convivio* he wishes to interpret allegorically the love songs of the *Canzoni* by stating that he was speaking of his love for philosophy and not of his love for

women. To a political accusation he gave a political explanation. Even more specifically, he refers to his exile and to the accusations of his political enemies in this passage: "Ah! piaciuto fosse al dispensatore de l'universo che la cagione de la mia scusa mai non fosse stata! Chè nè altri contra me avria fallato, nè io sofferto avria pena ingiustamente, pena, dico, d'essilio e di povertate." (*Convivio* I, III, 3). Barbi's discussion is in the Introduction to the *Convivio* edited by Busnelli and Vandelli (p. xxxix). Dante, while in exile and under threat of death should he fall into the hands of the Florentine Blacks, was on the defensive as is proven by his statement in the circle of the sinners of simony in which he declared that he did not break a baptismal font at the baptistry at San Giovanni out of irreverence, but only because a child was drowning in it. Comparing the fiery tombs of the sinners to the circular baptismal font, he wrote:

> L'un delli quali, ancor non è molti anni,
>   Rupp'io per un che dentro v'annegava:
> *E questo sia suggel ch'ogni uomo sganni.*

> One of which, not many years ago,
>   I broke on account of one who was drowning in it:
> And let these words be a seal that may undeceive every man.

The last line certainly expresses the attitude of a man protesting his innocence.

17. *Convivio*, II, I, 8.
18. *Ibid.*, II, I, 10.
19. *Ibid.*, II, I, 5.
20. *De Vulgari Eloquentia*, II, IV, 5.
21. *Ibid.*, II, II, 5.
22. *Purgatorio*, I, 7.
23. *Ibid.*, XXIV, 49–62.
24. Dante described Matelda thus:

> Una donna soletta, che si gìa
>   Cantando ed iscegliendo fior da fiore
>   Ond'era pinta tutta la sua via.

> A woman all alone, who walked slowly
>   While singing, and picking one flower from another
> With which all her path was painted.
>   *Purgatorio*, XXVIII, 40–42

and Chaucer: "in the garden at sunrise she walked up and down gathering the red and white flowers at will to make a delicate garland for her head; and she sang heavenly like an angel." *Complete Poetical Works of Geoffrey Chaucer*. New York, Macmillan, 1926, p. 18.

25. *De Vulgari Eloquentia*, II, II, 1.
26. *Inferno*, XXXII, 1–12.
27. Sì che dal fatto il dir non sia diverso, *Inferno*, XXXII, 12.
28. *Purgatorio*, IX, 70–72.
29. *Paradiso*, I, 127.

30. *Ibid.*, XIII, 78.
31. *Purgatorio*, XXXIII, 141.
32. *Ibid.*, X, 58–64.
33. *Ibid.*, XII, 67–68.
34. *Convivio*, II, I, 13; II, IV, 28.
35. *Inferno*, IV, 63; *Purgatorio*, VIII, 20.
36. *Purgatorio*, XV, 115–117.
37. Bonagiunta Urbiciani, in his "tenzone" with Guido Guinizelli, gives the latter the credit for having changed "la manera de la forma e de l'essere" of love lyrics. Monaci, *Crestomazia*, Città di Castello, Lapi, 1912, p. 303. A study of these "tenzoni" would be a useful field of investigation for further study of this problem. See also N. Zingarelli, *Dante*, Milano, Vallardi, 1931, p. 197. For the text of the "tenzoni" see *Sonetti Burleschi e Realistici dei Primi Due Secoli*, a cura di Aldo Francesco Massera. Two volumes. Bari, Laterza, 1920.
38. "E a vituperio di loro dico che non si deono chiamare literati, però che non acquistano la lettera per lo suo uso, ma in quanto per quella guadagnano denari o dignitate; si come non si dee chiamare citarista chi tiene la cetera in casa per prestarla per prezzo, e non per usarla per sonare." [And to their shame I say that they must not be called *literati*, since they don't pursue study for its own use, but in that through it they can gain money or honors; just as one must not call harpist one who has a harp in his home in order to rent it out for money, and not to play it himself.] *Convivio*, I, IX, 3.

He flays them even more pitilessly when he states that, had he written the comment of his canzoni in Latin, only one in a thousand among the men of letters of Italy would have been capable of reading it in that noble language. *Convivio*, I, IX, 2.

His bitterness toward the "literati" is found also in the *Divine Comedy*. He placed them among the sodomites, which group he identified with "clerks and literati." He referred to them with burning words:

> In somma sappi che tutti fur cherci,
> E letterati grandi, e di gran fama,
> D'un peccato medesmo al mondo lerci.

> In short, know that they were all clerks
> And great literati, and of great fame,
> Of the same sin filthy in the world.
>
> *Inferno*, XV, 106–108

Among them he placed the grammarian Priscian and Francesco d'Accorso, son of the jurist who had renewed the study of Roman law at the University of Bologna, and himself a great humanist.

THE HISTORICAL REALITY OF THE *DOLCE STIL NUOVO*

1. *Vita Nuova*, XX; *Purgatorio*, XI, 97–99.
2. *Purgatorio*, XI, 97–99.

3. *De Vulgari Eloquentia*, II, 4.

4. The line *"Sì che dal fatto il dir non sia diverso"* in *Inferno*, XXXII, 12, is one of the most luminous anticipations of modern realism that can be found in the past.

5. *Rimatori del Dolce Stil Nuovo*, edited by Luigi di Benedetto. Bari, 1939, pp. 7–8.

6. *Vita Nuova*, XX.

7. *Rimatori*, pp. 25–27.

DANTE AND COURTLY LANGUAGE

1. *Estetica*, Bari, 1922, p. 193.

2. *History of Criticism*, Edinburgh, 1900, p. 445.

3. *Convivio*, I, IX, 3.

4. *Inferno*, XV, 106–108.

5. *De Vulgari*, II, IV, 6: "Dum nullo accidente vilescant."

6. *Ibid.*, II, I, 6: "bona dignis, meliora dignioribus, et optima dignissimis convenient."

7. *Ibid.*, I, III, 1: "Cum igitur homo non naturae instinctu sed ratione moveatur."

8. *Ibid.*, II, IV, 6: "Stilo equidem tragico tunc uti videmur, quando cum gravitate sententiae tam superbia carminum, quam constructionis elatio, et eccelentia vocabulorum concordat."

9. *Vita Nuova*, II: "E pero che soprastare alle passioni ed atti di tanta gioventudine pare alcuno parlare fabuloso, mi partirò da esse; e trapassando molte cose verrò a quelle parole, le quali sono scritte nella mia memoria sotto maggiori paragrafi." [And since to dwell on passions and on acts of excessive youthfulness seems to be a kind of diction worthy of the *fabula*, I shall depart from them; and, neglecting many things, I shall come to those words that are written in my memory under greater headings.]

10. *Purgatorio*, XXIV, 52, 54.

11. *Inferno*, XXXII, 12.

12. *Purgatorio*, XII, 68.

13. *Inferno*, XXXII, 1–6.

14. *Purgatorio*, I, 7.

15. *Ibid.*, IX, 70–72.

16. *Inferno*, XI, 91–93.

17. *Ibid.*, II, 79–80.

18. *Ibid.*, II, 72.

19. *Paradiso*, I, 95.

20. *Ibid.*, XVIII, 21.

21. *Ibid.*, XVI, 5–7.

22. This thesis, identification of Beatrice with Christ, has been proposed by Charles Singleton in his *Essay on the* Vita Nuova, Cambridge, Mass., 1949.

23. *Paradiso*, V, 4.

DANTE'S "THE COURT OF HEAVEN"

1. E donna mi chiamò beata e bella,
   Tal che di comandare io la richiesi.

   And a lady called me, blessed and beautiful,
   To such an extent that I requested her to command me.

2. E cominciommi a dir soave e piana
   Con angelica voce in sua favella.

   And she began to tell me quietly and smoothly,
   With an angelic voice in her manner of speaking.

3. Tanto m'aggrada il tuo comandamento,
   Che l'ubbidir, se già fosse, me'è tardi;
   Più non t'è uo' ch'aprirmi il tuo talento.

   So much you command pleases me,
   To obey you, if I had obeyed you, it is late for me.
   You need only to reveal your desire to me.

4. In the first canto of the *Inferno*, Virgil refers to Paradise with the simple expression *beate genti* (blessed persons), and Dante with that of *porta di San Pietro* (door of St. Peter), where to the generic expression is added also the echo of the popular manner of considering Paradise.

5. Without wishing to make a pedantic enumeration of this motif, we can recall in Chapter XIV of the *Vita Nuova* the place in which one reads that "questa gentilissima venne in parte ove molte donne gentili erano adunate" (this most gentle lady came in a place where many other gentle ladies were gathered). In the sonnet *Ne li occhi porta la mia donna Amore* (My Lady carries Love in her eyes), Dante begs women to do honor to Beatrice. Chapter XX shows us the women who go to console Beatrice for the death of her father. The second sonnet of Chapter XVI, *Vede perfettamente onne salute* (He sees perfectly every salvation), presents Beatrice to us in the midst of other ladies like her. Chapter XXIV shows us Mona Vanna, shining with beauty, who follows Beatrice in the streets of Florence. The poet was so deeply struck by their beauty that he wrote a sonnet to his friend Guido Cavalcanti, concluding

   E si come la mente mi ridice,
   Amor mi disse: Quell'è Primavera,
   E quell'ha nome Amor, sì mi somiglia.

   And as my memory recounts to me,
   Love said to me: That is Spring,
   And that one has the name of Love, so much she is like me.

6. I' vegno il giorno a te 'nfinite volte
   E trovoti pensar troppo vilmente.

   I come to you infinite times during the day
   And I find you thinking in a very lowly manner.

   (*Tutte le opere*, Florence, 1921, p. 175)

7. "Io mi credea del tutto esser partito."

"I believe to have departed entirely."

(*Ibid.*, p. 178)

"I' ho veduto già senza radice."

"I have seen already without any root."

(*Ibid.*, p. 176)

DANTE'S CONCEPT OF LOVE

1. *Il Convivio*, edited by G. Busnelli and G. Vandelli, with an introduction by Michele Barbi. Florence, 1934, pp. LX–LXVIII.
2. "Il problema storico dello stile nuovo" in *Nuova Antologia*, I, October, 1896, p. 388.
3. "Amore intellettivo nell'evoluzione filosofica di Dante" in *Raccolta di storia e critica letteraria dedicata a Francesco Flamini*, Pisa, 1918, pp. 450–51.
4. *Ibid.*, p. 450.
5. *Vita Nuova*, edited by Kenneth McKenzie, New York, Heath, 1922, II.
6. *Ibid.*, III.
7. *Ibid.*, III.
8. *Ibid.*, IX.
9. *Ibid.*, XIV.
10. *Dante Forschungen*, I, pp. 1–65 and 141–82.
11. *Die Göttliche Konödie*, Heidelberg, 1907–1910. Translated by William Cranston Lawton under the title of *Medieval Culture*, New York, 1929.
12. "Dalla scuola di Virgilio alla scuola di Beatrice" in *Raccolta di studi dedicata a Francesco Flamini*, pp. 65 ff.
13. *Il Convivio*, XXVIII.
14. *Ibid.*, II, II, 1–2.
15. *Ibid.*, III, II, 11.
16. *Vita Nuova*, XXXVIII.
17. *Il Convivio*, I, III, 5.
18. *Ibid.*, I, III, 6–8.
19. *Ibid.*, I, II, 13.
20. *Ibid.*, I, II, 16.
21. *Ibid.*, II, III, 12.
22. *Ibid.*, II, XV, 3.
23. *Ibid.*, II, XVI, 8.
24. *Ibid.*, II, XII, 7.
25. *Purgatorio*, XXX, 124–32.
26. *Ibid.*, XXXI, 28–30.
27. *Ibid.*, XXX, 41–42.
28. *Il Convivio*. Introduction, pp. XXXIV–XXXV.
29. *Purgatorio*, XVII, 101–3.

30. *Paradiso*, III, 1–3.
31. *Ibid.*, XXXIII, 85–90.

FRANCESCA DA RIMINI AND THE *DOLCE STIL NUOVO*

1. Quoted by Francesco De Sanctis, *Nuovi Saggi Critici*, Naples, 1872, p. 14.
2. *Ibid.*, p. 1.
3. *Ibid.*, p. 14.
4. Dante, *Inferno*, XIV, 63–66.
5. Francesco De Santis, *op. cit.*, p. 15.
6. Benedetto Croce, *Poesia di Dante*, 1921, p. 77.
7. *Vita Nuova*, X.
8. *Ibid.*, II.
9. *Purgatorio*, XVIII, 19–39.
10. *Ibid.*, XXXI, 49–52.
11. Benedetto Croce, *op. cit.*, p. 78.
12. G. G. Parodi, *Poesia e Storia nella Divina Commedia*, 1920, pp. 70, 72.

SALUTATI'S LETTERS TO THE ARCHBISHOP OF CANTERBURY

1. *Epistolario di Coluccio Salutati a cura di Francesco Novati*. Tipografia del Senato, Rome, 1892–1911, Vol. III, pp. 360–363.
2. "viri quidem sanguinis sumus et iniurarum ultores crudelissimi," *op. cit.*, p. 362.
3. "cuncti sunt saccis induti, hymnos canunt, loca sancta visitant et penitentiae mira conversione simul omnes intendunt, abstinent carnibus atque ieiunant; nec est aliquis tantae nobilitatis et status, qui loca sancta non visitet, qui pedibus nudis per civitatem non incedet, quem non videres in humilitate et devotione flere super peccatis suis." *Op. cit.*, pp. 361–62.
4. "ceci quidem vident, claudi ambulant, audiunt surdi et quasi preter resurrectionis gratiam quicquid ex evangelio legitur, renovatur." *Op. cit.*, p. 362.
5. *Op. cit.*, Vol. III, pp. 380–82.
6. *Op. cit.*, Vol. III, p. 362, note 3.
7. These two books and the preface have been translated into English by Charles G. Osgood in a volume with a very thorough introduction that bears the title of *Boccaccio on Poetry* (Princeton University Press, 1930). Boccaccio directed a bitter attack against the enemies of poetry of his time whom he divided into four groups. The first group was that of the libertines and materialists who were interested only in the gross pleasures of life (Book XIV, 2). The second group was formed by pseudo-scholars who displayed as their own knowledge what they had learned by occasional and superficial contacts with those who really knew (Book XIV, 3). The third group was that of the jurists, lawyers, and judges, for whom truth had the same value as falsehood. In this connection Boccaccio deprecated the venal

character of the realists who were concerned only with making money (Book XIV, 4). The fourth group was formed by false philosophers (Book XIV, 5). The testimony of Boccaccio centered in condemning the worldliness and materialism of his contemporaries who failed to understand that money getting was not the aim of speculative sciences. Only applied sciences, according to Boccaccio, accrued monetary rewards to men. This distinction between speculative and applied sciences is of the utmost value, for it expresses the central characteristic of the fourteenth-century Humanism by stressing the moral nature and goal of learning in general and of classicism in particular. This statement by Boccaccio raises the question whether it is not unfair to make of the author of the *Decameron* a happy and debonair sensualist. It raises an even more important question concerning the theory of the Renaissance as repudiation of the transcendentalism and asceticism embodied in the Gothic spirit. If so, those whom Boccaccio called the enemies of poetry would represent the Renaissance, and Boccaccio, Petrarch, and Salutati would represent the Gothic civilization. To such a paradoxical conclusion one is led if one arbitrarily removes transcendentalism and asceticism from the civilization of the fourteenth century.

8. The orthodoxy of fourteenth-century Humanists has been very carefully investigated by the American scholar Paul Oskar Kristeller in two very thorough articles: "Humanism and Scholasticism in the Italian Renaissance." *Byzantion*, Vol. XVII, 1944–45, pp. 346–74, and "Augustine and the Early Renaissance," *Review of Religion*, May 1944, pp. 339–58.

9. See his letter to an unidentified Giovanni in *Epistolario*, Vol. III, pp. 221–31. A clearer document of Coluccio's transcendental leanings is found in his four letters to Pellegrino Zambuccari in which he discusses Platonic love. *Op. cit.*, Vol. III, pp. 3–52.

10. *Op. cit.*, Vol. III, pp. 497–501.

11. A contemporary of Salutati, G. Sercambi, speaking of the relation of his city of Lucca with England, stated: "il paeze d'Imghilterra . . . è utilissimo a ciptadini. . . . e a merchadanti per li lavori che quine si spacciano e per li molti guadagni che in quelli paezi si fanno." Quoted by Novati, *Epistolario*, Vol. III, p. 361, note 1.

12. *Op. cit.*, Vol. III, pp. 499–500, note 1.

13. Terent. Eun. I, II, pp. 193–96, quoted by Novati, *Epistolario*, Vol. III, p. 501, note 1.

14. *Op. cit.*, Vol. III, pp. 618–21.

15. See D. Vittorini "*I Dialogi ad Petrum Histrum* di Leonardo Bruni Aretino (Per la storia del gusto nell'Italia del secolo XIV)." *PMLA*, Vol. LV, N. 3. September, 1940, pp. 714–20.

LEONARDO BRUNI ARETINO AND HUMANISM

1. The *Dialogi* were published in a new edition, more complete and accurate, by Giuseppe Kirner, Livorno, Giusti, 1889. Two other editions appeared in the same year: *Beiträge z. Leonardo Bruni von Arezzo* by T. H.

Klette, and *Leonardi Bruni Aretini de tribus vatibus florentinis* by K. Wotke. The quotations in this essay refer to Kirner's edition.

2. Apostolo Zeno (in *Diss. Voss.* 1, p. 82); Lorenzo Mehus (in *Vita Leonardi Aretini*, in the volume of his epistles). Giammaria Mazzuchelli (in *Scrittori italiani* 11, 1v, 2196) had already studied Leonardo Bruni, when Girolamo Tiraboschi, at the end of the eighteenth century, evidenced a great interest in the Florentine author with the depth and accuracy that distinguish his writings. *Storia della letteratura italiana*, xiv, vi, p. 911.

3. Giuseppe Kirner, *Dialogi ad Petrum Histrum*, pp. viii and 8, basing himself on the fact that in the *Dialogi* there is a reference to Luigi Marsili's death, concludes that the book was written in the year 1401. We believe that the year 1401 refers to the time when Bruni imagined that the discussion here recorded took place and not to the year in which the book was written. We believe that the *Dialogi* were published in 1406, for Bruni refers here to a work of his, the *Laudatio Urbis Florentinae*, that appeared in 1406. How could Bruni refer in the *Dialogi* to a work not published until 1406, had the *Dialogi* been written in 1401? All the more that the reference to the *Laudatio* is made by Pietro di Ser Mino, a fact that suggests that the work had been released at the writing of the *Dialogi*. For the date of publication of the *Laudatio*, see Giuseppe Kirner, *Della Laudatio Urbis Florentinae di Leonardo Bruni*, Livorno, Giusti, 1866, p. 6.

4. De Franco E., *Dialogi a Pietro Vergerio*, Catania, 1929, p. 4, says that discussion took place on Easter Day of 1401. The text explicitly declares that it took place during the Easter week of that year: "Cum solemniter celebrarentur ii dies qui pro resurrectione Jesu Christi festi habentur." *Dialogi*, p. 4.

5. *Ibid.*, p. 11.

6. Giuseppe Kirner, *op. cit., Introduzione*, pp. 1–xxvi. E. Santini, "La Produzione Volgare di Leonardo Bruni," *Giornale storico della letteratura italiana*, lx, 289. E. De Franco, *I Dialogi al Vergerio di Leonardo Bruni*, Catania, Filippini, 1929.

7. Kirner, *op. cit.*, p. 47.

8. *Op. cit.*, p. 25.

9. Kirner, p. xiv, and Santini, "La Produzione Volgare di Leonardo Bruni," p. 289, believe that Niccoli definitely and bluntly assumes a hostile attitude against the poets of the past generation. De Franco, too, although he tries to blend together the Niccoli of the first day and that of the second day, gradually ends by accepting the conclusions of Kirner and Santini (p. 19). In fact, he concludes that the *Dialogi* "represent a moment of doubt and uncertainty concerning the three great fourteenth-century authors" (p. 24).

10. Kirner, *op. cit.*, p. 2.

11. *Op. cit.*, p. 12.

12. *Op. cit.*, p. 13.

13. *Op. cit.*, p. 15.

14. This attitude is also found in *Vita di Dante*, in which Bruni places the author of the *Commedia* among those poets who stand out through their doctrine, science, art, and prudence. Solerti, G., *Vite*, p. 105.

15. See the polemic on Platonic love between Salutati and Pellegrino Zambeccari, *Epistolario del Salutati*, edited by Francesco Novati, III, 3.
16. See A. Schiaffini, *Tradizione e Poesia*, Genoa, Emiliano degli Orfini, 1934, pp. 11–21; E. Faral, *Les Arts poétiques du XIIe au XIIIe siècle*, pp. 40 and 378; C. S. Baldwin, *Mediaeval Rhetoric and Poetry*, New York, Columbia University Press, 1928, p. 191.
17. Kirner, *Op. cit.*, p. 30.

REALISTIC ELEMENTS IN TASSO'S *AMINTA*

1. *Il Cinquecento*, Milano, Vallardi, 1929, p. 608.
2. *Storia della letteratura italiana*, Milano, Vallardi, 1924, p. 327.
3. Solerti, A. *Vita di T. Tasso*, Torino, Loescher, 1891, Vol. I, pp. 180–185.
4. *Aminta*, con introduzione e commento, a cura di Luigi Fassò, Firenze Sansoni, 1932, p. 16, note on lines 122–66.
5. Act I, 7; I, 39; I, 176.
6. Act I, (115–116).
7. Critics are agreed that this episode is borrowed from Achille Tazio's *Amori di Clitofonte e di Leucippo*, Book II. See Fassò, *op. cit.*, pp. 28–30.
8. *Le opere di G. Galilei*, edizione nazionale, Firenze, 1890–1909, Vol. IX.
9. *Tutte le opere di Alessandro Manzoni*, Firenze, Barbera, 1928, p. 860.
10. *Vita Nuova*, II.
11. *Ibid.*, II.
12. *Ninfale Fiesolano*, Bari, Laterza, 1937, pp. 302–304.
13. P. E. More, *Platonism*, Princeton University Press, 1931, p. 231.

GIAMBATTISTA VICO AND REALITY

1. The text of Vico's oration is found in *J. B. Vici Opera Latina*, edited by Giueseppe Ferrari (Milan, 1852), I, 1–55. There is a translation into Italian by Giuseppe Scerbo with an introduction by A. Aliotta, published by F. Perrella (Naples, 1937). Both the Latin text and the Italian free translation have been perused in writing this article.
2. See *Giambattista Vico nella vita domestica* by Fausto Nicolini, Naples, 1927.
3. G. Tiraboschi in his *Storia della letteratura italiana*, Venice, 1823, VII, 381, gives a flattering picture of Cardinal da Vio, but his conventional approach should not rob Vico's statement of its significance.
4. Republished by Laterza, Bari, in 1936, in the Latin text, bearing the Italian title of *Il diritto universale*, a cura di Fausto Nicolini, in three volumes. The original edition had been published in Naples in 1720 by the publishing house Mosca in one volume in quarto.
5. See introduction to *Purismo e romanticismo* by Edmondo Cione, Bari, 1936.
6. In *La cena delle ceneri*, edizione Gentile, Bari, Laterza, 1925, p. 31.

7. In *Pensieri*, Book X, Lanciano, Carabba, 1918, first complete edition, 1627.

8. *Estetica*, Bari, 1922, pp. 242–58.

GIACOMO LEOPARDI'S *L'INFINITO*

1. Francesco De Sanctis, *Studio su Giacomo Leopardi*, 8th ed., Naples, Marano, 1923, pp. 118–21.

2. A similar feeling, when confronted with infinite space, is confirmed by what Leopardi expresses in *Canto notturno di un pastore errante dell'Asia* (Nocturnal Song of a Wandering Shepherd in Asia). Here the poet addresses a series of disconsolate questions to the moon, very similar to his reaction in the *Infinito:*

> E quando miro in cielo arder le stelle,
> Dico fra me pensando:
> A che tante facelle?
> Che fa l'aria infinita, e quel profondo
> Infinito seren? che vuol dir questa
> Solitudine immensa? ed io che sono?
> Così meco ragiono: e della stanza
> Smisurata e superba,
> E dell'innumerabile famiglia;
> Poi di tanto adoprar, di tanti moti
> D'ogni celeste, ogni terrena cosa,
> Girando senza posa,
> Per tornar sempre là donde son mosse;
> Uso alcuno, alcun frutto
> Indovinar non so.

> And when I see the stars burning in the sky,
> I say within my own thoughts:
> Why so many lights?
> What is the purpose of this boundless air, and that deep
> Infinite serene sky? What does this
> Boundless solitude mean? and what am I?
> So I reason with myself:
> And of the boundless and proud room
> And of the innumerable family.
> Then I cannot find any use, any fruit
> Of so much doing, of so much moving
> Of every celestial thing, of every mortal,
> That whirl unceasingly
> To return there whence they came.

3. We find this same theme in *La sera del dì di festa*, where the tragic sadness of the poet, who thinks of the ever-fleeting world, is compared to the unconscious happiness of the worker who comes home after the festivity,

late at night, whistling after having enjoyed a holiday. We find the theme of the serenity of everyday life in other poems, such as *La Quiete dopo la tempesta* (The Quiet after the Storm) and *Il Sabato del villaggio* (Saturday Night in the Village).

4. In *Zibaldone* (Collection of Thoughts) with date of August 12, 1821, there is a brief reference to *L'Infinito*. Leopardi studies the effect of the feeling produced by a countryside, so steep that, at a distance, one is unable to see the valley. In *Tutte le opere,* edited by Francesco Flora, Milan, Mondadori, 1937, p. 953.

THE REALISTIC APPROACH IN THE EVALUATION OF ROMANTICISM IN MODERN ITALIAN CRITICISM

1. *La Letteratura italiana nel secolo XIX. Scuola liberale. Scuola democratica,* Lezioni raccolte da Francesco Torraca e pubblicate con prefazione e note da Benedetto Croce, Napoli, F. di Gennaro e A. Morano, 1898.

2. *Ibid.,* Part II, lesson 1, p. 377.

3. The characteristic phrase that he aptly used was "la scuola come decomposizione del caposcuola." This method is also applied to the study of the imitation of Petrarch in the sixteenth century. See *Saggio critico sul Petrarca.* Napoli, Morano. Nuova edizione a cura di Benedetto Croce, 1924, p. 58. The book first appeared in 1868.

4. *Ibid.,* Part I, lesson IV, p. 41.

5. *Storia della letteratura italiana dalla metà del Settecento ai giorni nostri,* Milano, Vallardi, 1880.

6. *Ibid.,* p. 217.

7. *Del Rinnovamento letterario* in *Prose,* Bologna, Zanichelli, 1906, pp. 377-767.
Del Risorgimento italiano. Ibid., pp. 1268-1312.

8. *L'Ottocento.* Milano, Vallardi, 1938, p. 194. The first edition appeared at the beginning of the century, 1913.

9. *Storia d'Europa nel secolo XIX,* Terza edizione riveduta, Bari, Laterza, 1932.

10. *Storia della critica romantica in Italia,* Bari, edizioni *Critica,* 1905.

11. *Il Romanticismo italiano non esiste.* The listed date of publication, 1908, is not the correct one, since Borgese, whose work appeared in 1905, refers to it as having already been published.

12. *Storia della critica romantica in Italia,* Milano, Treves, 1920, p. vi.

13. *Il senso della letteratura italiana,* Milano, Treves, 1931, p. 15.

14. *Storia della critica romantica in Italia,* p. x.

15. *Ibid.,* p. x. In 1920, when a new edition of his book was made, Borgese was fully conscious "of having mistaken for fog what was the port, and of having continued to wander on the sea like a slumbering, diminutive Ulysses," p. xxiii.

16. *Lettre à M. Chauvet* in *Opere,* a cura di Giuseppe Lesca. Firenze, Barbera. 1928, p. 241.

17. *Storia della critica romantica*, p. 127.

18. *La carne, la morte, e il diavolo nella letteratura romantica*, Milano, La Cultura, 1930.

19. *Dal Romanticismo al Futurismo*, Milano, Mondadori, 1925.

20. *Poesia e non Poesia*, Bari, 4th edition, 1950.

21. *"Lettera a Cesare D'Azeglio"* (1823) in *Opere.*, Firenze, Barbera, 1928, pp. 423–36.

22. *Il Settecento*, Milano, Vallardi, 1944.

23. *Ibid.*

24. See especially *Estetica*, quinta edizione riveduta, Bari, Laterza, 1922, pp. 260–67; 471–533.

25. *Italy and the Rise of a New School of Criticism in the XVIIIth Century*, Perth, 1921.

26. *Studies in the Genesis of Romantic Thought in the XVIIIth Century*, Cambridge, 1923.

27. *L'eredità del Rinascimento in Arcadia*, Bologna, Zanichelli, 1923. Toffanin, more than any other critic of today, clings to the humanistic illusion of the dependence of Italian literature on classicism, a belief based on the fact that he fails to distinguish between art and culture in the evolution of literature.

28. *Il Settecento*, pp. 620–30.

29. *Il Romanticismo nel mondo latino*, Torino, Bocca. 1927.

30. *Il Romanticismo e la poesia italiana dal Parini al Carducci*, Bari, Laterza. 1935.

31. *Ibid.*, p. 96.

32. *Ibid.*, p. 98.

REALISM DURING THE ROMANTIC AGE

1. *Conciliatore*, Turin, Utet, 1927, p. 149.

2. *Ibid.*, p. 160.

3. *Ibid.*, p. 266.

4. *Ibid.*, p. 209. Of the education received at Berne he stated: "... tutta la nostra istruzione è niente faticosa: somiglia a una scala sopra cui escendiamo a gradi a gradi." And also: "Costì (in Italy) mi si faceva parere lo studio uno spaventevole fantasma; qui invece è frammezzato da molte ore di ricreazione, ed è reso ameno per la varietà e facile pel metodo." Of the education imparted to Italian youth he stated: "... lo studio ... mi costa milioni di sospiri, e di sbadigli. Sono otto anni che mi s'insegna al latino, e capisco di non saperlo ancora.... Circa all storia, finora non ho inteso parlare che dell'assedio di Troja, degli amori di Enea e Didone, e del re Dejotaro."

5. *Ibid.*, p. 118.

6. *Lettera Semiseria*, Lanciano, Carabba, edited by A. Galletti, p. 10.

7. *Ibid.*, p. 121.

8. *Ibid.*, p. 119.

9. *Conciliatore*, p. 77.

10. See G. Toffanin, *L'eredità del Rinascimento in Arcadia*, Bologna. Zanichelli, 1923. Toffanin presents the thesis that every progress made then in Italian cultural life was in the direction of the classical pattern, a thesis with which we beg to differ.

11. *Conciliatore*, p. 41.

12. *Tutte le opere*, Firenze, Barbera, 1928, p. 421.

13. *Ibid.*, p. 424: "Quanto alla mitologia, i Romantici hanno detto, che era cosa assurda parlare del falso riconosciuto, come si parla del vero, per la sola ragione, che altri, altre volte, l'hanno tenuto per vero; cosa fredda l'introdurre nella poesia ciò che non richiama alcuna memoria, alcun sentimento della vita reale."

14. *Conciliatore*, p. 160: "Omero cantò l'inestinguibile riso degli Dei e le sciagure di Priamo, i giuochi dello stadio e lo strazio di Ettore."

15. *Ibid.*, p. 157: "Washington e i membri delle Cortes sono gli eroi che fanno al caso nostro, non più Sacripante e Amadigi."

16. *Ibid.*, p. 218: "Cercatela ora quella lingua nel gran Toscano registro dei suoi elementi, e nei mille codici dei modi suoi: ridotta la troverete, per le due terze parti, a sommario di stolide e basse formole; conversa in un serbatojo infinito di abbominevoli scurrilità, di bestemmie, di vituperj, di ribalderie canagliesche. Squallida la ritroverete, priva di vera sostanza, povera di concetti essenziali, d'idee madri, di sensi profondi, ricca e gonfia in vece di false idee, di erronee dichiarazioni, di nozioni equivoche; ridondante di voci identiche, di maniere striscianti, di popolari goffaggini, di pretti barbarismi, di frivolezze, di quisquiglie d'ogni sorta."

ALESSANDRO MANZONI AND THE REALISTIC NOVEL

1. *Tutte le opere*, edited by Giuseppe Lesca, 2d edition, Florence, 1928, pp. 831–72.

2. Caterina Re. "Di alcune pagine inedite del *Discorso del romanzo storico e dei componimenti misti di storia e d'invenzione* di A. Manzoni" in *Raccolta di studi dedicata a Francesco Flamini*, Pisa, 1918, p. 587.

3. *Tutte le opere*, p. 834.

4. *Ibid.*, p. 834.

5. *Estetica*, Bari, 1922, 5th edition, p. 398.

6. *Ensayo sobre la novela histórica*, Instituto de Filología, Buenos Aires, 1943, pp. 88–126.

7. Galletti, A., *Manzoni, il pensatore e il poeta*, Milan, 1927. II. p. 394: Alonso, A., *Ensayo*, p. 89.

8. De Simone, J. F., *Alessandro Manzoni*, New York, 1940, p. 123.

9. *Da "Sposi Promessi" ai "Promessi Sposi,"* Florence, 1926, p. 120.

10. "Notizie Storiche," in *Tutte le opere*, p. 59.

11. *Carteggio*, edited by G. Sforza and G. Gallavresi, Milan, 1912–21, Vol. I, p. 520.

12. Goethe had disagreed with Manzoni over the excessive importance that the latter gave to historical truth and the scrupulousness with which he

used historical themes in fiction. Senigaglia, E. "Relazioni di Goethe e Manzoni" in *Rivista contemporanea* (1888), I, p. 361. See also Allen C. Clark, *Literary Criticism—Pope to Croce*, New York, 1944, pp. 137–38.

13. *Tutte le opere*, p. 839.
14. *Ibid.*, p. 848.
15. *Ibid.*, pp. 842–43.
16. *Ibid.*, p. 840.
17. *Ibid.*, p. 870.
18. *Ibid.*, p. 870.
19. De Sanctis, F., *Zola e l'Assommoir*, Milan, 1879, p. 36; Morandi, L. *Voltaire contro Shakespeare, Baretti contro Voltaire*, Città di Castello, 1884, p. 121; D'Ovidio, F. *Discussioni manzoniane*, Città di Castello, 1886, pp. 45–46.
20. De Sanctis, F., *Zola e l'Assommoir*, p. 36; Tonelli, L., *Manzoni*, Milan, 1928, p. 430.

GRAZIA DELEDDA AND HER EARLY LITERARY CONTACTS

1. Published by *Treves*, Milan, 1938.
2. Published by *La Prora*, Milan, 1937.
3. *La Nuova Italia Editrice*. Florence, 1938.
4. January 1936, p. 16.

HIGH POINTS IN THE HISTORY OF ITALIAN LITERATURE

By DOMENICO VITTORINI

This collection of essays deals, as the title indicates, with the most outstanding points of Italian literature. Its parts are chronologically arranged, and they span the development of the literature of Italy from Dante to Benedetto Croce, Luigi Pirandello, and other twentieth-century writers.

Several of the essays bear on Dante: his contribution to aesthetics, the historical reality of the *Dolce Stil Nuovo*, Dante and courtly language, lights and shadows in the *Vita Nuova*, and Dante's concept of love. Among writers and subjects discussed in other essays are Francesca da Rimini, Aretino and humanism, realistic elements in Tasso's *Aminta*, realism during the romantic age, the modern Italian drama, and the development of the Italian novel.

Domenico Vittorini combines learning and critical perception with a style as simple as it is graceful. These studies will be of keen interest to scholars and students of Italian literature. In addition, because the author considers his